Speaking Back

Discourse Approaches to Politics, Society and Culture

The series includes contributions that investigate political, social and cultural processes from a linguistic/discourse-analytic point of view. The aim is to publish monographs and edited volumes which combine language-based approaches with disciplines concerned essentially with human interaction — disciplines such as political science, international relations, social psychology, social anthropology, sociology, economics, and gender studies.

The book series complements the *Journal of Language and Politics*, edited by Ruth Wodak and Paul Chilton

General editors

Paul Chilton and Ruth Wodak
University of East Anglia/University of Vienna

Editorial address: Paul Chilton
School of Language, Linguistics & Translation Studies
University of East Anglia
Norwich NR4 7TJ, UK
P. A.Chilton@uea.ac.uk and ruth.wodak@univie.ac.at

Advisory board

Michael Billig
Loughborough University

Jan Blommaert
University of Gent

Pierre Bourdieu †
Collège de France

Bill Downes
University of East Anglia

Mikhail V. Ilyin
Polis, Moscow

Teun A. van Dijk
University of Amsterdam/Pompeu Fabra, Barcelona

Jacob L. Mey
University of Southern Denmark

George Lakoff
University of California at Berkeley

Jim R. Martin
University of Sydney

Luisa Martin-Rojo
Universidad Autonoma de Madrid

Christina Schaeffner
Aston University

Volume 1

Speaking Back: The free speech versus hate speech debate
by Katharine Gelber

Speaking Back

The free speech versus hate speech debate

Katharine Gelber

University of New South Wales

John Benjamins Publishing Company
Amsterdam/Philadelphia

^{TM} The paper used in this publication meets the minimum requirements of American National Standard for Information Sciences – Permanence of Paper for Printed Library Materials, ANSI z39.48-1984.

Library of Congress Cataloging-in-Publication Data

Gelber, Katharine
 Speaking back : the free speech versus hate speech debate / Katharine Gelber.
  p. cm. (Discourse Approaches to Politics, Society and Culture, ISSN 1569-9463 ; v. 1)
 Includes bibliographical references and index.
  1. Oral communication--Social aspects. 2. Hate speech. 3. Freedom of speech. 4. Speech acts (Linguistics) I. Ttile. II. Series.

P95.54.G45 2002
302.2'242--dc21   2002016316
ISBN 90 272 2691 1 (Eur.) / 1 58811 188 1 (US) (Hb; alk. paper)

John Benjamins Publishing Co. · P.O. Box 36224 · 1020 ME Amsterdam · The Netherlands
John Benjamins North America · P.O. Box 27519 · Philadelphia PA 19118-0519 · USA

for Lou

Table of contents

Acknowledgements

I have been lucky enough to have the support of many other people while writing this book. I am deeply indebted to those who provided me with a framework for intellectual debate and a truly "free exchange of ideas"; Lisa Hill, John Fossum, Helen Pringle, John Braithwaite, Duncan Iveson, Andrew Fitzmaurice, Graeme Gill, Diarmuid Maguire, Ariadne Vromen, Martin Painter, Darryl Jarvis, Peter Dauvergne and Lou Stanley. Many thanks are due to the Series Editor Paul Chilton, for incisive and helpful remarks on the draft. Any errors remain, of course, my own.

I am grateful to the Research Committee of the Discipline of Government and International Relations, University of Sydney for providing me with a grant to conduct my empirical research, and to the NSW Anti-Discrimination Board which provided me with its own research grant. During my work at the Board, the staff were incredibly helpful and made my work there a pleasure. In particular I would like to thank Chris Puplick, Angelene Falk, Murray Burke, Kevin Williams and Catherine Duff. My thanks are also due to the Ethics Committee of the University of Sydney, for providing approval for me to gain access to confidential case study material essential to complete my research.

Some of the material that is drawn on in Chapter 1 has appeared in another form in (2000) "Implementing Racial Anti-Vilification Laws in New South Wales, 1989 to 1998: A Study", *Australian Journal of Public Administration*, Vol. 59, No. 1, March: 13–23. I am grateful for permission to use that material here.

Abbreviations

ADA	*Anti-Discrimination Act 1977* NSW (as amended)
ADB	Anti-Discrimination Board of NSW (Australia)
ADT	Administrative Decisions Tribunal NSW (Equal Opportunity Division) (Australia)
ALRC	Australian Law Reform Commission
CPDHR	Commonwealth Parliamentary Debates, House of Representatives (Australia)
CPDS	Commonwealth Parliamentary Debates, Senate (Australia)
EOT	Equal Opportunity Tribunal NSW (renamed in October 1998 as the Administrative Decisions Tribunal, Equal Opportunity Division) (Australia)
FCC	Federal Communications Commission (United States of America)
HREOC	Human Rights and Equal Opportunity Commission (Australia)
HRC	Human Rights Commission (Australia)
ICCPR	International Covenant on Civil and Political Rights
ICERD	International Convention on the Elimination of All Forms of Racial Discrimination
NSWPDLA	New South Wales Parliamentary Debates, Legislative Assembly
NSWPDLC	New South Wales Parliamentary Debates, Legislative Council
UDHR	Universal Declaration of Human Rights
UNCERD	United Nations Committee on the Elimination of Racial Discrimination
UNCHR	United Nations Centre for Human Rights
UNHRC	United Nations Human Rights Committee
VPDHA	Victorian Parliamentary Debates, House of Assembly

Abstract

What is hate speech? How does a person suffer when they are vilified? What can public policy do to redress it? In this book, I make a proposal for a new type of hate speech policy. I propose a policy of "speaking back" — providing institutional, material and educational support to enable the victims of hate speech to respond. By responding with their own counter speech, victims can contradict the messages contained in the hate speech and counteract the disempowering and silencing effects of the hate speech, at one and the same time. This policy is justified by integrating elements of Habermas' theory of communicative action, which allows the development of an understanding of what hate speech *does*, with Nussbaum's capabilities theory, which justifies the provision of assistance to those whose capabilities may be harmed by the hate speech of others. This policy is designed to overcome the shortcomings of existing policy approaches, which tend to counterpose the two goals of securing free speech rights and ameliorating the harms of hate speech. In the policy proposal outlined in this book, these two goals are viewed as mutually collaborative and able to be achieved simultaneously. The argument that existing policy tends to counterpose these two goals is supported by outlining a comprehensive and original study of an existing hate speech policy in practice in New South Wales, Australia over a period of ten years.

Introduction

"Really, now you ask me", said Alice, very
much confused, "I don't think ..."
"Then you shouldn't talk", said the Hatter.
Lewis Carroll, *Alice in Wonderland*

What is hate speech?[1] How does a person suffer when they are vilified? What
can public policy do to redress it? In Australia today, as in a growing number of
Western liberal democracies,[2] laws designed to ameliorate hate speech have
been put in place. I will argue that these laws, although well-intentioned, do
little to address the real problems of hate speech, because they unnecessarily
counterpose the goals of securing free speech and ameliorating the harms of
hate speech. Secondly, these laws tend to invoke a private and individualised
resolution process for what is essentially a public problem, which means there
is little scope for directly addressing the broader harms enacted by hate speech,
and resolution depends on the identification of individuals willing and able to
pursue a complaint to finalisation over a significant period of time. Thirdly,
these laws tend to rely on a statutory definition of hate speech which is either
vague and difficult to enforce, or is too restrictive and renders much hate
speech immune from regulation. To overcome these shortcomings, I propose
an alternative hate speech policy — a policy of "speaking back", where institutional, material and educational support are provided to the victims of hate
speech to enable them to respond.

Hate speech laws have become unexceptional in Western liberal democratic
orders. In 1948, in response to the horrors perpetrated by Nazi Germany, the
General Assembly of the United Nations ushered in a new era of human rights
protection in international law by adopting the Universal Declaration of
Human Rights. During the intervening half century Western liberal democracies have embraced the ideals of non-discrimination and equal protection
before the law. In this context "vilification", or "hate speech", is regarded as
speech which is particularly harmful because it contributes to a climate of
hatred and violence towards marginalised and disempowered sectors of the
community. It violates the basic human dignity of its victims.[3] Justifications for

hate speech legislation include claims that it might reduce the incidence of hate-speech, which might in turn reduce or ameliorate hatred, contempt or violence towards specifically identifiable groups.

In opposition to such legislation, defenders of free speech argue that "hate speech" may more productively be countered through the maintenance of principles ensuring the freest speech possible, for as many people as possible. Indeed, historically speech has been accorded pride of place among personal liberties. This means the development of an appropriate, efficacious or useful response to hate speech must weigh up two interests: the interest of maintaining free speech conditions, and the interest of regulating to prevent the harms of hate speech. Rodney Smolla describes the endeavour to cater for these two competing interests as the most intractable and difficult problem in speech theory (1992:151). These two interests tend to be conceived of as necessarily counterposed. On the one hand, a free speech principle — that speech ought to be as free from interference by the state as possible — has been maintained by many scholars. On the other hand, it can be acknowledged that many types of speech are already subject to regulation, including defamation, obscenity, commercial speech and incitement to commit a criminal act. Insofar as it can be demonstrated that hate speech is harmful, some writers argue that state regulation of this particular exercise of the speech liberty[4] is justifiable. Writers including Frederick Schauer, Cass Sunstein, Owen Fiss, Mari Matsuda, Judith Butler and Catharine MacKinnon all argue that some regulation appears justifiable, although they disagree as to the form and content of such regulation.

However, any regulation of hate speech, comes immediately into conflict with the free speech principle. How is it possible to devise a policy capable of acknowledging that speech in general ought to be free from restriction, and at the same time capable of defining hate speech precisely enough to allow its regulation? These competing policy demands tend to be framed by policy makers on speech in terms of striking a proper "balance". That is, hate speech policy makers tend to express a desire to achieve a "balance" between the right to free speech and the right to live a life free from harassment and intimidation. This can also be expressed as a "balance" between the policy demand to restrain from interfering in the exercise of the speech liberty and the policy demand to interfere in some instances of the exercise of the speech liberty to prevent or moderate the harms of hate speech.

It seems important to ask, then, whether in practice this "balance" is being achieved, or even whether it is able to be achieved in a policy environment. Is it possible (and if so how and to what extent) to *reconcile* a theoretical defence of free speech with a recognition and understanding of the harms of hate speech? In order to answer this question, an in depth, qualitative assessment has been carried out of the first anti-hate speech statute in Australia, the New South Wales (NSW) racial[5] anti-vilification legislation enacted in 1989.[6] The study which I conducted over a three month period involved exhaustive examination of all material on file in relation to 568 complaints lodged under the New South Wales (NSW) racial anti-vilification statute. The material included letters of complaint, follow up correspondence between the complainant and the NSW Anti-Discrimination Board, answers to the allegations provided by the respondent, and evidentiary material. In accordance with statutory requirements, all information derived from the study must remain anonymous. I am legally prohibited from providing any reference numbers, names or personally identifying information when discussing individual complaints. As a way of overcoming this constraint I have identified particular cases by letters.

The results of the study indicate that the NSW legislation has attempted both to maintain free speech conditions and to respond to the harms of hate speech. This has been done by providing, on the one hand, for wide-ranging exemptions to the kinds of instances of hate speech which are subject to the legislation. These exemptions include matters of scientific or academic debate, or any matter "in the public interest". On the other hand, where an instance of hate speech is not subject to exemptions, the legislation provides for actionable recourse by a victim of hate speech. This recourse takes the form of civil remedies, including apologies, retractions, educational programs or fines. Thus, the legislation can be seen as an example of policy-makers seeking, in practice, to implement a "balance" between the free speech principle and the harms of hate speech.

However, information derived from the study tends to suggest that a reconciliation between the goal of balancing the free speech principle and ameliorating the harms of hate speech was difficult to achieve. In some complaints it seemed an instance of hate speech had occurred; however, the expression was rendered inactionable due to inconsistencies in application of the law. In other cases, where it seems an instance of hate speech had occurred, the resolution appeared to go only a little way towards ameliorating the harms of the hate speech. I suggest that these inconsistencies in application of the law arise from the policy's reliance on an individualised, private complaint resolution process, conducted between the complainant and the respondent and facilitated by the NSW Anti-Discrimination Board. The private nature of the resolution process does not seem to fit with the public nature of the hate speech itself. This is a crucial criticism that can be made of the NSW legislation. Hate speech is — both by NSW statutory definition and in accordance with the phenomenology which will be suggested in this book — a public act. Yet the resolution process is overwhelmingly private; an apology or agreement to desist facilitated between two individuals in a closed setting. I will suggest that the public, broad impact of hate speech is not sufficiently ameliorated by a private and confidential resolution mechanism, because such a mechanism does not allow for a broader, public initiation or generation of a response to the hate speech. Another question raised by the study was that of the difficulty of drafting, and implementing, a workable statutory definition of hate speech which would not lead to over-regulation of speech, but would still allow action to be taken in response to the harms of hate speech.

Chapter 1, which outlines the study undertaken into the operation of the NSW racial anti-vilification law, presents three empirical problems. The first of these is the problem of understanding why the legislation has been framed with wide-ranging exemptions to the kinds of instances of hate speech subject to regulation, and with an emphasis on a private and individualised resolution process. The second problem is that of explaining apparent inconsistencies in the policy's application. The third problem raised is that of searching for a workable statutory definition of hate speech, because the NSW legislation relies on a strict statutory definition of hate speech which renders many instances of hate speech immune from regulation. These problems suggest shortcomings in the ability of the policy to reconcile two important, yet competing, principles of maintaining free speech conditions and also ameliorating the harms of hate speech.

In order to show how current understandings of free speech and speech theory may have led to inadequate policy responses to hate speech, Chapter 2 examines contemporary dominant arguments in defence of free speech and suggests they share the common feature of being unable to consider how it might be possible to ensure all citizens are able to *participate* in the exercise of the speech liberty. The question of how to make participation in the speech liberty possible leads directly to a questioning of the conception of liberty assumed in the four major free speech arguments. I argue that currently dominant liberal and utilitarian arguments in defence of free speech tend to emphasise the maximum absence of restraint on the speech liberty as a central policy goal. That is, they tend to assume that an increase in the amount of speech made free from interference will produce the most beneficial policy outcome. In other words, more is better. In contrast, this book advocates a different, broader conception of the speech liberty. I will suggest that the speech liberty may be conceived of in a manner which includes a consideration of how citizens might be empowered to participate and engage in the exercise of the speech liberty should they be inhibited from so doing. This conception of the scope of the speech liberty includes a consideration of what the exercise of, or ability to exercise, the speech liberty might be capable of doing in and for people's lives.

This alternative framework for conceptualising speech policy is derived from capabilities theory, an Aristotelian based theory derived from Martha Nussbaum's work. Capabilities theory aims to provide a framework for policy-making which emphasises not the maximum provision of goods as a policy goal, but instead the manner in which those goods may be used to improve quality of life. A corollary to this consideration is that the maximum provision of the speech liberty need not be the central goal for policy-makers. Instead, a consideration of what the exercise of the speech liberty is able to do in and for people's lives is called for. According to capabilities theory, it is the role of an "excellent lawgiver" (to use Aristotle's term) to ensure that goods are used to *improve* people's quality of life. This implies policy-making on speech ought to be concerned with assessing how the exercise of the speech liberty might be capable of improving or degrading people's quality of life. The application of capabilities theory to the arena of speech policy in this book is an original one. Capabilities theory seeks to provide a comprehensive, and embedded, account of "good human functioning", which means being capable of making and acting on decisions in universal spheres of human activity in a manner informed by one's own conception of a good human life. To each sphere of human functioning correspond human "capabilities", the means by which choices may be made as to how to function within those spheres. Spheres of human functioning include cognitive capabilities such as perceiving, imagining and thinking, planning and managing one's own life, and affiliation with others. The capabilities which correspond to these spheres include being able to imagine, to think, to reason, being able to form a conception of the good and be involved in planning one's life accordingly, and being able to live with other people (Nussbaum 1990: 219–225). It is the responsibility of excellent lawgivers to ensure citizens receive the requisite institutional, material and educational support to become capable of choosing to function well within each sphere (Nussbaum 1990: 228).

Capabilities theory, therefore, provides an embedded and holistic approach to a consideration of human needs, and a guide to policy-making. This means an application of capabilities theory to the arena of policy-making on speech may serve to overcome the weaknesses of current hate speech policy approaches. For example, capabilities theory is able to take a range of competing goods into account when determining social policy goals, because the aim of social policy is to move as many citizens as possible across the "capabilites threshold" (Nussbaum 1990:229). Consideration of what constitutes the capabilities threshold involves the consideration of a range of human needs. It is also possible that an application of capabilities theory to the arena of policy-making on speech may provide assistance in moving towards a successful reconciliation between a theory in defence of free speech and a recognition and understanding of the harms of hate speech. Capabilities theory provides a justification for free speech policy insofar as the exercise of the speech liberty is identified as central to the development of important human capabilities. Capabilities theory may also be capable of integrating an assessment of the harms of hate speech into considerations of the development of policy around speech if, and to the extent that, it is possible to demonstrate, that hate speech impacts negatively on the development of human capabilities among victim groups. It appears a consideration of people's ability to participate in, or even be harmed by the participation of others in, the exercise of the speech liberty is a logical application of the capabilities framework.

But in order to begin an assessment of people's capabilities with regard to policy-making on speech, it is necessary to examine the role speech might play within a good human life. If it is suggested speech may be capable of contributing to, or detracting from, a good human life, an analytical framework within which it is possible to examine what speech *does* becomes necessary. In Chapter 3 I undertake this task by examining speech-act theory, which suggests that speech may be conceived of as a kind of conduct. By contrast, in the arguments in defence of free speech discussed earlier, a distinction between speech and conduct is utilised. I argue that a speech-conduct distinction is highly challengeable, and that theories in defence of free speech tend to de-emphasise or ignore speech-act theories, because the maintenance of a speech-conduct distinction is regarded as central to justifying the free speech principle. A principle of preserving speech from regulation to the greatest degree possible is able to be justified when it can be argued that the speech is "special", able to be differentiated from acts. Conceding that speech is a kind of conduct is often opposed by theorists in defence of free speech on the grounds that to do so would render speech vulnerable to regulation on the same grounds as other conduct, and could easily lead to over-regulation. However, concerns of over-regulation of speech are also able to be addressed in the context of capabilities theory. It is suggested in this book that speech is an activity which is central to the exercise of many human capabilities. As such, it is an activity which people must be able to engage in, in a manner conducive to the development of their own capabilities and ability to choose to function well. The reasons for enhancing speech opportunities are therefore sufficiently powerful to avoid over-regulation. The argument in this book integrates speech-act theory with considerations of speech policy, because this allows for the integration of a considerable body of scholarly work into the arena of policy-making on speech. Speech-act theory enables the development of an understanding of what it is one does when one speaks that appears to accord with many people's experiences.

In Chapter 4, Austin's distinction between locutionary, illocutionary and perlocutionary speech-acts is combined with elements of Habermas' theory of communicative action, namely the validity claims. For Habermas, language is a medium of communication which has structures, rules by which agreement may be reached on the meaning of a communication, embedded in it (1984: x). He sought to unearth the communicative rationality of those structures in order to develop a theory of how communicative actions may be understood by others. He argues that when a person speaks, they do more than produce grammatical sentences. They claim to be saying something comprehensible, to listeners who will comprehend it, and in a comprehensible manner (1979: 1). For Habermas, uncovering the structures by which this comprehension may be mutually achieved provides a theory of communicative rationality. This theory provides a framework within which it becomes possible to develop rules which would enable communication to be oriented to reaching understanding. Reaching understanding, Habermas argues, is the "inherent *telos* of speech" (Habermas 1984: 285–287).

Habermas' theory of communicative action is a general social theory, a normative theory of social democracy. Within this book, however, I intend to make use only of a small part of this theory; namely, the validity claims. The validity claims are the rules by which agreement may be reached on the meaning of a communication, the claims raised by a speaker in communicative action. Utilising a validity claims framework makes it possible to understand what kind of an act is performed when an utterance is made. When a speaker, oriented to reaching mutual understanding, is able to raise validity claims which are agreed upon by the listener, communicative competence can in principle be achieved. A speech situation in which this has been achieved is "ideal" (Habermas 1984: 42). The comprehensiveness of Habermas' theory of communicative action raises the question of why the complete theory has not been utilised as a central theoretical framework for this book. It may be argued that the Habermasian approach on its own is comprehensive enough to deal with the problems I moot here. Why is Nussbaum needed? Both Habermas' theory of communicative action and Nussbaum's capabilities theory appear to be normative theories of social democracy.

The answer to the question of why only a small part of Habermas' theory of communicative action is integrated with capabilities theory lies in an understanding of Habermas' "ideal" speech situation. For although Habermas provides a framework and set of rules within which it becomes possible to reach understanding via communication, the theory of communicative action suffers in that it does not provide a framework within which it is clear what might be done to assist some individuals to engage in communicative action should they be inhibited from doing so by the speech of others. Nussbaum's capabilities theory is able to overcome this limitation of Habermas. Capabilities theory provides a framework within which it is possible to recognise that some people might not yet possess human capabilities, and to suggest the kinds of social policy (institutional, material and educational support) which might help them achieve the capabilities essential to choosing to function well. In other words, providing the requisite institutional, material and educational support to enable people to engage in communicative action, should their participation be hindered by the speech-acts of others, becomes a justifiable and justified policy goal.

At the same time, it is possible to reach an understanding of how some people might be prevented from engaging in communicative action by the speech of others, via an application of a validity claims model for assessing the phenomenology of hate-speech-acts derived from Habermas' theory of communicative action. This model enables an assessment to be made of the validity claims raised by speakers in uttering hate-speech-acts, and also provides a framework for suggesting how a communicative response might begin to address those claims. Utilising a Habermasian model in these two ways enables the development of a model within which to differentiate hate-speech-acts from other speech-acts, and also a model within which to suggest how a response might be framed. Generating a response enables participants to engage in argumentation, and criticise and question the validity claims raised by others in uttering speech-acts. This model is also augmented with a discrete analysis of the perlocutionary effects of hate-speech-acts on others, because a discrete analysis of the perlocutionary effects of hate-speech-acts appears to offer assistance in identifying how the speech-acts of some might be able to prevent others from engaging in communicative action. I will argue that hate-speech-acts are able to prevent others from engaging in communicative action by perpetrating, perpetuating and maintaining discrimination against its victims, in a manner which prevents them from participating in speech which would develop their individual capabilities.

Synthesising aspects of these theories enables an answer to the dilemma of hate speech to be reached. From Nussbaum's capabilities theory, I have developed the idea that a theory in defence of free speech can take into account an understanding of how and why speech is important, by viewing speech as important to the development of human capabilities. Speech *per se* no longer remains the goal for policy makers. Instead, making possible the *exercise* of speech conducive to the development of human capabilities becomes the primary policy goal. From Austin, I have utilised the idea that when a person speaks, they are doing more than making a statement. They are acting through a discursive utterance, with force and meaning as an act. From Habermas, I have utilised the validity claims model in order to investigate the specific force and meaning of a hate-speech-act. By analysing the claims to objective truth, intersubjective norms and values and subjective sincerity made by a speaker in an utterance, it is possible to develop a multilayered and embedded understanding of the force and meaning of a hate-speech-act. I will argue that a hate-speech-act is a discursive act of discrimination, which in its very expression perpetuates, propagates and maintains discrimination. Utilising the validity claims framework also allows for the development of a policy designed to *counter* hate speech acts. This analysis will argue that hate-speech-acts impair the development of human capabilities among victim groups. This argument belies the view that speech may be "only words" (MacKinnon 1993). It also demonstrates how free speech policies, when applied, do not result in equal opportunity to speak.

I argue that a validity claims model provides a framework within which it is possible to identify hate-speech-acts. One of the most important perlocutionary effects of hate speech identified is that of silencing. This is important in considerations of speech policy, because it is susceptible to correction by a capabilities-oriented hate speech policy, oriented to maximising the opportunity to speak. I also suggest in this chapter that if hate speech victims were provided with the opportunity to respond to the claims raised in hate-speech-acts, other negative perlocutionary effects of hate speech might also be minimised. A policy approach of "speaking back" provides a framework within which it becomes possible to view the two goals of securing free speech and ameliorating the harms of hate speech as mutually collaborative, facilitated simultaneously via a hate speech policy designed not to punish, but to provide assistance to speak to those who seek to respond to, contradict and counteract the effects of hate-speech-acts.

It is impossible to undertake a comprehensive examination of hate speech laws around the world. Nevertheless, it is useful to expand the remit of the argument in this book. Are these problems in hate speech policy limited to the particular Australian case study selected? Does the proposed remedy have wider applications? In Chapter 5, I adopt a comparative method and investigate whether the reasons for the weaknesses in the application of hate speech policy identified in NSW apply in other jurisdictions also. I examine and compare hate speech policies in Australia, the United Kingdom and the United States. I identify considerable variances between these countries' means of implementing treaty obligations, the specific mechanisms by and extent to which free speech is protected in law, and the nature of attempts that have been made to respond to the problem of racist hate speech. This chapter suggests that, despite these variances, an examination of these countries' approach to hate speech policy share weaknesses in policy implementation. These include a reliance on a conception of hate speech policy as necessarily restrictive or punitive, a related reliance on private, individualised sanctions, and reliance on a policy approach which counterposes the goals of free speech and responding to hate speech. This suggests the analysis presented in this book may be particularly fruitful, because other jurisdictions may benefit from adopting a capabilities approach to hate speech policy.

In the final chapter, the operationalisation of a capabilities-oriented hate speech policy is considered. In order to ameliorate hate-speech-acts, capabilities theory suggests that adequate institutional, material and educational support be provided to enable all citizens to reach a threshold of capabilities. In concrete terms, I make the suggestion that this might be achieved by devising hate speech policy aimed at the provision of an assisted response to those who would seek to contradict and counter the effects of hate-speech-acts. That is, a hate speech policy designed to assist in the initiation and generation of a response to hate-speakers, by those who are otherwise rendered unable to speak back by the hate-speech-acts of others. The final chapter explores the operationalisation of this policy via the provision of support to encourage and enable a process of "institutionalised argumentation", or "speaking back". This opens up the possibility for an exchange of ideas. In this manner, it might over the longer term be possible to achieve changes in attitude and behaviour. As Habermas acknowledges, change can be achieved via the discursive, collective construction of desired goals (1987:271). The process of institutionalised argumentation could constitute a discursive construction of the goal of eliminating racist discrimination. I also answer potential objections to the hate speech policy proposed in this chapter, and canvass other scholars' proposals for hate speech policies and compare them with the proposal I make in this book. Finally, I consider the potential application of the hate speech policy proposed to some well known "hard cases".

In conclusion, the argument of this book is that a capabilities-oriented hate speech policy represents a viable and comprehensive intervention into the arena of speech policy. This kind of policy provides an answer to those who declare that speech one doesn't like ought not to be banned, but ought to be answered, by allowing for the first time for public policy to assist in the generation of that response. The policy proposed in this book thus seems capable of truly reconciling a recognition of the importance of speech to individual development, the importance of speech to the discursive, collective, social construction of debate and goals (an understanding which implicitly rests at the "core" of any free speech principle), and the harms of hate speech.

CHAPTER 1

The problem

An example of racial anti-vilification laws in practice, 1989-1998

> "You're nothing but a coon ... I've shot worse coons than you."

The first anti hate speech statute enacted in Australia was a racial anti-vilification law,[7] enacted in 1989. A qualitative empirical study conducted of all finalised complaints (568 cases)[8] under the NSW legislation, from its inception in 1989 to December 1998 is outlined here. These findings provide access to previously untapped primary source material on a legislative attempt to respond to hate speech. First, I attempt to deduce the rationale behind the introduction of the legislation, which was not very clearly stated by its drafters. Then I outline the structure of the legislation in light of its rationale, and provide qualitative empirical evidence which suggests the legislation may not be meeting its declared objectives. Thus, I reveal empirical problems in the implementation of this hate speech law, problems which I will explain in later chapters by investigating the dominant theories around free speech.

The legislation

Aims and objectives

New South Wales, as a state within the Australian federal system, holds responsibility for developing its own criminal and civil laws. In the late 1980s, pressure was being brought to bear from a range of sources on the NSW legislature to introduce racial vilification legislation. Public concerns about expressions of racial hatred were increasing. In 1983 the federal Human Rights Commission noted that approximately one-quarter of the complaints it received regarding racial discrimination were about "racially derogatory comments" (HRC 1983:1), yet such "comments" remained outside the scope of all existing anti-discrimination legislation at both federal and state levels. The Commission expressed concern at this lack of a legislative response to the incidence and effects of racial vilification (HRC 1982; HRC 1983). In the NSW Parliament, advocates of anti-vilification legislation cited relevant provisions of the International Covenant on Civil and Political Rights (NSWPDLA, 4 May 1989: 7488–89; NSWPDLC, 10 May 1989: 7810). Prior to a 1988 NSW state election, Liberal Party leader Nick Greiner promised to enact "legislation making incitement to racial hatred a criminal offence" (Liberal Party NSW 1988). Later, the NSW Parliamentary Secretary on Ethnic Affairs, James Samios MLC, visited France and the United Kingdom to discuss measures to curb racial hatred in those countries (Samios 1998; NSWPDLC, 10 May 1989: 7816). Samios wrote a *Discussion Paper on Racial Vilification and Proposed Amendments to the Anti-Discrimination Act 1977* justifying the legislation as necessary to ensure the "right to a dignified and peaceful existence free from racist harassment and vilification" and "its attendant harms" (NSW Government 1988: 1, 3). The discussion paper also noted that "the Government is concerned to address *serious* forms of racial vilification and does not intend to cover trivial matters" (NSW Government 1988: 1) [my emphasis].

An impressive range of community organisations supported the introduction of anti-vilification legislation as well, including the Ethnic Communities Council, the Jewish Board of Deputies, the Federation of Ethnic Communities, the Labor Council of NSW, the Catholic Bishops Committee for Justice, Development and Peace, the Uniting Church and the Greek Orthodox Church (NSWPDLC, 10 May 1989: 7813). In parliament, the legislation received bipartisan support. Only one member, Marie Bignold, voted against it, claiming that it would be counter-productive and would exacerbate racial differences rather than tend to remove those differences (NSWPDLC, 10 May 1989: 7839). The decision was made to incorporate anti-vilification legislation into the *Anti-Discrimination Act* (NSW) 1977, because this provided a framework within which punitive resolution mechanisms, and referral to the Administrative Decisions Tribunal[9] for hearing and orders for redress, were made possible.[10]

Later reports and inquiries have provided ongoing evidence of racial hatred in Australia. The *Report of the National Inquiry into Racist Violence in Australia* (1991) noted high levels of hatred-induced violence and recommended the enactment of both civil and criminal offences for racial vilification. The report of the Royal Commission into Aboriginal Deaths in Custody (1991: 38, 116) included the recommendation that governments legislate to proscribe racial vilification with a view to providing conciliation mechanisms. This report recommended against the use of criminal sanctions. Office of Ombudsman NSW (1993) and Chan (1992) also cite high levels of racial hatred and racially-induced violence. All these reports argued that enacting racial vilification legislation might reduce the incidence and ameliorate the harms of hate speech by sending a message to the community that it is unacceptable, and by providing redress for individual complaints.

The racial anti-vilification legislation enacted in 1989 in NSW created an offence of "racial vilification" (Section 20C), with civil remedies, and a criminal offence of "serious racial vilification" (Section 20D). Since to date not a single case of serious racial vilification has been prosecuted, the focus of this study is on the civil provisions of the legislation.[11] Section 20C states:

> it is unlawful for a person, by a public act, to incite hatred towards, serious contempt for, or severe ridicule of, a person or a group of persons on the ground of the race of the person or members of the group.

An individual member of the allegedly vilified group, or a representative organisation[12] on behalf of an individual,[13] must lodge a complaint in writing. The Anti-Discrimination Board (ADB) may not initiate complaints itself. The complaint must refer to an incident that occurred in NSW. A complaint may be referred to the Tribunal on the request of a complainant, either after declination by the ADB or because attempts at resolution had failed. Tribunal rulings are enforceable via Sections 115 and 116 of the *Act* which impose a fine for non-compliance.

Remedies

If the ADB finds a complaint to constitute an offence of racial vilification, it may assist in resolution of the complaint by facilitating agreement on, or enforcing, a range of civil remedies. Potential remedies include:

a. obtaining written apologies
b. obtaining undertakings from an individual to cease vilifying a complainant
c. a workplace agreeing to the ADB holding information sessions to inform groups of staff about what constitutes unlawful racial vilification
d. ordering a respondent to develop and implement a program or policy aimed at eliminating unlawful discrimination
e. requesting the publication or broadcast of an apology or retraction contradicting the racially vilifying view.

Orders to perform these activities may also be made by the Tribunal. Under the civil provisions of the legislation, the Tribunal can order payment of compensation up to a maximum of $40,000 (Twomey 1994c: 3).[14]

Statutory definitions

The drafters of the legislation intended that the term "race" was to have a broad meaning, to include ethno-religious groups such as Jews, Sikhs and Muslims (NSWPDLA 1989:7921). A later Tribunal hearing reinforced this interpretation[15] and a 1994 amendment to the *Act* clarified this definition.[16] The definition of "race" for the purposes of interpreting the NSW legislation is therefore consonant with the definition used elsewhere in this book.

A "public act" is defined in Section 20B as:

a. any form of communication to the public, including speaking, writing, printing, displaying notices, broadcasting, telecasting, screening and playing of tapes or other recorded material, and

b. any conduct (not being a form of communication referred to in paragraph (a)) observable by the public, including actions and gestures and the wearing or display of clothing, signs, flags, emblems and insignia, and

c. the distribution or dissemination of any matter to the pubic *with knowledge* that the matter promotes or expresses hatred towards, serious contempt for, or severe ridicule of, a person or group of persons on the ground of the race of the person or members of the group [my emphasis].

Interpretation of the meaning of the term "public" is derived from Australian and international case law, which determines that any act done otherwise than in a purely domestic setting, and in which it is reasonable to foresee that members of the public could be capable of hearing or seeing the act, would probably be regarded as public. The "potential" of some members of the public to "receive the communication" is important, not whether they actually saw or heard the act.[17] To reiterate, it is

not the actual number of people who hear or see the communication that is significant; rather it is the openness and potential for members of the public 'casually passing by' to be likely to see or hear it that is relevant.[18]

This interpretation renders the "public act" distinction generally unproblematic for the purposes of the discussion here, since it allows for the immunity from regulation of private conversations.

Exemptions

A number of exemptions exist (Section 20C(2)) including fair reporting, material subject to absolute privilege and acts done reasonably and in good faith for academic, artistic, scientific or research purposes, or "for any other purpose in the public interest". In parliamentary debates preceding enactment of the Bill, then NSW Attorney-General John Dowd made the general statement that "legislation against racial vilification must involve a *balancing* of the right to free speech and the right to a dignified and peaceful existence free from racist harassment and vilification" (NSWPDLA, 4 May 1989: 7488) [my emphasis]. He added, the "exceptions have been included in the Bill to achieve a balance between the right to free speech and the right to an existence free from racial vilification and its attendant harms" (NSWPDLA, 4 May 1989: 7490). The idea of "balance" was repeated during parliamentary debate by other members, including Carr and Zammit (NSWPDLA, 4 May 1989: 7921, 7923), and Kaldis and Nile (NSWPDLC, 4 May 1989: 7813, 7833). In a discussion paper prepared for Parliament by Samios prior to the enactment of the legislation, the idea of "balance" was also emphasised, both in the preface and in specific discussion on the exceptions (NSW Government 1988: 1, 3). However, the discussion paper is somewhat vague on the rationale for the extent of the exceptions, noting only that

> the Government is concerned to protect works of art, religious activities and scientific and academic debate and so has included exceptions to cover these and other activities (NSW Government 1988: 3).

In interview, Samios described the rationale for the inclusion of these broad-ranging exemptions as that they were "seen to be virtually motherhood" protections of freedom of expression, implying that they were considered so broadly within the general community to be expressions warranting protection that their exemption from vilification provisions was necessary (Samios 1998). In a 1994 assessment of the legislation it was noted that despite bi-partisan parliamentary support for the Bill, some members of the public had opposed it, worried about the slippery slope potential for the legislation to curb speech which would not warrant censure (Hennessy and Smith 1994: 249). This paper noted that the exceptions "accommodated" these views and that they were "designed to strike a balance between freedom of expression and freedom from racist abuse and hostility" (Hennessy and Smith 1994: 249; 257). It has even been claimed that the public interest exception was necessary because Australia lacks specific constitutional protections of freedom of expression (Hennessy and Smith 1994:257–258).[19] However, there is no concrete evidence in the form of parliamentary debate or transcripts which supports the idea that there is a direct link between the lack of a constitutional free speech protection in Australia and the inclusion of the public interest exception in the legislation (Samios 1998; Dowd 1998; NSW Government 1988; NSWPDLA 1989; NSWP-DLC 1989). Except for very general comments in parliamentary debate, very little concrete evidence exists that the specific terms or breadth of the exemptions were discussed in detail before the racial anti-vilification legislation was enacted in NSW.

Changes to the draft while the legislation was under consideration included raising the standard defining vilification from an action to "promote or express" racial hatred to the more stringent standard of "incitement" (Hennessy and Smith 1994:252). Definitions of the terms "incite", "hatred", "serious contempt" and "severe ridicule" for the purposes of the Act have been developed by ADB and Tribunal deliberations over individual complaints. The ADB's interpretations of the terms were initially drawn from their ordinary meaning in the Macquarie Dictionary. At the first Tribunal hearing into a racial vilification matter, *Harou-Sourdon v TCN Channel Nine Pty Ltd* (1994), the Tribunal concurred with the ADB's interpretations, which were then confirmed in a subsequent homosexual vilification case.[20] In its deliberations over *Harou-Sourdon*, the Tribunal specified that these terms were to be interpreted in accordance with their plain meaning, derived from the Macquarie Concise Dictionary. Hatred was defined as "the feeling of one who hates; intense dislike; detestation". Contempt was defined as the "feeling with which one regards anything considered mean, vile or worthless; the state of being despised; dishonour; disgrace". Ridicule was defined as "words or actions intended to excite contemptuous laughter at a person or thing; derision". Contempt and ridicule were to be read in the context of the intensifying adjectives "serious" and "severe" respectively. As a result, the threshold required for the ADB or the Tribunal to uphold a complaint as harmful, and therefore actionable, is relatively high (and is hereinafter referred to as the "hatred threshold") (see also Hennessy and Smith 1994).

Also, in *Harou-Sourdon*, the Tribunal adopted an objective standard to determine whether an utterance was considered an offence. The test was whether the utterance *could incite an ordinary, reasonable person not immune from susceptibility to incitement nor holding racially prejudicial views, to hatred, serious contempt or severe ridicule* (not that they *had been* so incited). The context of the statement was taken into account in determining the incitement potential, including such factors as the length of the vilifying utterance compared with other utterances, and the tone of the discussion and whether repetition of the vilification occurred.

1989–1998: The problems

In this section, I provide an overview of the operation of the NSW law in practice.[21] The examples I use here reveal weaknesses in the legislation's implementation. I cite typical examples, not exceptional ones. I have provided each case with a title, and a summary of the cases cited is provided in Appendix A.

Complaint procedures — an individual, private resolution to a public problem

The practice at the NSW Anti-Discrimination Board (ADB) is first to determine whether a complaint is actionable, that is whether it falls within the procedural limitations and the statutory hatred threshold described above. Once a complaint is regarded as probably actionable, the statute requires that the ADB contact the respondent (the person alleged to have uttered the vilification) to gather further information. If the complaint warrants action, the ADB then tries to facilitate an agreement between the complainant and the respondent. When the respondent is contacted they are provided with the name and address of the person who made the complaint. All information about complaints, complainants and respondents is statutorily confidential, which means members of the general public do not know when complaints have been lodged or whether complaints have been lodged in regard to certain events, and are not able to be involved in the resolution process. Resolution usually involves seeking an undertaking from the respondent to cease uttering vilifying remarks, and/or the extraction of an apology from the respondent to the complainant. If the respondent refuses to apologise or retract their statement, they can be ordered by the Tribunal to pay a fine.

All vilification, by NSW statutory definition, is a "public act". Some vilification, however, occurs via a medium in which it is possible for greater, rather than lesser, numbers of people to have heard the utterance. If the vilification occurred, for example, in a newspaper column, on radio or in a workplace, resolution may involve the printing of an apology or retraction in the newspaper, the broadcasting of an apology or retraction in the same radio program, or the holding of a workplace seminar to inform staff of the provisions of the *Anti-Discrimination Act NSW (1977)*. For example, a complaint was lodged alleging vilification of Jewish people in a newspaper article. The newspaper subsequently printed another article correcting the errors of the first article, and printed a third article by a Jewish organisation discussing vilification. The newspaper also conducted a workplace seminar with the Federal Race Discrimination Commissioner to explain legal obligations to their staff. In this instance the resolution process generated a discussion within the organisation which had permitted the vilifying statements to be made, in an effort to prevent further occurrences. However, not all complaints of actionable vilification in a broader medium such as a newspaper necessarily result in these resolution procedures being carried out. In some cases, where the vilification has occurred in the hearing of a broader audience, resolution may still occur via a private apology and/or retraction from the respondent to the complainant. The resolution process is, therefore, by and large a private one, despite the legislative provision that actionable vilification must be a "public act".

Some examples help illustrate these points. In Case A, a complaint was lodged against a person with a long history of anti-Semitic vilification in an amateur radio broadcast. Comments made on air included, "I'm not racist, I just hate Jews", "Hitler had the right idea ... the trouble is he missed a few", and a reference to "diseased Jews". The complainant felt that, despite an ADB finding that the vilification was actionable under the hatred threshold,[22] because the respondent was a committed anti-Semite orders to desist would be unlikely to curb the respondent's remarks. Also, since the respondent was poor, the complainant felt that a fine imposed in a Tribunal hearing would be unlikely to be paid. The complainant felt that even if an apology was forced from the respondent, it would be meaningless as s/he would not desist from future acts of vilification. In short, the complainant felt that the individualised and private nature of possible remedies, which required an apology or the payment of a fine by a committed anti-Semite, were of little use. The complainant withdrew.

In another instance, Case B, a complaint was lodged of alleged vilification of Aborigines and Torres Strait Islanders by a well-known public figure with a history of comments prejudicial towards the indigenous community. In this instance, the respondent had described Aboriginal religion as "bizarre", "primitive" and "animalistic", adding that "lots and lots of Aboriginal people are educated enough to understand that". The respondent, when contacted by the ADB for comment, described the remarks as "accurate" and accused the ADB of threatening free speech and of demonstrating a "zeal for social engineering". The complainant, who holds a doctorate, pointed out that s/he disagreed with the respondent's claims and was of the opinion that a private, protracted dispute with the complainant would be of little use in discouraging future, similar utterances. The complaint was withdrawn. Interestingly, the complainant entered into discussions with the President of the ADB, who noted that he was pursuing the production of educative television programs on Aboriginal culture with various media outlets. The complainant felt this broader, educative approach could be beneficial. However, this kind of imaginative and innovative response — the generation of a public television program — was only noted on one complaint file in the ten year period of the study. It was not a regular occurrence, nor was it provided for in the legislation. Furthermore, the complaint file contained no reference to the successful broadcasting of such a program, nor was it possible to find evidence that the issues raised in this complaint were linked in any way with subsequent television programs discussing Aboriginal culture.[23]

In another instance, Case C, a complaint was lodged regarding a flyer distributed in a neighbourhood. Although the ADB found that the flyer racially vilified some residents, they noted that writing directly to the respondent, a committed anti-Asian community group, would be of little use. In this instance, because the complainant was not from the vilified group, no action could be taken and the complaint was declined. This case again raises the problem that the resolution mechanism invoked by the NSW legislation relies on the receptivity of the perpetrator to redress. How does this approach ameliorate the harms of hate speech? What happens to those affected by the utterance? Cases A, B and C demonstrate a serious failing of the NSW legislation, which relies for resolution on the corrigibility of the vilifier. The incorrigibility of the perpetrator ought not to provide a basis for not proceeding against actionable vilification, yet in practice this has occurred.

In some cases, the complainant withdrew their complaint because they did not have the time to pursue it. In other cases, after a period of time the complainant became uncontactable and the file therefore had to be closed, regardless of the merits of the complaint itself. The resolution process is dependent on a complainant being willing to sustain a process that frequently takes 6 months or more. Even if the vilification is actionable under the terms of the legislation, nothing can be done to pursue action if the complainant withdraws from the process. According to anecdotal evidence provided in interview (Williams 1999), withdrawal of some complaints lodged by members of the Aboriginal and Torres Strait Islander communities in particular reflects a difference between community perceptions of the use of the law and statutory limitations on the use of the law. Those community members prepared to lodge complaints were often involved in other community activities as well. This meant they did not always have time to pursue vilification complaints within the time period specified by law, and it was difficult to explain to these communities the importance of statutory requirements. Furthermore, their negative historical experience of dealing with government bodies tended to engender skepticism in the law's ability to deliver benefits to their community.

An example of a complaint that was withdrawn for time reasons, Case D, was a complaint alleging racial vilification in a pamphlet distributed by a minor political party. The pamphlet, *inter alia*, blamed "ethnics" for crime and advocated reduced immigration to Australia. The ADB found the pamphlet did amount to actionable vilification, but the complainant decided not to proceed with the complaint because full-time employment did not leave enough time. The file was therefore closed. An example of a file closed after contact was lost with the complainant is Case E, a complaint about a radio broadcaster who made comments in a talkback program criticising Islamic practices and Muslim people. The ADB found the broadcaster did not make sufficient distinction between the two. On balance, the ADB found the complaint to constitute vilification. When the radio station was contacted for comment, they expressed disagreement with the ADB's finding. Furthermore, the individual broadcaster cited the Australian Prime Minister's general promotion of free speech and criticism of "political correctness" in defence. The ADB attempted to organise a conciliation conference between the parties, but when the complainant did not respond the file was closed and no further action was taken. In Case F, a woman at a service station was the target of the following comments from occupants of another vehicle: "You black slut", "you're nothing but a coon", "I've shot worse coons than you". In this case, the complainant first went to the police who took no action.[24] Then the complainant moved residence and was uncontactable, so the ADB closed their file.[25]

In other cases the complainant withdrew for an unspecified reason or due to fear of reprisals from the respondent, a fear exacerbated by the statutory requirement that complainants must be identified to the respondent by name and address. In one complaint, Case G, a complainant was racially vilified by a service station proprietor. The complaint was withdrawn due to fear by the complainant of violent reprisals from the proprietor, who had threatened the complainant with a crowbar. In Case H, a person of Chinese descent was told, in public, to "go back to China", which led another person in the vicinity to say, "we let you into this country and you destroy it". After receiving threatening phone calls, the complainant withdrew her/his complaint.

Identification of the complainant raises another problem which has been discussed elsewhere (Gelber 2000a). Under the NSW legislation, a complainant must be a member of the allegedly vilified group to be allowed to pursue a complaint (or a "representative body" on behalf of a member of the vilified group). In Case I, a complaint was lodged about poems in a club newsletter vilifying people of Asian descent. The ADB had received previous complaints regarding the same poems, which were considered actionable. However, the complainant was not of Asian descent, so the complaint had to be declined. In Case J, a complaint was lodged regarding a cartoon in an industry magazine which vilified indigenous Australians. However, because the complainant was of Chinese descent, the complaint was not actionable and had to be declined. In Case K a complaint was lodged regarding an edition of an erotic magazine containing pictures of women of Asian descent. The caption on the magazine cover named the edition, "Dirty Orientals Value Pack". Again, because the complainant was not of Asian descent the complaint was inactionable and had to be declined. And in Case L, a complaint was lodged by a community organisation about a booklet distributed to legal studies students in NSW which was critical of immigration by people of Asian descent, and of Aboriginal land rights. The ADB agreed to accept the complainant as a "representative organisation" and purse the complaint, if the organisation could fulfil statutory requirements and provide the names of individuals from each racial group vilified on whose behalf they could lodge the complaint. Because the organisation failed to provide these names, the complaint could not be acted on. The identification by the ADB of both an individual complainant who is willing to take the complaint to resolution over a potentially long period, and the identification of the complainant and the respondent to each other are procedural limitations which appear to circumscribe the legislation's effectiveness. These procedural limitations arise directly from an individualised resolution process, which requires the identification of individuals willing and able to pursue a complaint to finalisation over a significant period of time.

The need to identify an individual respondent raises some other problems. For example, if the name and address of a respondent are unable to be determined, the ADB does not have an individual against whom to pursue a complaint and, if warranted, obtain an apology or retraction. This renders some instances of vilification automatically inactionable. Where vilification happens randomly, for example on the streets, it is often difficult to identify a respondent.

It is probable that these cases would not even be lodged as complaints with the ADB, because if would-be complainants were to ring the ADB for advice they would be told the vilification was inactionable. It is impossible, therefore, to quantify the number of instances in which this might occur. However, the fact that the legislation renders such complaints inactionable by default raises questions about the ability of the statute to respond adequately to the harms of hate speech. Insofar as these harms may occur, they are likely to occur whether or not the vilifier is identifiable. This procedural limitation arises directly from a resolution process dependent on the identification of an individual, against whom an action might be pursued. This also underlines the inadequacy of an individualised resolution process.

A further procedural limitation is the "with knowledge" qualification which applies to the distribution or dissemination of written material within NSW. The NSW legislation states that in order to commit the offence of racial vilification, the distributor must have possessed knowledge that the material promoted or expressed hatred towards, serious contempt for, or severe ridicule of, a person or group of persons on the ground of race. For example, in Case M a complaint was lodged against a fundamentalist Christian group distributing cartoon pamphlets in NSW. In these pamphlets, an Arab man was stereotyped as violent, a child abuser and irrational until he is converted and "finds Jesus". When the ADB wrote to the distributor, they replied that their intention in distributing the pamphlet had been to bring God's love to Muslim people. On this basis, the ADB recommended that the complaint be declined because the pamphlet had not been distributed "with knowledge" that it was racially vilifying, and therefore it did not fall within the legislative definition of a "public act". No further action was able to be taken. This is another example of the resolution mechanism invoked by the NSW legislation relying on the receptivity of the perpetrator to redress. In this instance, the perpetrator must be willing to confess that they knew their expressions constituted vilification. This demonstrates another failing of the NSW legislation, because where vilification has occurred, the harm has been inflicted regardless of whether the utterance was made with or without the knowledge that such harm would occur.

So it seems that cases do exist where a complaint which may constitute actionable vilification on substantive grounds, may be unable to be pursued due to weaknesses in the application of the law. This means that some utterances which inflict the "attendant harms" referred to when the law was introduced are inactionable. The inability of the ADB to pursue action in these cases appears to be inconsistent with the stated objectives of the legislation. These weaknesses of application arise directly from an individualised and private resolution process. Yet this resolution process has been applied to "public acts", acts of hate speech. Furthermore, even where the ADB *is* able to take action against utterances of hate speech, the empirical evidence suggests a disjuncture exists between the utterance of a public act of vilification on the one hand, and the facilitation by the ADB of an individualised and private resolution process on the other. Complaints "successfully" settled in the NSW study[26] tended to result in the facilitation of a private apology or agreement to desist between an individual complainant and respondent, or the payment of a fine by the respondent. This resolution process tends to occur behind closed doors. An exception to this is those complaints successfully lodged against a newspaper, where the outcome includes publication of a subsequent article contradicting the message of the first. Even where a settlement includes a commitment to develop and implement an anti-discrimination policy within an organisation which was the subject of a complaint, this resolution process does not allow for the broader involvement of the victim community. The settlement procedure, therefore, is often private, despite the statutory requirement that a hate speech act be a "public act".

Defining "hate speech"

The empirical data raise yet another question for discussion: the question of defining vilification in a way that is statutorily workable. The NSW statutory definition has been outlined above and is referred to as the "hatred threshold". A number of complaints lodged with the ADB during the ten year period of the study were found not to constitute vilification under the NSW statutory definition, and were declined. For example, in Case N a complaint was lodged by a person of Anglo-Saxon descent, about a mural painted on the wall of a school in an area characterised by a high ethnic mix and with a high population of indigenous Australians. The mural depicted a large Union Jack background, with a soldier of Anglo-Saxon descent standing in front of the flag holding a rifle. In the foreground, a black, manacled arm representing dispossessed indigenous Australians appeared. The mural was intended to convey the history of dispossession and disempowerment of Australian Aborigines. In rejecting this complaint, the ADB advised the complainant that although they might consider the mural offensive, British colonial dispossession and disempowerment of Aboriginal communities were a matter of historical record and their depiction did not amount to vilification. They also stated that the mural contained other positive images reflecting pride in Aboriginality as well as in broader issues related to multiculturalism.

Other complaints which were rejected by the ADB on the ground of not constituting vilification, however, were more difficult cases to assess. For example, in Case O a complaint was lodged regarding a pamphlet distributed by a community-based political organisation. The theme under discussion in the pamphlet was multiculturalism. Headlines included, "Multiculturalism threatens" (alleging that immigration policies permitting entry to people of a variety of ethnic backgrounds threatened social stability in Australia), "a conspiracy of silence" (alleging suppression of the immigration debate), "best migrants murdered" (an argument against abortion), and "the Asian issue" (a reference to alleged "Asian" inter-ethnic rivalries within Australia). The ADB found the material unlikely to pass the hatred threshold and declined it. In Case P, large articles were run in the weekend section of a major newspaper on the issue of immigration. The articles' headlines included: "The hidden costs of immigration" and "Quarter-Asian Australia". The article argued that increasing "Asian" immigration represented a threat to social cohesion and stability in Australia. Graphics accompanying the article included a stylised face, one quarter of which was coloured yellow, an aggressive Oriental dragon, and a scared white cockatoo surrounded by dark and sinister birds. The article argued that "soon", i.e. in 27 years' time,[27] Australia would be one quarter "Asian". This figure was based (as was pointed out in a subsequent letter to the editor by a multicultural expert)[28] both on unreasonably high estimates of immigration rates and on identification as "Asian" of anyone with Asian ancestry. The ADB found the material unlikely to pass the hatred threshold and declined the complaint, noting that even if it were held to pass the hatred threshold it would be likely to be exempt under the "public debate" provision in the legislation. These kinds of complaints raise an interesting question for policy-makers trying to enact legislation designed to ameliorate the harms of hate speech. How is it possible to reach a statutory definition of hate speech which both responds to appropriately harmful hate speech and permits free speech? How is it possible to determine which utterances constitute hate speech and which do not? An answer to this question will also be sought in the chapters which follow.

Conclusion

In this study, I present three empirical problems which warrant examination, in order to determine if it is possible to implement a hate speech policy capable of achieving the aims cited when the legislation was enacted. First, there is the problem of understanding why the legislation has been framed in the way it has, with wide ranging exemptions and with a statutory definition of hate speech which renders many instances of hate speech immune from regulation. Secondly, there is the problem of seeking to explain apparent weaknesses and inconsistencies in the application of the law. Thirdly, there is the problem of searching for a workable statutory definition of hate speech. It is also possible that these problems are not confined to the NSW legislation studied here, but that they apply more broadly to the problem of hate speech internationally. I will make this point more clearly in a later comparative section of the book.

For the moment, I will turn to an investigation of these three empirical problems by locating my argument within the broader context of debates around free speech, speech policy and hate speech. I will do this in the next chapter.

Chapter 2

Expanding speech liberties
A capabilities approach

The limitations of dominant contemporary arguments in defence of free speech when applied to the arena of speech policy have been discussed by other scholars (Schauer 1982; Barendt 1985), and only a brief overview of the relevant critiques is necessary. Below, I will argue that all these arguments suffer from a central weaknesses in terms of their application to free speech policy: they share an emphasis on a conception of free speech policy which posits an absence of restraint on the speech liberty as the central policy goal. This provides the basis for an argument that an alternative conception of speech and speech policy is warranted. I will then examine the question of the kind of liberty speech may be considered to be. Discussing the concept of the speech liberty allows a differentiation to be made between a policy designed to minimise restraint on individuals' exercise of the speech liberty, and a policy designed to ensure participation in the exercise of the speech liberty. I will argue that the integration of capabilities theory into considerations of speech policy invokes a policy oriented to ensuring people are able to participate in speaking. This provides a more effective approach to speech policy, because it means the goals of ensuring free speech and ameliorating the harms of hate speech are not counterposed. Instead, the two goals are viewed as mutually achievable objectives of speech policy.

Flaws in the major arguments in defence of free speech

According to the argument from truth, it is possible and even necessary that discussion of ideas and opinions may result in the acquisition of "truth"[29] in the sense of dissemination of new information and/or knowledge (Schauer 1982: 15). Although this argument has been derived from the work of John Stuart Mill,[30] the argument persists in the contemporary free speech debate. A descendant can be discerned in the concept of a "marketplace of ideas",[31] which holds that a free and open discussion amongst competing ideas and opinions ensures that individuals may choose those ideas which best meet the demands of rigorous contestation and hence are more likely to be true or contain elements of "truth". Jonathan Rauch also argues that the restriction of freedom of thought and expression is inimical to liberal science,[32] which "happily tramples [one's feelings] in the name of finding truth" (1993:19). However, the argument from truth appears vulnerable as a guide to policy-making on speech, because it rests on the assumption that the pursuit of "truth" is the highest good (Schauer 1982:17; Barendt 1985:9) and does not figure in competing goods whose provision might require restrictions or prohibitions on speech (such as commercial confidentiality or defamation). It assumes that "truth" is best capable of emerging under conditions of minimal restraint on speech, an optimistic assumption not borne out by history, because many "truths" may be elusive, in the sense that they are contextual,[33] and because many utterances are not sufficiently coherent to be considered a contribution to the search for "truth" (Barendt 1985:13; 8; 11) (cf. the example cited above of Case F, where an Aboriginal woman was called a "black slut" and "nothing but a coon").

The strongest criticism is that, as a guide to policy-making, it emphasises the importance of the search for "truth" over other, competing, values (which could include the need to protect citizens from harm), thus rendering the argument from truth vulnerable to competing demands when used as a defence for constitutional or legal protections of free speech. The hate speech policy examined in the first chapter attempted to maintain "free speech" conditions by providing exemptions from its applicability. It was difficult to pin down specific justifications for the introduction of these exemptions. In practice, the exemptions are designed to place policy priority on free speech by rendering some allegedly harmful utterances immune. It is possible that these exemptions, then, leave the policy vulnerable to charges that competing demands might be insufficiently met within the terms of the legislation — specifically the demand to ameliorate the harms of hate speech. To the extent that the exemptions may have been justified, even implicitly, according to the argument from truth, this inability to take competing demands into account might suggest that the policy has been poorly framed. Furthermore, the argument from truth implies that ideas which best withstand contestation do so because they elucidate a higher degree of "truth" than those less able to withstand contestation. Yet this is itself contestable. All this renders the argument from truth insufficient as a guide to policy-making on speech

The argument from self-development, or self-fulfillment (Barendt 1985), emphasises that the *process* of engaging in expressive activities is a necessary condition for the cultivation of individuality via self-development (Rees 1985:48; Gray in Mill 1991). Within this argument, as expressed by John Stuart Mill, opinions may only be considered harmful when their expression leads to immediate and causal harm, because of the high regard with which Mill viewed expression (Mill 1991:62). Mill's "harm principle" seems to err towards protecting freedom of expression, when applied to the contemporary problem of vilification, and would be unlikely to allow for the regulation of an expression such as that in Case F ("I've shot worse coons than you") or Case A ("Hitler had the right idea ... trouble is he missed a few"), since in these instances it is unlikely the expression would have led immediately and causally to someone shooting an indigenous person or murdering a Jewish person (although the possibility cannot be ruled out altogether).

Within Mill's argument, the benefits of permitting an expression to be heard are not contingent on content or viewpoint.[34] Mill makes the normative claims that all individuals ought to be engaged in a process of self-development, and that informed and contested speech is vital to this process. Mill does not differentiate, however, between "good" and "bad" or "higher order" and "lower order" speech. That is, Mill does not allow, as do some contemporary speech scholars, for the demarcation of a *sui generis* category of "low value" speech based on the form, content or viewpoint of the speech. The practical implication of this is that Mill's model would not automatically condemn racist speech, for example, as unhelpful in the process of debate and contestation required for self-development. Racist speech, if it were informed and contested, could be capable of contributing to self-development. Lewis calls this Mill's rule of neutralism (1997:3).

The argument from self-development can also be criticised on the grounds that the onus for engaging in and maximising self-development opportunities rests overwhelmingly with the individual, yet not all problems faced by individuals in their self-development are able to be solved by individuals, in isolation. Needs which may be identified as social and which may compete with or even be inimical to individual needs are not taken into account, because they do not figure in the argument. For example, it may be possible to identify the prevention of racist slurs (such as blaming "ethnics" for crime in a pamphlet advocating reduced immigration; Case D in the empirical study) within an entire community as directly conducive to the self-development of the intended victims of those slurs, and indirectly conducive to the self-development of all within the community via the promotion of tolerance.

It has been argued that, despite its flaws of application, the argument from self-development persists for pragmatic reasons. Because free speech is conceived of in negative terms, as a liberty that is enjoyed free from government interference, a free speech policy is maintained by government not restraining individuals (Barendt 1985:15). This makes the implementation of free speech policy relatively easy because government simply has to refrain from intervening in individuals' expressive activities, or in the case of NSW hate speech policy outlined earlier, allow for wide-ranging exemptions to the imposition of restrictions on speech. This negative liberty is counterposed to positive liberties,[35] which require from government a positive intervention in order to provide the facilities or means by which a liberty may be exercised. A contemporary example of the international operationalisation of this distinction is the division between civil and political rights (negative liberties) embodied in the International Covenant on Civil and Political Rights (ICCPR), and social and economic rights (positive liberties) in the International Covenant on Economic, Social and Cultural Rights (ICESCR). The distinction is in many ways unstable, but it is an imperfect tool with a significant history. The idea that free speech, conceived of as a negative liberty has an enforcement "edge" over competing positive liberties is a *practicalities justification* for free speech policy.

The argument from self-fulfillment is consequential, relying on the beneficial outcome to the individual of engaging in speech for its underlying rationale. But does this exhaust the possible grounds upon which speech, as important to the individual, may be assessed? It is possible to discern a discrete claim for the speech liberty, based not on a consequential approach, but instead on a deontological view of the relationship between individuals and freedom of expression. Such a deontological perspective could consist of the normative claim that free speech should be considered to be of intrinsic value to individuals, regardless of any consequences of its holding or its exercise. To the extent that this differentiation is possible, a rights-based argument exists[36] in favour of defending free speech; an individual has a "right" to freedom of speech in the same way s/he has a right to other basic and important liberties such as equality of opportunity and human dignity.

The most influential argument in defence of a free speech right, elements of which I find persuasive, is presented by Ronald Dworkin (1977a),[37] who makes the normative claim that individual rights act as political trumps, meaning that in a situation of competing objectives the rights held by individuals supercede other policy considerations such as general welfare. Individual rights trump utilitarian considerations because a successful claim of a right means it would be wrong for it to be denied an individual, even if it would be in the general interest to do so (1977a: 269). He argues instead for a defence of the speech liberty based on the concept of equality (1977a: 272–278), conceived of as the fundamental and inalienable right to "equal treatment" (1977a: 227).[38] Because Dworkin's concept of liberty is derivative from this equality right, government may be constrained to provide equal distribution of opportunity.

Dworkin posits free speech as an individual and inalienable right. This means that individuals have a right to the important and basic liberty of speech (1977a: 269–270), and any infringement of the right to free speech would risk contravening Dworkin's fundamental concern — that government must provide equal distribution of opportunity to all citizens (1977a: 272–273).[39]

However, if speech is understood as an unassailable right, this implies that the argument from rights provides little internal restraint against absolutist protections of speech, that is a policy framework which provides no justification for government intervention in individuals' right to speak. Applied to laws governing speech, the argument from rights implies a tendency towards absolutism. Indeed, First Amendment jurisprudence in the United States recognises the tendency towards absolute protections of speech, even where the speech under dispute is considered to have been offensive or harmful.[40] (I will examine First Amendment jurisprudence below.) However, no liberal-democratic jurisdictions provide absolutist protections of free speech. Restrictions on free speech rights do exist in liberal democracies. but are more likely to be justified by utilitarian considerations of general welfare than to derive their justification from the argument from rights itself. This is a problem in the application of the argument from rights to speech policy, because the argument requires considerable and constant qualification as a rationale for free speech policy where and when that policy is designed to allow for the restriction of *some* speech. A second weakness of the application of the argument from rights to protections of freedom of expression is its privileging of the rights of the speaker. For if some speech can be said to be offensive, hurtful or harmful,[41] then an emphasis on the rights argument to allow that speech to be expressed privileges some rights over others. Specifically, the rights of the speaker are privileged over the rights of those hearers who may find the speech hurtful or harmful. No consideration is provided within the argument from rights for the impact of speech. Since the argument from rights is deontological in nature, it does not consider the impact of speech or the distribution of the impact of speech (on individual hearers or on individuals affected by others who heard the speech). Dworkin argues that in a society infused with prejudice, preferences will inevitably be saturated with that prejudice (1977a: 237).

In the real world, it is often the case that hurtful speech is directed against those who suffer the effects of prejudice, for example people of colour. The cases cited in the NSW empirical study support this contention, because they demonstrate that it is marginalised and vulnerable social groups (for example indigenous Australians and immigrants of non-Anglo-Saxon descent) who tend to be subjected to racial vilification . To the extent that it can be established that racist prejudice exists, the protection of free speech as a right implies that marginalised, disempowered or oppressed sections of society must bear the burden of those protections, even where and when that burden may be disproportionate. This is noted by Schauer (1992:1355) and Matsuda (1993) and will be discussed in greater detail below. This problem is inherent to deontological claims for speech rights.

Finally, the argument from democracy maintains that effective democracy is dependent on citizens' ability to criticise government, and to develop their capacity for self-determination by participating actively in deliberation over issues. Democracy is defined, for the purposes of the argument here, as a system within which sovereignty, and control of the operation of government, rest with the people (Schauer 1982:36). The argument from democracy has been used as a justification for First Amendment free speech protections in the United States.[42] It was also evident in the reasoning underpinning the finding of an implied constitutional free speech protection on political matters in Australia,[43] where it was argued that guarantees of freedom of expression on political matters necessarily inhere in the practice of an effective representative democracy.

However, a model of majoritarian democracy could be used to support restrictions on speech. For example, a majority of people within a democracy, via a democratic process, could elect to restrict the speech of some members of society (Barendt 1985:21; Schauer 1982:40). Perhaps those with blue eyes.[44] Or a majority of people within a democracy, via a democratic process, could elect to restrict speech about some topics. The majority might regard the restriction of the speech of those with blue eyes or those debating particular topics as an enhancement of democracy (perhaps because all people with blue eyes intended imprisoning all brown-eyed people). In such a case, restriction may be justifiable according to a majoritarian argument from democracy. Dworkin points out that in a society where racism exists, majoritarianism may be flawed by preference formation which is saturated with racist prejudice (1977a:237).[45] This could mean that a speech policy conceived of within the framework of a majoritarian democratic argument could allow expressions of speech which the majority held to be worthy of protection, but limit some speech not so considered — and that these determinations could be made in such a way as to reinforce racist prejudice. This could preclude the expression of anti-racist dissent.

However, when the argument from democracy is based on a *participatory* model, this problem can be overcome. A participatory model of democracy invokes the right for all citizens to be able to participate in democratic debate and dissent, and to pursue self-determination. This includes dissenters, or those who hold unpopular views. This model of participation has been recognised by some speech scholars (e.g. Schauer 1982:41).[46] But even an argument for the defence of free speech which rests on a notion of the importance of speech to participation in democratic decision-making is not necessarily capable of explaining a related, but distinct, attribute. The argument from democracy, even participatory democracy, as a guide to policy-making on speech suffers from being unable to explain *how* participation in the exercise of the speech liberty might be made possible, or even why *encouraging* participation might be legitimate goal of speech policy.

These questions revisit the theme raised earlier, that of the kind of liberty that speech may be conceived to be. A discussion of how it might be possible to ensure people are able to participate in exercising the speech liberty raises questions of whether this is even an appropriate goal for government policy on speech.

The arguments discussed to this point support an assumption that the policy goal of ameliorating harmful speech can be integrated into hate speech policy as a *residual* policy goal. In other words, only the speech that is left after that speech considered necessarily immune from government restraint is removed, remains actionable. This "residualism" raises questions as to a gap between the legislation's stated aim — ameliorating hate speech — and the presumptions underlying its enactment which seek to preserve much speech from a legislative response. Applied to the NSW study, this answers the question of how the NSW legislation in practice adjudicated the competing policy goals of free speech and ameliorating the harms of hate speech. By rendering much speech immune from response, the legislation did not so much integrate these competing policy goals as *counterpose* them. This renders the legislation vulnerable to criticism that it does not sufficiently take the harms of hate speech into account, since it renders some hate speech immune from response. By utilising an alternative conceptual framework for speech policy derived from capabilities theory, it is possible to overcome the weaknesses identified here.

What kind of liberty?

The question of what is an appropriate goal for speech policy is intrinsically linked to assumptions about what constitutes the speech liberty. Since the emergence of contractarian thought in the 17th century, conceptions of liberty have tended to be "negative", conceived of as the absence of constraint (Skinner 1984: 194). I have suggested that the dominant arguments in defence of free speech discussed above inform a concept of speech policy which emphasises the absence of restraint as the paramount policy goal. Within this conceptual framework, the policy goal of rendering speech immune from regulation is then counterposed to the policy goal of ameliorating harmful speech. This emphasis on an absence of restraint epitomises a negative conception of the speech liberty. In some instances, a reliance on a negative conception of the speech liberty is explicit. This is the case, for example, in Mill's defence of the argument from self-development in which he claims that each agent should be left alone to the greatest degree possible to pursue their chosen ends, and that they alone are in a position to choose the ends that will best serve their own good (Hill 1999: 33). A limited concept of negative liberty is also explicit in the practicalities justification for the persistence of the argument from self-development (Barendt 1985: 15), which encourages free speech opportunities, because such policy requires only an absence of restraint. In other arguments a limited concept of negative liberty is *implicit*. This is the case in the argument from truth, for example, whose premise is an absence of restraint on speech in order that "truth" may be sought. Similarly, the argument from self-development is premised on a commitment to freedom from interference in order that individuals may undertake activities conducive to their self-fulfillment. The argument from rights can also be said to be supported by a negative liberty framework, to the extent that an individual's possession of a speech right is premised on an absence of external restriction, impositions or interference with that right. Similarly, to the extent that an ability to participate in democratic processes and decision-making implies freedom from restrictions on those activities essential to that participation, the argument from democracy also appears to rely on a conception of speech as a negative liberty. When a negative conception of liberty is assumed in arguments used to frame speech policy, the policy which results is inevitably conceived of as an absence of restraint on speech. Because the negative conception of liberty is dominant in contemporary liberal democratic orders (Skinner 1984: 194–5), this conception of the purpose and design of speech policy predominates.

Other conceptions of liberty, however, have been elaborated which challenge the dominance of the negative liberty concept and enlarge the conception
of liberty, such as the works of Harrington (1977), Gibbs (1976), Taylor (1979),
Baldwin (1984), Skinner (1984; 1997) and Berlin (1969). (It is an enlarged
conception of liberty which informs capabilities theory, hence its usefulness in
this context.) Charles Taylor, for example, regards freedom as not merely an
"opportunity", but as an "exercise" (cited in Skinner 1984:196). Taylor's
argument is that individuals are free when they are able to exercise certain
capacities, and that they are "not free, or less free, when these capacities are in
some way unfulfilled or blocked" (1979:179). Taylor's concept of liberty
suggests that something more than the absence of restraint might be called for
in devising policy, since not all individuals spontaneously or automatically
participate in the exercise of their capacities. Gibbs argues similarly that
freedom depends on an individual both attaining and being able to enjoy the
goods they have chosen (1976:22). Isaiah Berlin referred to the concept of
"positive" freedom as an "interference" to allow someone to do something. He
compared this to "negative" freedom, an area free from interference (1969:
121–122).[47] A broader, positive, conception of liberty invokes a consideration
of the conditions under which liberty may be exercised. As a guide to policy-
making, it implies more than the absence of restraint.[48] Applied to speech
policy, a positive conception of the speech liberty implies that policy ought to
consider the provision of conditions to ensure participation in speaking. To
conceive of speech as a positive liberty is unusual, but not impossible, and
indeed a positive conception of the speech liberty is not unheard of in the arena
of speech policy. For example, Owen Fiss notes that, historically, libertarian free
speech arguments view the state as an enemy of freedom. They therefore
presume free speech may be attained by the state refraining from interference
(1996:2). He criticises this presumption as misleading, arguing instead in
favour of a democratic theory of speech which incorporates the premise that
fostering full and open debate is a permissible role for the state (1996:17). The
critique raised in this book aims at a deeper and more comprehensive application of the positive liberty concept to speech than that attempted by Fiss (1996).
If government were to be involved in fostering full and open debate, this
implies a thicker conception of free speech than one informed by a limited,
negative conception of the speech liberty. This is because here the government
is being asked to intervene in providing conditions in which the speech liberty
may be undertaken, not simply to refrain from taking action in order that
citizens may individually and spontaneously do so for and by themselves. The

argument that fear of state power is anachronistic is also adopted by Sadurski (1994), who argues that nineteenth century liberals feared the growing and unchecked power of government since that power could be used to disempower minorities. But a century later, he suggests, the state may have a legitimate role to play in protecting minorities against majoritarian oppression.

When we apply this framework to speech, it raises new possibilities for speech policy. A positive conception of the speech liberty could invoke designing policy in such a way as to *enhance* debate, which would enhance participation in the speech liberty. In this way, the conception of the purpose of speech policy moves from restraining government from intervening, to invoking government action to enhance participation in the exercise of the speech liberty. In this way, the central question when developing speech policy undergoes a shift from consideration of *whether* government should intervene in the speech of citizens, to *under what conditions* and *in what form* government might intervene to assist the exercise of the speech liberty. The former question presumes a restrictive or prohibitive form of intervention, and implies a conception of speech as a negative liberty. The latter question allows for the possibility of an intervention that may enhance the exercise of the speech liberty. This possibility demands a further conceptual shift. If speech is able to be conceived of as a positive liberty, it is not necessarily free speech which ought to be the concern of policy makers. Instead, the maintenance of appropriate conditions conducive to the *exercise* of the speech liberty becomes important. These conditions would include, but not be limited to, permitting free speech. Conditions conducive to the exercise of the liberty of speech would also include maximisation of *participatory* speech conditions. At this point the integration of a capabilities theory framework into considerations of speech policy becomes salient, because capabilities theory provides a conceptually more satisfying framework within which to develop speech policy

A capabilities approach to speech policy

Capabilities theory, elaborated by Nussbaum (1990; 1993a; 1993b) and Sen (1993a; 1990), is an Aristotelian theory of ethics within which central human capabilities are posited as requisite for the pursuit of an objective human good (also called human flourishing). Aristotle argued that a well-ordered polity was one in which political planners ensured the provision of the conditions within which human flourishing is made possible. Nussbaum revives Aristotle's notion of the "excellent lawgiver", whose job it is to ensure that every individual is able to enjoy and engage in activities conducive to human flourishing:

> It is the job of the excellent lawgiver to consider, concerning a city and a class of human beings (*genos anthrōpōn*) and every other association, how they will partake in the flourishing living (*eudaimonia*) that is possible for them. (Nussbaum 1988:147, citing Aristotle, *Politics*, 1325a7ff).

The specific means by which this becomes possible involve making available to all citizens the concrete circumstances within which they may choose good human functionings, within which they may become sufficiently capable of choosing to live and function well. To understand the task of a political arrangement, therefore, it is necessary first to understand what good human functioning might be, because the political arrangement is defined in terms of achieving those functionings (Nussbaum 1990:203, 208).

Before discussing what these functionings might be, it is important to note that Nussbaum defends the universality of her theory of ethics against theorists who reject the possibility of rationally justifying transcultural norms with universalist claims (e.g. MacIntyre 1981). Her defence rests on the objectivity of an Aristotelian theory of ethics, which is located in its reference to "features of humanness that lie beneath all local tradition" (1993a:243). Nussbaum's theory defends a "thick, vague conception of the good" (1990:205, 217) as one which (a) provides a comprehensive conception of good human functioning ("thick"), but (b) at a high level of generality ("vague"). Thus, her conception provides for the development of policy objectives which provide for the capability of functioning in certain ways that are intrinsic to a good human life, but which yet allows that individuals may make informed choices for themselves about the ways in which they might function (Nussbaum 1990:214).[49] This means the Aristotelian conception of the role of social policy-makers does not "aim at producing people who function in certain ways"; rather it aims at "producing people *capable* of functioning" in certain ways, should they choose to do so (Nussbaum 1990:214). At the same time as Nussbaum's conception of the good is both thick and vague, it is also "broad" and "deep". This means her conception of the task of political arrangement is concerned with each and every member of the polity ("broad") and not just with the provision of resources such as money or land but with all the functionings that constitute a good human life ("deep") (1990:209). This enables her to overcome liberal objections to the notion of a list of human functionings as "paternalistic" or necessarily biased, since the list is both "thick" — dealing with all areas of human life

— and at the same time "vague" — providing an "outline sketch" of the good life without being prescriptive (Nussbaum 1990: 217).

Here, Nussbaum's theory is counterposed to both liberal and utilitarian arguments concerning the role of government, and it can be demonstrated that capabilities theory is able to incorporate a thick account of liberty. Liberal arguments concerning the role of a political arrangement tend to define good in terms of wealth (or "opulence", to use Nussbaum's term), and the task of government therefore as maximising the total wealth available. In crude versions of this argument, such as the ranking of nations according to GDP, no account is taken of the distribution of wealth within a nation, or how that wealth is used to impact on the quality of life of its constituents (Nussbaum 1990: 209). Utilitarian arguments about the task of political arrangement are also criticised by Nussbaum. That is, when decisions about the correct task of a political arrangement rely upon the satisfaction of individuals' desires or preferences, they are flawed by the malleability and unreliability of preferences. As noted earlier, Dworkin argues that in an environment saturated with prejudice, individuals' preferences will be affected by that prejudice and will therefore not be "ideal". Nussbaum makes a similar argument — that humans tend to adapt their preferences to prevailing circumstances and therefore may circumscribe their preferences unnecessarily, and also many people are not aware of the alternatives available to them. Preference-based decision making, therefore, is likely to shore up the status quo (Nussbaum 1990: 213), rather than to deliver change essential to improving quality of life. Capabilities theory, on the other hand, assesses resources, such as wealth, according to what they can do for human beings, as a tool rather than as an end in themselves. Nussbaum argues that even in liberal accounts which take some notice of the question of distribution (e.g. Dworkin 1981, 1985; Rawls 1971), the emphasis on a maximisation of those resources still blinds their theories to an adequate account of what those resources might do for human functioning (Nussbaum 1990: 209–211). For example, in some cases it may well be the case that more wealth is not better but in fact could have a negative impact on the quality of life of individuals, by encouraging excessive competitiveness or by being a distraction from other pursuits such as learning. Nussbaum's critique of liberal approaches to the task of political arrangement can be applied to speech policy. Her critique lends weight to the suggestion that the dominant free speech arguments discussed earlier in this chapter imply the policy goal of maximising speech (as a resource), without taking full consideration of whether people are able to engage in expressive activity, or what their ability or inability to speak might mean for their ability to live fully human lives. Her critique places this suggestion within a framework of a more general critique of liberalism and utilitarianism as guides to policy-making. If liberalism and utilitarianism demonstrate this general weakness of application to social policy, a suggestion that they also demonstrate weaknesses of application to speech policy carries greater weight.[50]

So, what are the "good human functionings" that it is the task of a political arrangement to make available? Nussbaum seeks to provide a comprehensive conception of good human functioning by identifying spheres of human life within which all people must make choices as to how to live (1990:219–223). These spheres of human functioning are derived from the "constitutive circumstances" of being human, the "commonness" of human experience across time and place (1990:217). The spheres of functioning within which people must make decisions, the things that make people human and form a common conception of a "human life", include mortality; the human body (including hunger, thirst, shelter, sexual desire, mobility); capacity for pleasure and pain; cognitive capability such as perceiving, imagining, thinking; early infant development; practical reason (in the sense of planning and managing one's own life and being capable of choosing and evaluating decisions about one's life); affiliation with other human beings; relatedness to other species and nature; humour and play; and separateness (1990:219–224; 1993a:263–265). Nussbaum argues that in all these spheres, humans must make decisions, they must choose how to function. To be denied the ability even to function in any of these spheres would mean in some way to deny a person's humanness, to deny them a full human life.

To each of these spheres corresponds a human "capability", the means by which a human being may make choices as to how to function within these spheres (1990:225). The capabilities which correspond to each of these spheres of human functioning are unsurprising. They include being able to live to the end of a complete human life; being able to have good health, nourishment, sexual satisfaction and being able to move about; being able to avoid unnecessary pain and to feel pleasure; being able to use one's senses, to imagine, to think, to reason; being able to form relationships, to love, to grieve, to feel gratitude; being able to form a "conception of the good" and be involved in planning one's life accordingly; being able to live with other people and with respect for nature; being able to laugh; and being able to live one's own life (Nussbaum 1990:225). These are basic capabilities, and they seem somewhat irrefutable in the sense that they appear central to a conception of what it means to be fully human.[51]

It has been noted that in the Aristotelian model, it is the role of the excellent lawgiver to ensure the provision of adequate institutional, material and educational support to make these capabilities possible for each individual to achieve. Nussbaum provides further assistance in identifying how this goal might be attained. She argues a "special" case of "interpenetration" of the human functionings of "practical reason" and "affiliation". These two capabilities distinguish humans from other animals and are both "ubiquitous" (they infuse all other capabilities) and "architectonic" (they provide a plan within which other functions may be realised) (1990:226–277). Practical reason is the function of deliberative and collective planning and managing of one's life circumstances. Nussbaum argues that a human life involves engaging in these functionings in a manner which informs and directs all the other capabilities, because humans are social beings who plan, manage and organise their lives in a manner distinguishable from all other animals. It is demonstrably the case that human beings have shaped the natural environment and developed complex social structures in a unique manner.

In light of this, it is highly likely speech could be regarded as central to a number of human capabilities, able to contribute to or detract from a good human life in various ways. Engagement in the functionings of practical reason and affiliation requires possession of the following capabilities, derived from Nussbaum's list above:[52] being able to imagine and to think; being able to form a "conception of the good" and to engage in "critical reflection" about the planning of one's life; being able to live for and to others, to recognise and show concern for others and to engage in social interaction (1990:225). Speech is clearly an important component of the realisation of all these capabilities. Participation in expression as a means of communicating ideas, knowledge and opinions is an activity central to human development. Here, a link may be made between capabilities theory and the argument from self-development as a defence of free speech, to the extent that both emphasise the importance of engaging in expressive activity for individual self-development.[53] There can be little doubt that engaging in speech assists in human development in almost innumerable ways. In cases where that expression is not via a spoken language, for example because a person is deaf or mute, other means of expression can be utilised in order that learning, engaging with others, a sense of self, and other cognitive abilities are developed. The speech liberty, then, appears crucial to the functionings of practical reason and affiliation, and also crucial to the capabilities of being able to imagine, think, reflect, plan and engage with others. Speech is therefore central to living a distinctively human life, and a speech policy commensurate with this understanding would prioritise making the exercise of the speech liberty available to all.

Furthermore, participation in expressive activity appears to apply to the development of both "internal" and "external" capabilities. "Internal" capabilities are traits of the person, of intellect, character and body, that enable a person to choose to function well, and which are developed by education in both youth and adulthood (Nussbaum 1988:160–161). However, a person may be in possession of internal capabilities, but externally constrained from choosing to function well. Therefore "external capabilities" are also important. They provide an individual with the "scope" to turn their internal capabilities into action, and include conditions which would not inhibit or prevent individuals from choosing to function well (Nussbaum 1988:162–164). Nussbaum notes this formulation of the definition of external capabilities is "negative" in the sense that it speaks of restraint from choosing rather than empowerment to choose (1988:164).[54] (This idea of an absence of restraint from choosing to function well is revisited later in the argument in the context of Habermas' ideal speech situation, which requires an absence of restraint from choosing to speak.) Nevertheless, this does not circumscribe her account of the goal of social policy and limit it to a negative conception of liberties, because the "total task" remains inclusive and holistic. It is to train and maintain internal capabilities, and simultaneously "create and preserve" the external circumstances in which developed capabilities can "become active" (Nussbaum 1988:164). Expressive activity would appear to be important both to internal and external capabilities. The role of speech in individual development appears more closely related to internal capabilities, because it concerns individuals' development of intellect and character.

The recognition of the dimension of external capabilities adds a depth to a consideration of the role of speech in people's lives which is absent from the four other arguments discussed earlier. By applying a capabilities theory analysis to an analysis of the role of speech in people's lives, the importance of speech to the development of human capabilities has been demonstrated. At the same time, a consideration of harmful speech has been integrated into the argument via the dimension of external capabilities. If it can be suggested that some speech is harmful in the sense that it inhibits or prevents others from speaking (and this question will be investigated later), then it becomes possible to assess some speech as counter-conducive to the development, maintenance and exercise of external, as well as internal capabilities. And if some speech is counter-conducive to the development, maintenance and exercise of individual capabilities, this would suggest the appropriateness of a response engineered to make the development of those capabilities possible.

I argue, therefore, that capabilities theory is able to integrate the two, previously counterposed, goals of speech policy. The goal of allowing free speech and the goal of ameliorating the harms of hate speech may both be considered when devising speech policy. Furthermore, they may both be ameliorated via the same mechanism — the provision of assistance to those whose ability to speak may be hindered by the speech of others.

The central role of speech in the development of human capabilities might lead an observer to conclude that virtually any speech that reflects a deliberative, imaginative or affiliative process of engagement is relevant to the development of individual capabilities. If this were the case, at first sight it would seem that capabilities theory implies that virtually all speech should be protected by a free speech principle. Indeed, Sunstein raises the question of whether an application of "contemporary ... Aristotelianism" (1993b: 248) to speech policy might imply that virtually all speech should be protected, since it reflects processes of deliberation and expression relevant to the development of individual capabilities. But to arrive at such a position is questionable in light of the differentiation between internal and external capabilities. Because insofar as the argument can be sustained that some speech might inhibit the development of and/or the ability to choose to exercise capabilities by others, that speech can be identified as counter-conducive to the development of some individuals' capabilities.

As noted above, Nussbaum discusses the sphere of separateness to which the capability of being able to live one's own life corresponds. She later expands this sphere into two spheres. The first is that of separateness, in the sense that each human being proceeds on their own path through the world. "We have no difficulty figuring out where one begins and the other ends" (1990: 223). The sphere of "strong separateness" invokes a sense of the context in which each individual lives their own life, including their history, friendships and location. This is a separateness of context. Although Nussbaum notes that the limits of these spheres are contestable, she argues that the spheres nevertheless invoke the need for privacy. She notes further that the Athenian interpretation of the content of this sphere included "almost all speech" and above all "political speech" (1990: 239). However, it has been suggested here that speech could be conceived of in terms of the role it is able to play in assisting the development of capabilities to choose a "good" human life. Nussbaum also emphasises that an Aristotelian approach is one which must be open to the possibility of change, one which does not "doggedly defend the status quo" (1986:371). On the contrary, she argues, laws should be revisable (1993a:249) because meeting human needs requires not always or necessarily conforming with the past, but developing an account of the good. When it has been agreed that change is good, it should be possible to change laws. It is possible, then, that if some speech is counter-conducive to the development and exercise of human capabilities in some people, then the development of an appropriate response within a capabilities framework appears justifiable. An appropriate response could seek to counteract the inhibiting effects of some people's speech, by seeking to maximise the benefits of engaging in speech activities. This role could include the provision of conditions to assist the targets of hate speech to participate in exercising the speech liberty, by generating a response to the hate speech.

Bearing in mind that it is the task of Aristotelian politics to ensure the provision of adequate institutional, material and educational support to make the central human capabilities achievable, Nussbaum describes the aim of social policy as a kind of "institutional" (as opposed to "residual") welfarism (1990: 228). This means that social policy ought not be designed as a safety net, to catch only those who fail to do well without institutional, material and educational support. Instead, social policy ought to be designed comprehensively, for all citizens in all the spheres of human functioning. Nussbaum draws an analogy with Aristotle's common meal plan, a plan designed not simply to assist those who could not otherwise afford to eat, but as a subsidised common meal program for all citizens. This plan was designed to ensure no citizen ever need reach a state of not being able to afford to eat; it was not designed to subsidise only those who could not afford to eat (1990:228). So a capabilities-oriented approach to social policy ought to be designed to provide adequate support to enable citizens to move, given available resources, across a "threshold" into possession of the capabilities to choose to function well (Nussbaum 1990:229). Maintaining this aim means that the focus of policy is on moving as many citizens as possible across the threshold of capabilities, and not on further enhancing the opportunities of those citizens who have already crossed it. So, a necessary and sufficient condition of benefitting from an Aristotelian social policy is that a person possesses a less developed capability to perform a functioning, a capability that would be able to be developed given appropriate material and social circumstances. On the other hand, once a person has reached a level of capabilities that makes them able to choose well, they are by definition in possession of capabilities which will enable them to continue to make choices and exercise capabilities in order to plan and manage their own lives in pursuit of their own conception of the good, and in affiliation with others (Nussbaum 1990:229). Therefore, the goal of an Aristotelian policy is not just to "spread some goods around", but to produce capabilities. Distribution must be adjusted to each person's current requirements (Nussbaum 1988:168–169).

The question of the goal of an Aristotelian policy is important, because it enables an answer to be reached to the question of who might be able to benefit from a capabilities-oriented speech policy, designed to provide assistance to develop the capabilities of those whose ability to speak may have been inhibited by the speech of others. I will return to this question in greater depth in the final chapter. For the moment, it is important to recognise that the framework elaborated by Nussbaum provides a justification for the development of an institutional welfarism which could provide assistance to citizens to speak, where and when those citizens possesses a less developed internal or external capability to perform a functioning, a capability that would be able to be developed given appropriate material and social circumstances.

In summary, capabilities theory provides a superior framework within which to develop speech policy for four reasons. First, capabilities theory provides a holistic approach to the development of social policy, an approach which seeks to provide individuals with the institutional, material and educational support to enable them to become capable of choosing to function well. This approach therefore appears capable of adjudicating competing demands, in a way that some of the other arguments discussed above do not. Competing policy demands are judged by examining whether they will assist in the development of capabilities in individuals who do not yet possess them. Secondly, a capabilities theory framework is able to integrate an argument concerning allegedly "harmful" speech into considerations of policy-making, to the extent that it is possible to establish that "harmful" speech inhibits some individuals from participating in expressive activity, and thereby developing their internal and external capabilities. Thirdly, capabilities theory seeks to move as many people as possible across a threshold of capabilities. It therefore provides a framework within which it is possible to justify a policy which provides assistance to those who do not yet possess capabilities, in the context of an overall goal of providing all citizens with equal opportunity to develop their capabilities. Fourthly, capabilities theory is able to incorporate considerations of providing the means for participating in the exercise of the speech liberty into policy-making. This overcomes a historical presumption against government intervention in the speech liberty as a policy goal. The policy goal is posited as ensuring that as many people as possible are able to participate in expressive activity, which implies that where some people are not able to participate in expressive activity, a role exists for the excellent lawgiver in making participation in the speech liberty possible. The policy goal of a capabilities-oriented speech policy, therefore, is *engagement* and *participation* in expressive activity, not restriction or punishment of aberrant speech. Historically, aberrant speech has been dealt with in punitive or restrictive ways: by the imposition of fines or jail terms, or censorship of some kind. A policy designed to deal with aberrant speech by providing assistance to *respond* to it stands in stark contrast to these policy approaches. It aims to *expand* human capabilities, not to contract them.

With this understanding of the *aim* of an Aristotelian social policy (institutional welfarism) and the *means* of achieving it (institutional, material and educational support), a consideration of what speech might be capable of doing becomes important. Because if the argument that some speech may be counter-conducive to the development and exercise of capabilities can be sustained, then not all speech is necessarily conducive to the development of individual capabilities. Considering speech within a capabilities framework does not generate a necessary argument for the immunisation of all speech from an institutional response. If some speech is counter-conducive to the development of other individuals' capabilities, this suggests some speech is counter-conducive to achieving the *aim* of an Aristotelian social policy.

The conclusion that the policy goal of a capabilities-oriented speech policy could be engagement and participation in expressive activity, not restriction or punishment of aberrant speech, relies on an as-yet untested premise: the premise that hate speech might be capable of causing harms, and specifically that it might be capable of causing the harm of inhibiting its victims' ability to speak. Inhibiting some people's ability to speak inhibits them from developing and exercising their individual capabilities, and therefore justifies a policy response. I will unpack the premise that some speech might be capable of inhibiting or preventing others from engaging in expressive activity in the next chapter.

CHAPTER 3

Speech as conduct

Is some speech capable of inhibiting or preventing others from engaging in expressive activity? If so, how? In this chapter, I will analyse conceptions of "speech" within the framework of examining speech-act theory, particularly the work of J. L. Austin's and Jürgen Habermas' theory of communicative action.[55] I will suggest that hate speech may be conceived of as a kind of conduct, and that the maintenance of a speech-conduct distinction within speech policy is challengeable. I advocate the integration of speech-act theory into considerations of speech policy, in order that speech may be conceived of as a type of conduct. Although it could be argued that this conception of speech renders expressive activity overly vulnerable to punitive and/or restrictive regulation, I will argue that locating speech policy within a capabilities-oriented approach overcomes this difficulty.

Thinking about what speech *is* raises the central question of whether, and how, speech may be differentiated from "acts".[56] Is speech a "special activity", more akin to the process of thought than to actions? To answer this requires an investigation, first of the philosophical origins of a conceptual speech-conduct dichotomy. Then, I will elaborate Austin's critique of the performative-constative distinction and canvas potential applications of this distinction in speech policy. This will include examining Austin's alternative distinction between locutionary, illocutionary and perlocutionary speech-acts noting that Austin himself acknowledged the difficulty of operationalising a differentiation between speech-acts within this tripartite model, due to overlapping between the categories. As a more successful means of developing a framework within which to assess specific types of speech-acts, I will then elaborate a validity claims analysis derived from Habermas' theory of communicative action. I will suggest that a combination of elements from both these theorists allows the development of a framework within which it becomes possible to assess both the meaning and the impact of an utterance. This framework permits a detailed analysis of speech-acts to take place, within which it might be possible to differentiate whether some types of speech-acts (hate-speech-acts) are particularly harmful, and in what way.

A speech-conduct dichotomy

Historically in free speech scholarship, a sharp distinction has been made between speech, or expressive activity, on the one hand, and overt acts on the other.[57] A speech-conduct distinction is implicit in the free speech principle — the idea that speech ought to be accorded "special" (i.e. different from other human activities) immunity from government intervention (Barendt 1985:1; Schauer 1982:xi). Bracken argues that the philosophical foundations of the free speech principle lie in Cartesian philosophy,[58] which rests on a mind/body dualism — the idea that the mind and the body are two very different substances (Bracken 1994:3), that there is a "vast difference" between them (1966:99). Applying this philosophy to the realm of speech enables speech to be conceived of as integral to the mind, and discrete from acts which are integral to the body (Bracken 1994:xi). According to this argument, speech is integral to the mind and the mechanics which are capable of explaining bodily motions are incapable of explaining the "creative aspect of language use" (Chomsky 1968:6), the human ability to develop new thoughts and create new meanings within the framework of already instituted and constituted patterns of speech. This aspect of language use implies a discrete world of the mind which cannot be explained in the same terms as the body. Applying this conception to speech places speech within the province of mental privacy, and thus provides a strong foundation for protecting speech from undue interference or restraint (Bracken 1994:4).

It is possible that the distinction between speech and action arises from a Cartesian understanding of the human condition. Cartesian philosophy was influential in the 17th century, and was radically challenged in the 18th century (Bracken 1994:11) and then the 19th century by scholars including Herder, Hegel, Marx and Darwin, who emphasised the historical, social and cultural influences on consciousness (Habermas 1984:viii). Accompanying developments in empiricist theories of human consciousness was a linguistic shift. The term "speech" began to be replaced with the term "expression", indicating the inclusion of non-verbal expressive activities within the conception of communicative activities (Bracken 1994:xi-xii).

Some dualist philosophical conceptions of speech have survived these critiques and endure, indeed dominate, in contemporary contributions to the debate around speech policy. This manifests itself in arguments including that speech is not a form of action, and it cannot coerce (Bracken 1994:8), that the maintenance of free speech is "only coherent to the extent that speech can be distinguished from other areas of human conduct and activity" (Barendt 1985:6), and that to equate the uttering of offensive words with committing an act of violence would be "falsely and mischievously conflating ideological dissidence with overt acts" (1994:51). United States First Amendment jurisprudence, although it shows evidence that a variety of expressive activities have been conceived of as "speech", has also tended to uphold the idea that expressive activity can only be considered to have occasioned harm, and therefore be considered a harmful act, when the expressive activity under consideration invokes a discrete and subsequent danger of "some imminent, non-rebuttable, and very grave secular harm" (Richards 1994:40).[59] In an important US free speech Supreme Court judgement, Justice Black noted that the First Amendment protected speech (or expressive activity) absolutely and conduct not at all (Schauer 1993:833).[60] So how sustainable is the speech-conduct dichotomy?

Performatives and Constatives

J. L. Austin, in his important work *How to Do Things with Words* (1975), was critical of the fact that "for too long" it had been philosophers' assumption that a statement either describes something or states facts (1975:1). He analysed the possibility that descriptive statements often include words which indicate that more is being undertaken than simply description. In exploring what it is we do when we speak,[61] Austin questioned the usefulness of the performative-constative distinction as a distinction between "doing" and "saying". Performatives consist of sentences in which saying something also constituted doing it (1975:5). For example, to say "I do" in a marriage ceremony is to undertake the act of marrying another person. Similarly, uttering the statements, "I name this ship", "I give and bequeath" and "I bet" is not to describe naming a ship or bequeathing one's estate or making a bet, but actually to do these things. The performative utterance is a necessary, but insufficient, condition for the act to conclude, since other requirements must also be met. Usually the performative is accompanied by another act altogether, such as the placing of a ring on another person's finger or the breaking of a bottle on a ship's bow. The circumstances under which the performative takes place must be appropriate to the act taking place or the act does not succeed. When a performative has failed the result is usually qualitatively different from that intended. For example, if someone says "I do" in a marriage ceremony and they are attempting to marry a dog, or if it is discovered that they have previously been married, the performative utterance does not succeed in achieving its aim. In a Hollywood movie, the female lead declares "I'm a federal marshall and you're under arrest" to two men in the process of abducting her.[62] The immediate result is hilarity, not incarceration. Austin describes the failure of a performative in this manner as unhappy, or infelicitous (1975: 14). Performatives, according to the logic of the constative-performative dichotomy, are not "true" or "false" in the sense that descriptive statements may be understood to be "true" or "false". A performative may be happy, which means the intended act has been carried out successfully; or it may be unhappy, which means the act "misfired" and did not take effect, or the carrying out of the act was an abuse of procedure (such as promising something one has no means of providing) (Austin 1975: 12–24). In this context, it is interesting to consider whether expressions such as "You're nothing but a coon" (Case F), describing Aboriginal religion as "bizarre" and "primitive" (Case B), or calling Jewish people "diseased" (Case A) would qualify as performatives. The answer is unclear.

Constatives, as opposed to performatives, are "sayings", descriptive statements. Would the utterances derived from the NSW empirical study be classifiable as just "descriptive statements"? According to the logic of the performative-constative dichotomy, descriptive statements may be "true" or "false", a matter which can be verified by other means. But here a problem is developing, since the happy-unhappy qualification of performatives and the true-false qualification of constatives do not withstand scrutiny. Austin demonstrates, in a sophisticated argument, that for many performatives to be happy, certain statements also have to be true (1975: 45). For example, if a person says, "I promise to give you this car" they must possess the rights to transfer ownership of the car. Whether or not they possess those rights is demonstrably true or false. Thus, some performatives may need to consider truth or falsity. Similarly and conversely, some descriptive statements may need to consider happiness and unhappiness, in the sense that considerations of success or failure may be applied to the speaker's achievement of agreement on his or her meaning (Austin 1975: 55). So the differentiation between performatives and constatives is not clearly definable. For these reasons, Austin argues that the performative-constative distinction is not a useful way of understanding the meaning of speech. A dualism between utterances which only "say" something and others which "do" something is unsustainable. The cases described in the empirical study in the first chapter also seem difficult to categorise as either performatives or constatives.

Austin argues that performative and constative elements of speech may be assimilated. To this end, he advocates consideration of the entire situation within which a statement is uttered in order to understand its meaning. This entails a consideration of utterances as "speech-acts". Searle describes Austin's "discovery" that statements are speech-acts as one of his "most important" (1973:157). Austin describes it as a "revolution in philosophy" (1975:3). He concludes,

> in order to explain what can go wrong with statements we cannot just concentrate on the proposition involved … we must consider the total situation in which the utterance is issued — the total speech-act … Thus we are assimilating the supposed constative utterance to the performative. (1975:52)

Austin made some proposals for alternative ways of differentiating what it is we do when we speak. But before considering these it is useful to look at the extent to which contemporary speech *policy* might be perceived to rely on a performative-constative theoretical distinction. This is important, because if this distinction is unstable, yet policy relies on it, the policy-making can be critiqued as resting on potentially unstable philosophical ground.[63]

Policy applications of the performative-constative distinction

Contemporary liberal-democratic legal regimes do not provide absolutist protections of free speech. A number of restrictions on speech exist including compensation for defamation, protection of commercial confidentiality, restrictions on the publication of matters of national security and obscenities, and abuses of privacy. Is it possible that the differentiation between those utterances subject to regulation and those utterances free from regulation may be explained through the performative-constative distinction?

It could be suggested that speech which conforms to the "performative" is, generally speaking, more easily subject to regulation than speech which conforms to the "constative" type. For example, the act of saying "I do" in a marriage ceremony is legally regulated. The performative is only considered to have been happy, i.e. successfully carried out, when the appropriate circumstances apply to its enactment. Regulations apply to the determination of these circumstances, including who may perform the ceremony, the gender of the two persons wishing to marry, their familial relationship, and their status as not already married. These circumstances are statutorily regulated. Furthermore, when the appropriate circumstances are satisfied, the act of saying "I do" becomes legally binding and has legal consequences which are also regulated via divorce statutes, family court provisions and taxation arrangements, for example. It is also possible to construe the offence of defamation as a performative utterance, since in making a defamatory statement a speaker is considered to have done more than state (true or false) facts about a person. It is considered that the speaker injured another's reputation — that is, caused harm to their reputation which could unduly affect the conduct of their life in future. This is what justifies a claim for damages. The upholding of an offence of defamation, an individual's ability to seek damages, and the level of allowable damages are statutorily regulated. Similarly, commercial speech in many liberal-democracies is subject to regulation. Commercial speech is restricted to protect confidentiality. The assumption behind the regulation of commercial speech may be that to permit such speech would not just be to allow statements of description of the operations or initiatives of a company, but in doing so to diminish that company's potential revenue from that operation or initiative by permitting its competitors to become aware of its achievements. Since the statements describing a company's achievements to its competitors have these effects, they become subject to restriction. To contravene confidentiality regulations means to become subject to further regulations in the form of compensation or apologies. Similar arguments can be made for other instances of utterances subject to regulation, including the hate speech policy described in the first chapter. In that policy, utterances which incite "hatred", "serious contempt" or "severe ridicule" are subject to regulation. It may be interpreted that the regulation is intended to curb not the statement *per se*, but the concomitant activity which the statement necessarily *does* in being uttered in its context. So, it is the performative component of the utterance that is subject to regulation.

On the other hand, speech which is conceived of as simply an expression of opinion may be interpreted as conforming to the constative type. The expression of opinion, dissent or criticism has historically been accorded protection from regulation. The regulation of performative speech and the protection of constative speech from regulation may be seen, in the context of this discussion, as not accidental. Perhaps the different regulatory approaches result from the adoption and implementation within liberal-democratic policy regimes of a reliance on a speech-act dichotomy, where "speech" conforms to the constative and "act" conforms to the performative. The interpreting of speech, in the sense of the communication and exchange of ideas, as constative[64] helps provide a theoretical and philosophical justification for its immunity from regulation.

But if it is possible, as Austin claims, that the performative-constative distinction is unstable, this has considerable repercussions for speech policy. If the performative-constative distinction is not considered stable, the idea that some utterances involve the performance of some act and other utterances do not involve the performance of some act is subject to challenge. If this is the case, it suggests a different justification for the immunity of some speech from regulation should be sought. Here, then, I will return to Austin's development of speech-act theory, only the first stage of which has thus far been discussed. Once Austin argued that the performative-constative distinction may be unstable, he proceeded to develop an alternative model for understanding what it is one does when one speaks. This alternative model will now be explored, for the potentialities it offers in understanding what it is one *does* when one speaks.

The illocutionary possibilities of speech

Once Austin had demonstrated that descriptive utterances, or statements, as much constituted the performance of an act themselves as utterances perceived as performative (Searle 1973: 142), he then sought to develop an alternative classification, not between "speech" and "act" or "constative" and "performative", but within the general category of "speech-acts".[65] Austin suggested that when an utterance is made, the speaker performs a "locutionary" act, an act of saying something. A locutionary act is defined as uttering a sentence with a certain meaning (Austin 1975: 109). In the act of speaking, when something is said, a locutionary act is performed. Austin's second type of speech-act is the "illocutionary" (Austin 1975: 94–101). When an act is performed *in* the saying of an utterance, a speaker performs an illocutionary act. For example, if someone shouts "fire" and, by making that utterance, warns people in a building that there is in fact a fire and by implication suggests that they exit the building, they have performed an illocutionary act. If they shouted "fire" and, by making that utterance, caused people in a building to fear that a fire existed even though none did, an illocutionary act may still be considered to have been performed. The illocution that has been performed is different from that performed in the first example. In the first example, the illocutionary act was a warning, and advice to act. In the second example, the illocutionary act was a joke at the expense of those whose anxiety levels were raised. Similarly, when someone is targetted with the comment, "You're nothing but a coon" and "I've shot worse coons than you", it might be possible to interpret the illocution of this utterance as a disparaging event, which warned the hearer they were held in low regard and that they might be subject to extreme violence on the grounds of their race. Other examples of illocutionary acts include informing someone of an event that has occurred, ordering someone to do something, or arguing with someone. In all these cases, a speaker does more than simply say something. In saying something, they are also doing something, performing an act which is identifiable as coincidental with the utterance.

Austin's third type of speech-act is "perlocutionary". Perlocutionary acts are those acts brought about by, or as a consequence of, saying something (Austin 1975:94–101; 109). In the perlocutionary instance, an act is performed *by* saying something. For example, if someone shouts "fire" and by that act causes people to exit a building which they believe to be on fire, they have performed the perlocutionary act of convincing other people to exit the building. The perlocutionary act was a consequence of the illocutionary act (the warning) that had also been performed, but may be discretely identified. It may have been possible to perform an illocutionary act, of warning people of a fire, in an unconvincing manner. In this instance people would not have left the building and either no perlocutionary act would be identifiable, or a different perlocutionary act would be identifiable. If the latter was the case, the perlocutionary act may have been convincing others in the building that the speaker who shouted "fire" was someone not to be trusted. Examples of perlocutionary acts, then, include convincing or persuading. In another example, if a jury foreperson declares "guilty" in a courtroom in which an accused person sits, the illocutionary act of declaring a person guilty of a crime has been undertaken. The perlocutionary act related to that illocution is that, in reasonable circumstances, the accused person would be convinced that they were to be led from the courtroom into a jail cell. Perlocutionary acts are acts intrinsically related to the illocutionary act which precedes them, but discrete and able to be differentiated from the illocutionary act. An example of a perlocutionary act arising from an utterance can be seen in Case I in the NSW empirical study, where cartoons were printed in a newsletter vilifying people of Asian descent, with the express purpose of provoking contempt and ridicule.

The close relationship between the three types raises some questions as to the viability of the distinction, questions Austin explores in great depth. For example, a locutionary act is defined as uttering a sentence with a certain meaning (Austin 1975:109) and an illocutionary act is one which is uttered with a certain force (Searle 1973:142). However, the meaning or force of an utterance cannot be interpreted in isolation from its context. In the example cited above, the shouting of "fire" may have different meanings, it may constitute different illocutions depending on whether or not a fire existed, the credibility of the speaker, and perhaps other external factors such as the presence of smoke. Similarly, the utterance may have different force (perlocution), depending on the context. If the credibility of the speaker is under question, the listeners may decide not to exit the building and the utterance may have the force of returning them to their desks. A great number of interpretive possibilities exist. The utterance may be interpreted as a threat, a warning, a prediction or even a promise. It is not possible to know which meaning is accurate without studying the context, or circumstances, under which the utterance was made. The meaning and force are related, to each other and to the context within which the utterance takes place. Searle regards the meaning and force of utterances as often inseparable (1973:147–148) because the force cannot be abstracted from the meaning of the utterance. Ultimately the meaning, in terms of the speaker's meaning in saying the sentence, the hearer's understanding of the meaning, and/or any consequences of the sentence, cannot be determined in the abstract — they are contingent on the circumstances of the utterance.

Austin in fact acknowledges that the locutionary/ illocutionary/ perlocutionary distinction is difficult to maintain, because undertaking all three types of speech-acts involves doing many different things at once. Understanding all three types of speech-acts embraces taking many different aspects of circumstance and context into account. Each speech situation represents a complex web of interactions. Uttering any of the three types of speech-acts, "embrace[s] doing many things at once to be complete" (Austin 1975:108). Austin concludes from this that understanding speech-acts requires much more than studying a sentence. What is needed to understand speech-acts is a study of each speech-act within a "speech situation" (Austin 1975:139). Within a speech situation, every utterance is an act of some kind. So Austin himself acknowledges some difficulty in demarcating the three types of speech-acts he set out to create. As well as the abandonment of the performative-constative dichotomy, and in order to understand the meaning of speech-acts, he advocates the examination of "general families of related and overlapping speech-acts" (Austin 1975:150; Searle 1973:149).

In spite of the complexities involved in interpreting these three types of speech-acts, a differentiation between locutionary (also called 'propositional'), illocutionary and perlocutionary speech-acts has remained central to speech-act theory. A differentiation between the two is often therefore maintained in consideration of the situated meaning of an utterance. Also, because the same expression of a locution can occur in different illocutionary acts, some speech-act theorists have found it necessary to maintain a locutionary/illocutionary distinction for this purpose (Searle et al eds. 1980: vii). Reaching an understanding of the situated meaning of an utterance requires understanding the potentialities of a speech-act to embody at least one, and often more than one, of these types. Differentiating between the complexities of the three types of speech-acts is an area subject to considerable contest within speech-act theory.[66] Theorists who have entered into this debate include Habermas (1979: 34–68; 1984; 1987); Searle, Kiefer and Bierwisch (eds.) (1980); Motsch (1980); Levinson (1983: 226–283); Langton (1993); Hornsby (1994); and Butler (1997).

However, a commonly held premise maintained by speech-act theorists is that utterances may be interpreted as "speech-acts" of some kind. Austin offers the locutionary/ illocutionary/ perlocutionary distinction as a means of differentiating the *types* of actions undertaken. Since all three types of speech-acts constitute actions, Austin argues that they therefore necessitate consideration as actions, capable of inflicting "ills" (1975: 105). Austin's finding here is significant. Since actions are readily subject to considerations of regulation, this implies that speech-acts (since they are types of action) may also be subject to considerations of regulation. This means the considerations that ordinarily apply when judging whether an action ought to be subject to regulation could apply also to speech-acts, for example a consideration of the degree of harm enacted in a speech-act. This is an important point, because it has profound implications for public policy. The idea that utterances may be capable of inflicting "ills" renders them vulnerable to regulatory considerations. The question for policy-makers is no longer one of *whether* speech-acts ought to be provided special immunity from regulation. This question may be answered in the negative. Instead, policy-makers might begin to consider (1) what kind of harm speech-acts might be capable of, and (2) what type of regulation might be appropriate to respond to, and attempt to minimise or eradicate that harm.

Some contemporary free speech scholars have begun to integrate a conception of speech as conduct into their arguments. Sunstein, for example, refers to the speech-act distinction in free speech theory as "discredited" (1993a: 826), preferring instead to differentiate between acts (verbal, symbolic or physical) intended as expressive conduct, to communicate a message in an exchange of ideas, and acts which are not so intended (1993: 833–840). Thomas Scanlon, similarly, argues that distinguishing speech from acts as a way of differentiating forms of expression is not very successful (1977: 156). He argues instead for a differentiation between speech which enables others to act via reasoning, and speech which enables others to act by providing them with the means to do what they want (1977: 159–160). Sadurski also acknowledges that the speech-conduct distinction is not useful, despite attempts by some legal scholars to render the distinction more sophisticated by regarding speech with a high "conduct ingredient" as "speech-plus" (1992:168). His reasons for declaring the distinction not useful include that any speech is accompanied by conduct of some kind or another, and that much conduct has the primary aim of communicating ideas (e.g. flag-burning). Joseph Raz defines freedom of expression as the right to communicate in public, where "communication" is interpreted broadly and includes expressive acts that are intended to be understood as such by others (1994:1). And Frederick Schauer critiques the use of the term "speech" without a clarification of what is meant by the author, since what is meant by each author is contingent on their underlying rationale — which is always contestable (1993:635–636). Schauer advocates the clarification by speech scholars of what they mean by the term "speech", in order to expose the underlying rationale and make debate more meaningful.

A conception of speech as conduct has also been integrated into speech policy. For example, the NSW legislation examined in Chapter 1 explicitly relies on a consideration that speech-acts may be harmful, by imposing penalties on those who incite hatred, serious contempt or severe ridicule on the grounds of a person's race. The justifications provided for the legislation's enactment include an acknowledgment that instances of vilification incurred "harms" (NSW Government 1988:3). The two questions — (1) what kind of harms some speech-acts may be capable of, and (2) the type of regulation which might appropriately respond to such harms — are closely related. A consideration of an appropriate response to harm can only be made when the extent and manner of the harm inflicted and sustained can be identified. I will do this in the next chapter. For the moment, it is important to note that conceiving of utterances as speech-acts renders them vulnerable to considerations of regulation of some kind.

This raises the concern of over-regulation. Free speech theorists who tend to uphold a speech-conduct dichotomy may be doing so on the basis that to elide the distinction could open up speech to a very great deal of regulation. Such concerns are valid, but are answerable in the context of the overall argument presented here. As I argued earlier, locating speech policy within a capabilities theory framework provides a strong justification for the maintenance of conditions where speech is possible, because speech is central to the development of a range of human capabilities. Participation in expression as a means of communicating ideas, knowledge and opinions is an activity central to human development. The speech liberty appears crucial to the functionings of practical reason and affiliation, which renders it central to the development of capabilities such as being able to imagine, think, reflect, plan and engage with others. The goal of social policy is to train and maintain internal capabilities, to which speech is central. Locating speech policy within this framework, therefore, provides ample argument with which to refute concerns that a conception of speech as conduct would render speech vulnerable to over-regulation, since over-regulation would directly contradict the goals of a capabilities-oriented social policy. Furthermore, a second aim of social policy is to "create and preserve" the external circumstances in which developed capabilities can "become active" (Nussbaum 1988:164). This implies that if some speech is harmful, then it becomes possible to regard some speech as counter-conducive to the development and maintenance of external and internal capabilities. This in turn would suggest that a policy designed to assist a response to such harmful speech would be warranted; a kind of regulation oriented towards enhancing speech opportunities, and not towards restricting or punishing speech. This type of policy does not raise concerns of over-regulation of the speech liberty.

Regarding speech as a kind of conduct is a necessary and initial step in assessing whether speech might constitute a harmful act. But it is not enough to sustain the premise that hate-speech-acts actually *are* harmful acts, or to explain what kind of harm they might constitute. For this to happen, hate-speech-acts more specifically need investigation — I will do this in the next chapter. For the moment, to continue the assessment of whether speech might be capable of constituting harm, a methodological framework within which speech-acts may be assessable remains important. To do this, I will now turn to an integration of Austin's tripartite distinction into elements of Jürgen Habermas' theory of communicative action.

Preliminary observations on the application of Habermas' validity claims to an analysis of speech-acts

Habermas has developed a theory of communicative action, within which language is conceived of as a medium of communication which has structures embedded in it (1984:x).[67] Habermas sought to unearth these structures, the rules by which agreement may be reached on the meaning of a communication, in order to develop a theory of communicative action oriented to reaching understanding. He argued that when a person speaks, they do more than produce grammatical sentences. They claim to be saying something comprehensible, to listeners who will comprehend it, and in a comprehensible manner (1979:1). Uncovering the means by which this comprehension may be mutually recognised requires uncovering the rules by which communication may be oriented to reaching understanding, the inherent *telos* of language use (Habermas 1984:285–287). He called his theory of speech-acts "universal pragmatics", where "pragmatics" is intended to mean the study of the conditions according to which speakers and hearers determine the context-dependent and use-dependent meanings of utterances. It is to be distinguished from the study of language abstracted from the user ("semantics") (Searle et al eds. 1980:viii–x; Habermas 1984:316–319).[68]

The rules by which agreement may be reached on the meaning of a communication are the claims raised by a speaker in communicative action. Habermas calls these "validity claims" (1984:305). When an utterance is made, a speaker makes claims regarding the truth of an objective world, the rightness of inter-subjective norms and values, and the sincerity of his/her subectivities. These three validity claims[69] are raised simultaneously with every utterance. Understanding them, that is reaching understanding on the three validity claims, means understanding the utterance. In a moment I will discuss the validity claims in more detail. However, first it is necessary to make some preliminary remarks concerning the relationship between Habermas' theory of communicative action and Austin's distinction between three types of speech-acts. It has been necessary to preface an application of Habermas' theory of communicative action with an elaboration of Austin's speech-act distinctions for two reasons. First, this ordering of an examination of speech-act theory accords with the chronology of developments in the philosophy of speech, and utilising this chronology here therefore aids in the development of an understanding of the subject matter. Secondly, Habermas utilises the terms "illocutionary" and "perlocutionary" in his theory of communicative action.

In moving at this point to an elaboration of elements of Habermas' theory of communicative action, it is important to note that Habermas incorporates the notion of an "illocutionary" speech-act as one which allows a speaker to motivate a hearer to reach agreement on the validity claims raised when an utterance is made (Habermas 1984:278).[70] Reaching agreement on the validity claims raised by a speaker means reaching agreement among speakers and hearers as to the content of an utterance (Habermas 1984:287). This use of language, oriented to the achievement of mutual understanding of the meaning of an utterance, is regarded by Habermas as the "original mode" of language use, meaning the use of language on which all other purposes or effects are "parasitic" (1984:288–289), or secondary. This means that a strategic or teleological use of language is derivative from language oriented to understanding. Habermas takes time to differentiate strategic-oriented language use from understanding-oriented language use (1984:285–286).

Habermas claims that, in Austin's framework, illocutionary acts can be understood via the meaning of what is said (1984:289). Perlocutionary effects, on the other hand, result where illocutionary acts are embedded in contexts of interaction (1984:289). The identification of perlocutionary effects of language use indicates that speech-acts have been integrated into contexts of strategic interaction, as opposed to contexts of reaching understanding (1984:292). Perlocutions, Habermas argues, are a

> special class of strategic interactions in which illocutions are employed as means in teleological contexts of action (1984:293).[71]

So Habermas differentiates between illocutionary acts which are closely connected with language use oriented to reaching understanding on the one hand, and perlocutionary effects of language use which are closely connected with language used strategically on the other.

This bifurcation implies that an application of Habermas' validity claims to speech-acts enables the development of an analysis of illocutionary speech-acts (to the extent of course that Austin's tripartite distinction is viable), and I will do this below. However, this bifurcation also implies that an application of Habermas' validity claims may not be appropriate where the speech-act to be examined is one with perlocutionary effects. Habermas makes the claim that when at least one participant in communication wants to produce perlocutionary effects, the utterance becomes classifiable as linguistically mediated strategic action (1984:295). Does this imply that where a speech-act has perlocutionary effects, the validity claim analysis ought not be applied because validity claims are raised in contexts of utterances oriented to reaching understanding, not utterances used strategically?

The bifurcation itself between strategic language use and language use oriented to reaching understanding appears problematic. Habermas himself argues that illocutionary acts are the form of language use from which other uses are derivative. This would appear to imply that *all* speech-acts are vulnerable in the first instance to analysis as language use oriented to achieving understanding. After this analysis has taken place, it would seem possible to build upon that by *also* examining any possible perlocutionary effects of language use. This question of the type of language use being examined is important because if the premise that speech is conduct is sustainable, it should become possible to analyse what kind of conduct some speech-acts are. The focus of this book is on a particular type of speech-act, namely hate-speech-acts. On face value, an observer might be tempted to conceive of hate-speech-acts as speech-acts used with a strategic purpose: to offend, to humiliate, to degrade, to discriminate, to insult, to hurt, or to threaten. The wording of the NSW racial anti-vilification legislation studied for this book similarly implies that hate-speech-acts are utterances used with a strategic purpose: to incite hatred, serious contempt or severe ridicule. The idea that hate-speech-acts are utterances used strategically would particularly be the case with unsophisticated, "crude" hate-speech-acts. If hate-speech-acts were to be conceived of in this way, an initial reading of Habermas' theory of communicative action might lead a reader to conclude that the analytical framework being proposed here is inappropriate. If hate-speech-acts are utterances used strategically, then it would seem inappropriate to analyse them within a framework developed to explain and reach agreement on the meaning of utterances used with an orientation of reaching understanding. But Habermas provides his own solution to this perceived problem. The solution is to understand the strategic use of language as derivative from or secondary to, understanding-oriented language use. This means all speech-acts may first be analysed from the perspective of understanding-oriented language use, because to achieve perlocutionary effects, an utterance must *originally* have been oriented to reaching an understanding of some kind. Habermas clarifies,

> [i]f the hearer failed to understand what the speaker was saying, a strategically acting speaker would not be able to bring the hearer, by means of communicative acts, to behave in the desired way. (1984:293).

The use of elements of the theory of communicative action to analyse hate-speech-acts, therefore, is appropriate.

In the analysis which follows I will be utilising Habermas' framework for understanding the means by which agreement may be reached on the meaning of language use oriented to reaching understanding. This will involve an analysis of the three validity claims raised by a speaker when an utterance is made; claims to be representing an objective truth, of appealing to intersubjective norms and values and of sincerely representing the speaker's subjectivities. A validity claims analysis, therefore, provides a comprehensive, multilayered approach to understanding the illocutionary force of an utterance. This analysis will be applied to speech-acts generally in this chapter, and hate-speech-acts in particular in the next chapter, which also will examine the secondary, perlocutionary effects of the use of hate-speech-acts.

Habermas' validity claims

Habermas argues that humans' ability to communicate has a universal core, made up of the basic structures and fundamental rules that all people become competent in when they learn to speak a language (1984: x). Speech-act theory, argues Habermas, allows the development of a method for reaching agreement by thematising the elementary units of speech (utterances) in the same way that linguistics thematises the elementary units of language (sentences). It is a theoretical framework within which Habermas has attempted to develop rules of "competent speech". These rules, if followed, might enable utterances to be "happily" or effectively employed (Habermas 1979: 26), in such a manner that the speaker and hearer would be able to agree on what was meant.[72]

Habermas derives these rules from the performance of successful speech-actions. In his model, a speech-action is successful — that is, agreement is reached on what has been communicated — when "validity claims" are recognised by both the speaker and the listener/s (1979: 1–3). Since full agreement between the speaker and listener/s on what has actually been communicated is rare, Habermas sets about imagining the circumstances under which agreement may successfully be reached (1979: 3). A speech situation in which these conditions are satisfied, so that participants reach agreement motivated by a discussion on what the validity claims mean,[73] is "ideal". An ideal speech situation also presupposes the absence of constraints on participation (Wodak 1996: 30). So when agreement on validity claims is reached, the general pragmatic presuppositions of argumentation have been met (Habermas 1984: 42, 25). This enables communicative action to be "oriented to reaching understanding". Reaching understanding is important, because understanding is the "inherent *telos* of speech" (Habermas 1984: 285–287).

Habermas goes on to describe the "validity claims" by which rationally motivated agreement may be reached. For agreement to be reached on the meaning of an utterance, an utterance must fulfil more than the traditional statement-requirement of "truth", because the "truth" requirement is inadequate to assess the embedded meaning and force of a speech-act. Instead, the speech-act may be assessed by a hearer in a manner which means the hearer either accepts or rejects three levels of validity claims. First, a speech-act may be assessed in terms of its "truth", in the sense of representing knowledge that both the hearer/s and speaker can share. This represents states of affairs in an objective world, "the world around us". The truth claims are assessable via empirical investigation. Secondly, a speech-act may be assessed in terms of its "rightness", in the sense that both hearer and speaker agree on shared and recognised norms and values. These norms and values establish and maintain interpersonal relations, and are inter-subjective. When a speaker raises claims of the rightness of certain norms and values, s/he is appealing to social norms and values that are linked to a community. The rightness of these norms and values may be assessed either in terms of whether the norms and values do exist within the community being appealed to (often implicitly) by the speaker, or in terms of whether the norms and values are considered appropriate within the "lifeworld" (Lebenswelt)[74] in which the utterance takes place (Habermas 1984:374). Finally, a speech-act may be assessed in terms of it being "truthful", or sincere, in the sense that the speaker represents what s/he intends. Here, the speaker's subjectivities (feelings, intentions, desires) are taken into account. This level of validity claim raised by a speaker is the most difficult to assess, because it involves an assessment of the manifest intention of the speaker. Such claims may be assessable by investigating whether a speaker and hearer are able to establish mutual trust in the subjective sincerity of the speaker (Habermas 1984:308), or by examining the consistency of the speaker's behaviour (1984: 303). The third validity claim, therefore, as an assessment of each individual's subjectivities, is not universalisable. The first two, however, are universalisable in the sense that they may be tested against shared propositional knowledge and normative accord. Insofar as it is possible to establish an objective case for knowledge and for the existence and rightness of shared norms and values, the first two validity claims are more easily assessable.[75] A competent communicative action is one in which agreement is able to be reached on three levels which correspond to the three validity claims: the objective world, the social world and the speaker's subjective world (1979:29–33, 67; 1984:x–xi, 38–42, 279–337).

In a Habermasian model, all speech-acts which are oriented to reaching understanding may be accepted or rejected under any of the three validity claims (1984:307). For example, if a person were to say to a colleague, "you're an idiot", the colleague can reject the utterance on the grounds of the three validity claims. First, the colleague can understand yet reject the speaker's claim to be representing truth in the objective world by saying, "no, I passed all my exams this year". Secondly, the colleague can reject the rightness of the inter-subjective norms and values represented in the speaker's utterance, and reply, "you have no right to talk to me like that". Here, the colleague is rejecting the rightness of intersubjective norms and values within which the utterance was considered a reasonable manifestation of the relationship between the speaker and the hearer, in the lifeworld context in which the utterance took place. Thirdly, the colleague may reject the sincerity of the speaker's subjectivity and answer, "I know you don't really think that I'm an idiot". These three alternative responses each reject a different validity claim made by the speaker in uttering the speech-act. Communicative actions are speech-acts containing validity claims, in response to which hearers can take a "yes" or "no" position (Habermas 1984:306),[76] in light of the reasons or grounds provided by the speaker. These reasons or grounds are often, indeed "normally", raised *implicitly*, and not explicitly, by a speaker (Habermas 1984:38). This, however, does not lessen the prospect of assessing the validity claims raised.

Content-neutrality?

Habermas' theory allows for a multi-dimensional analysis of the meaning of speech-acts within the context in which they were uttered. The grounding of the interpretation of speech-acts in the context within which they are uttered suggests that interpretation of the meaning of an utterance need not, indeed can not, be "content-free". This raises a challenge to free speech theorists who argue in favour of content-neutrality in speech policy. Many defences of free speech lay claim to neutrality and do not differentiate between protecting the speech of the Ku Klux Klan and protecting the speech of anti-racists. Speech, whose interpretation is not context-bound, is regarded by proponents of content-neutral free speech arguments as having an equivalent impact, regardless of who does the speaking and who does the listening. However, I have raised the challenge that a content-neutral free speech policy does not take account of the unequal distribution of the impact of speech on listeners, and groups of listeners. This is of concern if policy objectives (including speech policy objectives) are to be organised around ensuring opportunities to *all* for the advancement of human capabilities. If the impact of speech is unequally distributed among hearers, a case might be able to be made for the provision of benefits to those listeners who might be harmed by that speech. In order to make this case, it is necessary to sustain an argument that speech is capable of constituting a harmful act. The integration of a speech-act theory analysis (derived from Austin and Habermas) to the argument adds a new dimension to the challenge to content-neutrality. For it means that where some hearers bear a disproportionate burden of speech, the burden they bear is not simply that of hearing words which disparage them. The hearers in this case are bearing a burden of *acts* which are not regulated, indeed are perceived as being beyond regulation. If these acts are capable, as I will suggest in the next chapter, of being harmful on a number of levels, the burden is both disproportionate and one which could be subject to regulation on the basis of the harm inflicted. Here, no claim is being made as to the form of regulation. But if to speak is to act, a response of some kind would seem justifiable.

The need for a response

The Habermasian validity claims provide a framework within which it is possible to assess what a person means when they make an utterance. At the same time, they provide a framework within which mistakes, in the sense of an intersubjective dissonance between communicative intent and communicative understanding, may be able to be identified and, conceivably, corrected. Argumentation around the meaning of validity claims allows participants in a discussion to test the meaning of utterances. It also allows participants to respond to their understanding of the meaning of an utterance by responding with their own validity claims. Speakers can modify their claims in subsequent utterances, if they become convinced to do so by the claims of others (Habermas 1984:25). In this way, participants can enter into a "discourse", an ongoing discussion within which it should become possible to achieve agreement on the validity claims raised, "if only the argumentation could be conducted openly enough, and continued long enough" (Habermas 1984:42). An ongoing discourse would constitute his constraint-less ideal speech situation.

The goal of a capabilities-oriented speech policy is to provide the conditions under which those whose speech capabilities have been harmed by others are able to respond. This means the policy goal is to provide assistance to the victims of hate speech to raise alternate validity claims which seek to contradict the claims made by the hate speaker/s. Habermas' validity claims framework, therefore, is being used in two ways. First, an analysis of the validity claims raised by speakers provides insight as to the meaning of speech-acts, and hate-speech-acts. In the next chapter, the validity claims analysis will be developed in order to examine specifically what kinds of acts hate-speech-acts are. The second way in which a validity claims analysis will be used, is to provide a framework for developing an appropriate communicative response to hate-speech-acts. The use of a validity claims framework enables the development of a model of *institutionalised argumentation*, a process whereby the victims of a hate-speech-act can raise their own validity claims in response to the hate speaker/s. In this model, the validity claims raised in the hate speaker's utterance are able to be understood, and a response to hate-speech-acts (in which speakers would raise countering validity claims) is able to be generated. In this way, the model of hate speech policy I propose can be seen as the institutionalisation of argumentative discourse, with the aim of exposing the implicit and explicit validity claims raised in a hate-speech utterances and raising alternative validity claims in response. This will be elaborated in the final chapter.

In this chapter I have argued that speech may be conceived of as conduct, which implies that speech ought not be accorded automatic or special immunity from government regulation,[77] which in turn implies that speech might to be subject to considerations of regulation in a similar manner to other human activities. However, this does not expose the speech liberty to over-regulation, because locating speech policy within the framework of a capabilities-oriented social policy means prioritising the development of individual human capabilities, a process to which speech is central. Finding that speech is a kind of conduct does, however, expose the speech liberty to considerations of non-punitive, or non-restrictive types of regulation, including the type of regulation I propose in this book — the provision of assistance to generate a response to hate-speech-acts. However, a conception of speech as conduct is on its own insufficient to explain the phenomenology of hate-speech-acts. The integration of a validity claims framework makes such a specific investigation possible, and will be undertaken in the next chapter. Developing this model will help to provide answers to the second and third questions posed in Chapter 1: the problem of seeking to explain apparent weaknesses and inconsistencies in the application of the law and the problem of searching for a workable statutory definition of hate speech.

CHAPTER 4

Hate speech as harmful conduct

The phenomenology of hate-speech-acts

Is it appropriate, as Rauch suggests, to say to a victim of vilification, "Too bad, but you'll live" (1993:27)? In this chapter, I will revisit some of the examples of alleged (racist[78]) hate speech utterances identified in Chapter 1, and analyse them in terms of the validity claims raised by the speaker/s,[79] and the identification of perlocutionary effects of the utterance. This analysis will show that hate-speech-acts can be identified as raising validity claims which *enact* discrimination and support inequality. So a hate-speech-act is an utterance which perpetrates, perpetuates and maintains discrimination. The effects of this discrimination on members of the victim groups include that they are silenced, in the sense that a response is rendered "unspeakable" (Langton 1993:311). Understanding hate-speech-acts in this way has momentous implications for hate speech policy, because it suggests that an appropriate policy ought to be able to respond to this specific harm. Understanding hate-speech-acts in this way also provides some answers to the questions raised at the beginning of this book concerning the feasibility of an existing hate speech policy approach, because it supports the idea that a punitive and private resolution to hate-speech-acts does not address the specific harms enacted by such utterances.

The first example I will assess is an example of an alleged racist hate-speech-act against an individual perceived to be an indigenous Australian. This example has been selected in part because this group suffers a high incidence of racial vilification in Australia (Royal Commission into Aboriginal Deaths in Custody 1991; Human Rights and Equal Opportunity Commission 1991). Case F concerns a woman, as we saw in Chapter 1, who was the target of the following comments from occupants of another vehicle at a service station: "You black slut", "You're nothing but a coon", "I've shot worse coons than you". This speech-act can also be described as crude, a speech-act exhibiting patent evidence of the holding of prejudicial and racist ideas on the part of the speaker, so it may therefore provide clear guidance to assist in the identification of a racist hate-speech-act. Also, analysis of this utterance will enable an investigation to be carried out of the degree or types of harms enacted by the utterance of such a crude and overt hate-speech-act. I will argue that although this utterance is crude, it is also capable of constituting and perpetuating significant harm.

The second example I will discuss is a more sophisticated utterance. Case P concerned newspaper articles on the issue of immigration. Headlines included "The hidden costs of immigration" and "Quarter-Asian Australia". Graphics used to illustrate the articles included a stylised face, a quarter of which had been coloured yellow; an aggressive oriental dragon; and a scared white cockatoo surrounded by black and sinister birds. The articles claimed, among other things, that "soon" (in 27 years' time) Australia would be a "quarter Asian".[80] A complaint alleged that these utterances constituted vilification of people of Asian descent. These speech-acts are less crude than those investigated in Case F. Analysing this speech-act will enable an investigation to be carried out of how more sophisticated hate-speech-acts might also be identifiable as hate-speech-acts which constitute acts of harmful discrimination. This analysis will help to provide an answer to the question raised earlier, of devising a workable statutory definition of hate-speech-acts.

A third example warrants scrutiny here, namely the case of an alleged hate speech utterance which, upon investigation, might be found *not* to constitute a hate-speech-act. Under any policy model designed to respond to hate-speech-acts, it is as important to be able to identify hate-speech-acts as it is to be able to identify speech-acts which may offend or insult a hearer, but which do *not* constitute hate-speech-acts. An example which will help to illustrate this difference is Case N, in which a complaint was lodged by a person of Anglo-Saxon descent about a mural depicting a large Union Jack background, with an Anglo-Saxon soldier standing in front of the flag holding a rifle. In the foreground, the manacled arm of an Aboriginal man appeared.[81] The complainant alleged the mural vilified white people.

These three examples of allegations of hate-speech-acts will now be analysed in terms of the validity claims raised by the speakers, and the identification of perlocutionary effects of the utterances. In the section which follows, I will assume the position of a critical hearer, in order to assess critically the legitimacy of the claims made in the utterances.

A straightforward case

The first level on which a speaker makes claims in making an utterance is on the level of claiming to represent a state of affairs in the world around us. Implicitly or explicitly, a speaker raises "truth" claims when an utterance is made. These truth claims may be assessable via empirical investigation. What were the truth claims raised in Case F? In this case, the utterance sought to convey a state of affairs within which the recipient was posited as inferior. The speaker's use of the word "coon" reflected a derogatory, culturally racist meaning of the word. There seems little doubt that the term "coon" is understood by members of the speaker's and hearer's community as an offensive slang term for a person of colour. The use of the word also suggested that the recipient was comparable with a "racoon", an animal assumed to be of a lower order than human beings, and furthermore an animal which may be hunted, trapped, killed and regarded as a pest. The use of the word "slut" indicated a claim that the recipient was sexually promiscuous. The use of this personally derogatory term implied that her sexual activities were morally denounceable, a claim which reinforced the inferior state the perpetrator held the recipient to be in. There is an intersection in this utterance between an epithet used to make truth claims regarding the inferiority of the recipient on the grounds of her race, and an epithet used to make truth claims regarding the inferiority of the recipient on the grounds of her gender. By linking their claims to the threat of shooting — both people of colour and racoons — the speaker linked his/her own truth claims with historical evidence regarding the treatment of indigenous people in Australia. The claim that indigenous people have historically been hunted, shot and killed, is empirically sustainable (HREOC 1998a). The truth claims embodied in this utterance included the claim that the speaker/s engaged in such behaviour ("I've shot"), and furthermore that the shooting of people of colour would constitute a continuity with the historical perpetration of such behaviour against indigenous Australians.

The truth claims raised in this case, then, reach beyond the claim that inequality exists. They reach beyond the claim that indigenous Australians have historically been hunted and killed, and treated as inferior to people of Anglo-Saxon descent. These elements of the truth claims raised in the utterance are empirically defensible, because they are verifiable via documentation and historical record. The truth claims raised in this case, however, try to augment the historical record by placing the unequal treatment of indigenous Australians and women in the context of contemporary behaviour. The speaker claims that the hearer is to be treated as inferior due to her identification as an Aboriginal person. The speaker claims the hearer is "nothing but" a creature with a derogatory name. This is an empirically contestable claim. The victim of this utterance is a person who, according to international and Australian law,[82] possesses an inalienable right to be treated with dignity. Empirical evidence does not in any way substantiate a claim that indigenous Australians warrant treatment as animals. Furthermore, the speaker claims to have "shot worse coons" than the hearer. It is possible that the truth claim of having committed murder here is literal, although the presence of the speaker at the service station implies the potential falsity of this statement. It is much more likely that the speaker's claim here was not a literal claim to have shot indigenous Australians, but a claim to have treated other indigenous Australians in a similar manner as the hearer was being treated in this case. In either interpretation, the truth claim is difficult to verify empirically although the demonstrable prejudice on the part of the speaker renders their maltreatment of indigenous Australians likely.

The truth claims made by the speaker in this instance are claims of an objective world suffused with inequality. Within this power asymmetry, the speaker is placed in a position of power over the hearer. The utterance raises the claim that this unequal relationship is "true" and in so doing not only describes inequality, but also seeks to carry out and reinforce inequality. When a person in a position of relative advantage over another person, as persons of Anglo-Saxon descent are over indigenous Australians in terms of health, access to education, income and incarceration rates (HREOC 1997b), engages in an utterance which claims inequality exists, and at the same time claims to the hearer that they are in a relatively dominant position, and at the same time claims to the hearer that they are prepared to act to perpetuate their dominance, the utterance does more than *describe* an unequal relationship. In this instance, the utterance can be seen to have the illocutionary force of claiming the inequality to be "true" in a manner which reinforces and reinscribes the unequal relationship between the speaker and the hearer. Inequality is therefore *carried out* in the utterance of the speech-act. In this example, the inequality enacted is based on racial identity, intersecting with gender. The utterance therefore constitutes more than simply name-calling. It constitutes an *act* of discrimination.

At the same time as the utterance raises the claim of representing a state of affairs in the world the speaker raises a claim on shared and recognised norms and values, norms and values which establish and maintain interpersonal relations. This second level of validity claims raised is one of defining intersubjective values and norms within a social world. When a speaker makes an utterance, s/he appeals to values in the lifeworld, and this appeal may be accepted or rejected on two grounds. First, a hearer may assess the "rightness" of the claim in the sense of whether or not the intersubjective values appealed to by the speaker actually exist within the community to which the appeal is made. Secondly, a hearer may assess the "rightness" of the claim in the sense of the legitimacy or appropriateness of the appealed-to values within the lifeworld within which the utterance takes place.

What norms and values may be identified as being appealed to by the speaker in Case F? The utterance in this sense appears fairly straightforward. The speaker raises truth claims which reinforce inequality on the grounds of race, and simultaneously raises the validity claim that inequality on these grounds is appropriate. The speaker is appealing to norms and values which *support* inequality on the grounds of race. In other words, the speaker is appealing to norms and values which support racist discrimination — norms and values which support the propagation, perpetuation and maintenance of an asymmetrical power relationship within which powerful racially defined groups circumscribe less powerful racially defined groups to limit the way they are able to participate in society. The norms and values raised are exclusive, they support a differentiation on the grounds of race, and in a manner which supports power asymmetries in favour of the dominant racial group, with which the speaker is implicitly and explicitly identified.

The "rightness" of these norms and values, in the sense of whether they exist within the community to which the appeal is made, is assessable insofar as it is possible to assess community attitudes. As noted previously, numerous reports have cited the existence of racially discriminatory attitudes within sections of the Australian community (HRC 1982; HRC 1983; National Inquiry into Racist Violence in Australia 1991; Royal Commission into Aboriginal Deaths in Custody 1991, Office of Ombudsman NSW 1993). In this sense, then, the "rightness" of the appeal can be affirmed. It is possible to say that the utterance was appealing to norms and values which support racist discrimination and that these norms and values do exist to some degree within the community at large to which the speaker was appealing. This makes the utterance comprehensible. A hearer knows what the speaker "means" because the norms and values called upon can be recognised by both speaker and hearer. Both speaker and hearer are aware that norms and values which support racist discrimination exist. Both speaker and hearer are able to understand the utterance as located within that dialogue.

However, the "rightness" of these norms and values may be challenged in the sense of whether they are regarded as appropriate or legitimate within the lifeworld-context in which they were raised. Here, the question can be raised of whether the norms and values appealed to by the speaker cohere with certain standards. The question of measuring community standards is, of course, a difficult one. Nevertheless, within the framework of international and Australian law, numerous conventions and statutes advocate the treatment of all human beings with dignity and respect (for example, the Universal Declaration of Human Rights) and condemn differential treatment and maltreatment on the grounds of race (for example the International Convention on the Elimination of Racial Discrimination). Australia is signatory to these conventions, and possesses domestic legislation at both the federal level (*Race Discrimination Act 1975; Racial Hatred Act 1995*) and state levels (for example *Anti-Discrimination Act NSW 1977*), which upholds these standards. It seems, then, that the "rightness" of the speaker's appeal to norms and values which support racist discrimination is challengeable on this ground.

An assessment, then, of both the claims to represent an objective state of affairs and the claims to represent shared norms and values reveals an utterance which may be characterised as reinscribing inequality in a manner which supports racist discrimination. Furthermore, the appropriateness of such claims within the Australian context is questionable, in light of verifiable standards in law. The utterance appears to be one which perpetrates, perpetuates and maintains racist discrimination. The act of discrimination constituted by the utterance inflicted harm on the hearer, the harm of suffering discrimination.

What of the third level of validity claims raised in the claim to be truthfully, or sincerely, representing the speaker's subjectivities? As noted earlier, this level of validity claim is the most difficult to assess because to do so relies on an evaluation of the speaker's sincerity in expressing his/her intentions. On this level an analysis of the meaning of an utterance begins to take the speaker's intent into consideration. It is possible, of course, that the speaker in this case had no sincere intention of shooting the hearer, in spite of the threat to do so implicit in the utterance. It is also possible that the speaker did not in fact hold the hearer in as low regard as the utterance implied, but that the utterance was nevertheless made. Although it seems some hurt was intended, the question of assessing the sincerity of the speaker in raising the validity claims identified here appears difficult. As a methodological approach to assessing the meaning of an utterance, the difficulty of assessing the sincerity of the speaker's expression of their subjectivities might suggest that "intent" or "motive" are much less important elements to take into account than the empirically examinable (to use Habermas' term, "universalisable") claims raised in the first two validity claims. Habermas suggests that the third validity claim may be assessable by investigating whether a speaker and hearer are able to establish mutual trust in the subjective sincerity of the speaker, or by examining the speaker's consistency of behaviour. In this case, no opportunity existed to establish "mutual trust" or to examine consistency. The communication was unidirectional, and performed in such a manner as to cut off possibilities for retort. The exchange was brief, although powerful. In utilising a validity claims framework to assess the meaning of an utterance, then, it may be appropriate to place an emphasis on the first two validity claims which may be tested against shared propositional knowledge and normative accord. The third validity claim may be used for guidance, but may not be decisive in assessing the meaning of an utterance.

So, employing a validity claims-based analysis enables the utterance to be categorised as one which made claims which supported inequality, and constituted an act of discrimination on the grounds of race. The utterance is therefore assessable as a hate-speech-act, a speech-act which perpetrates, perpetuates and maintains discrimination. This speech-act did more than describe something, and it did more than insult the hearer. It was more than an expression of opinion or a statement. It constituted an act of discrimination in itself. In the face of an act of discrimination, it seems inappropriate and insufficient to adopt Rauch's suggested response of, "too bad, but you'll live".

A more sophisticated, and difficult, example

The second example to be examined is Case P. Run over two issues of the newspaper, the articles' headlines included "Asian Australia: It's closer than you think", "Quarter-Asian Australia: Why it's coming soon", "Australia's population: the Asian component" and "The hidden costs of immigration". The articles questioned whether Australia was "moving too far, too fast on Asian migration" and suggested that high rates of Asian migration could lead to social tensions and violence. The suggestion was made that Asian migrants don't "mix easily" with other ethnic groups, and that immigration placed welfare and health services under strain, as well as increasing crime rates. The articles conceded that definitions of "Asian" varied, but utilised a definition broad enough to include any person of "Asian" or "Middle Eastern" descent as Asian in the figures cited in the headlines. How may the validity claims raised in these articles be understood? Did these articles represent a genuine contribution to ongoing public debate about immigration policy, or did they represent something else? I will first examine the truth claims raised.

The articles raised a number of truth claims which are empirically assessable. First, the claim was made that Australia is being "Asianised" faster than anticipated. The figures cited to back up this claim were derived from a "respected demographer" who claimed that immigration rates had increased from 62,000 per year in 1985 to 142,000 per year in 1986–1991, and that from 1986–1991 roughly half those immigrants were "Asian". The article suggested these rates of immigration were likely to continue. In *Face the Facts*, a report released by the Australian Human Rights and Equal Opportunity Commission (HREOC 1998a), it was noted that in the period 1993 to 1998, migration had been lower than during most of the post World War II period. In 1991–92, 98,900 migrants entered Australia, in 1994–95 the figure was 87,428 and in 1995–96 the figure was 82,000. The highest post World War II immigration rate occurred in 1969–70. Furthermore, in 1995 4.8% of the population was born in Asia. The largest groups of migrants in 1995–96 were 12.4% from New Zealand, 11.4% from the United Kingdom and 11.3% from China. These figures contradict the claims of "Asianisation" made in the articles.

Furthermore, the article utilised a definition of "Asian" inclusive of any person with "Asian" ancestry, regardless of country of birth or length of residence or citizenship status in Australia. The articles cited a political commentator who argued that someone's appearance was the feature that "stays with you" when deciding their ethnicity. In a letter to the editor of the same newspaper, printed a few days later and written by leading researchers in the field, this definition of "Asian" was criticised as a "recessive ethnic gene theory of demography", one akin to that employed in population policies used in apartheid South Africa and Nazi Germany. The "truth" of this definition of "Asian" is therefore highly contestable.

The articles suggested further that high rates of Asian immigration had generated signs of social unrest, including high unemployment among Indo-Chinese and Lebanese migrants, and the existence of "migrant crime, especially triads". In *Face the Facts* (HREOC 1998a), it was reported that although levels of unemployment were relatively high amongst recently arrived migrants, those levels dropped dramatically with length of residency. In 1993, for example, unemployment among migrants who had been in Australia for less than three years was 24.9%, but among migrants who had been in Australia for between 3 and 8 years the figure dropped to 14.2%. This drop implies the causes of unemployment in migrant communities were related less to their ethnicity than to factors around their arrival and settling in, which are amenable to improvement over time. *Face the Facts* reported that migrants in general were less dependent on social welfare than people born in Australia. The report also stated that in 1983 fewer criminal offences were committed by migrants than those born in Australia, and that the longer migrants were in Australia, the closer their offending rates began to resemble those of the rest of the population. Furthermore, in 1991 the rate of prisoners per 100,000 population was 127.5 for Australian-born residents and 82.9 for those born in non-English speaking countries.

These figures suggest the articles misrepresented many facts. The truth claims made regarding rates of immigration, behaviour of immigrants and definitions of "Asian" immigrants are highly contestable. The articles attempted to link substantive truth claims concerning immigration numbers and crime rates with imputed truth claims of poor social attributes among the targetted group. By focussing on attributes such as unemployment, lack of social cohesion and the generation of fear among the non-Asian population, the articles attempted to make truth claims that went further than saying people of Asian descent were numerous in Australia. The truth claims in this instance were claims of an objective world in which Asian immigrants represented a threat to non-Asian Australians — a threat to social cohesion, stability and quality of life.

The truth claims of the article were claims of an objective world in which a targetted group represented a threat to the speaker. This is empirically challengeable, on the basis that "Asian" migrants do not, as a specific sub-group of immigrants, represent a threat to the quality of life of non-Asian Australians. The claim was made that an unequal relationship existed between the speaker and the racially-defined targetted group, a relationship in which the speaker had something to fear from the targetted group, and therefore needed to protect themselves by shutting the targetted group out (denying them the ability to migrate to Australia). In this relationship, the speaker was in a position of power over the targetted group, who may wish to migrate but could be prevented from doing so.

The shared and recognised norms and values called upon by the speaker in this instance buttress the truth claims made. The norms and values appealed to by the speaker are ones according to which the exclusion of some would-be migrants on the basis of their (curiously defined) ethnic heritage is appropriate. The speaker is appealing to norms and values which support differential treatment on the grounds of race. The speaker is appealing to norms and values which support the protection of a racially-defined dominant group against the potential harms of a racially-defined threatening group. In this instance, the "threatening" group is placed in a position of powerlessness, because if they are excluded from migrating they have no ability to participate in the social system and lifeworld to which the speaker is appealing.

As in the previous example, the "rightness" of these norms and values may be questioned on two grounds. First, they may be assessed in the sense of whether they exist within the community to which the appeal is made. An anti-immigration sentiment, including a specific sentiment against "Asian" immigration, has been documented within Australia (Jayasuriya 1999:21–29). Two letters to the editor published in the weeks following the articles' publication praised their tone, demonstrating further the existence of the values and norms within the community appealed to. In this sense, and in the same manner as the previous example, the utterance is comprehensible. The norms and values called upon can be recognised as those which support differential treatment of migrants on the basis of their perceived racial heritage.

However, the "rightness" of these norms and values may also be challenged in the sense of whether they are regarded as appropriate or legitimate within the lifeworld-context in which they were raised. Here, two responses can be made. First, it is possible to refer to statutes including the *Race Discrimination Act (Cth)* 1975 to demonstrate that attempts are being made to combat racist attitudes within the Australian community. Secondly, the appropriateness of the norms and values raised in relation to immigration policy specifically may also be questioned. Australian immigration policy does not differentiate between would-be migrants on the basis of race, and has not done so since the abolition of the "White Australia Policy" in 1973 (Jayasuriya 1999:21; Parkin and Hardcastle 1997:488–490; Ozolins 1994:206–207).[83] Indeed, the articles themselves acknowledged that because the specific exclusion of "Asians" from immigration was not permissible, the only solution would be to halt all immigration. The "rightness", therefore, of the norms and values raised is questionable in light of verifiable standards in Australian law and public policy.

This utterance, then, raised truth claims which are highly challengeable but which appear to represent an objective state of affairs based on exclusivity on the grounds of race. Furthermore, the appropriateness of this exclusion is challengeable. As a whole, the utterance can be interpreted as one seeking to carry out inappropriate inequality (in the sense of exclusion from migration on the grounds of race). In this sense, the utterance can be analysed as one which perpetrates, perpetuates and maintains racist discrimination. The third level of validity claims raised here, the claim to be truthfully or sincerely representing the speaker's subjectivities, is again difficult to assess. It is difficult to assess whether the speaker intended to utter a racist speech-act, or whether s/he intended to engage in a genuine discussion about immigration policy. In any case, the two verifiable validity claims already discussed shed considerable light on the illocutionary force of the articles. The claims of representing an objective state of affairs and appealing to shared norms and values are assessable, and provide ample evidence to support the argument that the article constituted a racist speech-act. This means the articles constituted more than a contribution to a public discussion over immigration policy, and to regard them as only that would be to misunderstand the meaning of the utterances. A validity claims analysis has made it possible to assess these utterances as acts of racial discrimination.

This is an example, then, of a sophisticated utterance which may nevertheless be interpreted as a racist speech-act. This is an important finding, because a significant and growing body of evidence exists which suggests that some racist dialogue is seeking to avoid prohibition or contest by becoming increasingly sophisticated or "sanitised" (Matsuda 1993:23). The moderation of some racist propaganda may render it capable of reaching, and convincing, a wider audience (Lester and Bindman 1972:374). Van Dijk argues that the reproduction of racism is facilitated not by "popular racism", but by a more moderate racism which — due to its very moderation — may be legitimised and validated by large segments of the population (1995:24). He terms this discourse "elite racism", and describes it as articulate, moderate and superficially sophisticated. Such discourse therefore carries the appearance of being humane (van Dijk 1995:25), while it maintains and legitimises the racism of the dominant ethnic group/s within a polity. A similar argument has been made in the United Kingdom, in the context of implementing legislation designed to deal with racist hate-speech-acts.[84] During reviews of UK racial vilification legislation, it was noted that following the introduction of such legislation, racist propaganda, in a bid to render itself immune to prosecution, had become more sophisticated (Twomey 1994a:238). Utterers of the more sophisticated racist hate speech claimed that they had no intention of stirring up racial hatred, but instead wished to make a contribution to public education and debate. It was noted that policy makers felt that hate speech legislation was unable to target such racist speech, despite concerns that a more moderate message was able to have a more powerful effect in terms of perpetuating racism (Twomey 1994a:238). The issue of "sophisticated" racist expressions will be discussed in greater depth below.

The analysis presented here of Case P demonstrates that, regardless of the speaker's claimed intentions in making an utterance, the validity claims of representing an objective state of affairs and appealing to shared norms and values remain assessable. The speech-acts are assessable as acts of discrimination. Understanding the validity claims raised allows this conclusion to be drawn. They were not simple contributions to a policy debate about immigration, but discursive acts of discrimination. If a validity claims assessment is able to demonstrate that an utterance has the illocutionary force of perpetuating racist discrimination, protestations by speakers that that was not their intention carry less weight in determining the need for a policy response. Sophisticated, or sanitised, instances of hate speech may become vulnerable to a policy response if the method proposed here were to be operationalised into a hate speech policy. This would render a greater number of utterances potentially vulnerable to a policy response. If that policy response is designed to enable targetted individuals or groups to speak out against the utterances which discriminate against them, the policy might be capable of responding to important but hitherto policy-immune instances of hate speech.

"An undeserving complaint"

An example which will help to illustrate the difference between speech-acts which may offend or insult a hearer, and speech-acts which constitute hate-speech-acts is that of Case N. The truth claims raised by the section of the mural which was subject to the complaint were that British troops had manacled Aboriginal people, and used arms against them. The record of British colonial and later administrations towards Aborigines in Australia is well documented, and includes massacre, dispossession of land and servitude of indigenous people (Reynolds 1995; HREOC 1998a). The truth claim, then, that indigenous Australians suffered the treatment depicted in the mural appears sustainable. The mural could also be interpreted as making the truth claim that such practices are still occurring. At the time this complaint was lodged, the issue of imprisonment of Aborigines and Aboriginal-police relations were being publicly discussed. The report of the Royal Commission into Aboriginal Deaths in Custody (1991) noted disproportionately high rates of incarceration of Aboriginal people, including incarceration of juveniles and incarceration for minor offences. It appears, then, that a claim that the mural depicted current practices towards Aboriginal people is also sustainable.

The suggestion that the image in the mural represents an empirically assessable "truth" is one consideration in identifying whether or not the expression constituted a hate-speech-act. But other factors, which have featured in the other two cases examined, also should be considered. A key criterion appears to be whether the mural makes a truth claim that bolsters inequality on the ground of race. It is possible to construe the mural as portraying a derogatory image of people of Anglo-Saxon descent, implying that they are aggressive, militaristic and involved in the oppression of indigenous people. Even if this interpretation were made however, the power asymmetry between Anglo-Saxon and indigenous Australians in this instance does not rest in favour of the speaker making the truth claims. The mural was constructed by members of a community with a high representation of indigenous Australians and migrants. It contained images representing the history of these sectors of the Australian community. The speakers in this case were indigenous Australians and members of the local multicultural community, groups historically marginalised and discrimination against in Australian society. The complainant was of Anglo-Saxon descent however, no evidence exists of discrimination in Australia against Anglo-Saxon people on the basis of race. On the contrary, institutionalised racist discrimination in Australia — including the aforementioned White Australia Policy — was designed to *benefit* people of Anglo-Saxon descent. A claim, therefore, that the makers of the mural claimed to represent an objective state of affairs in which people of Anglo-Saxon descent are discriminated against on the ground of their race is unsustainable. Empirical investigation denies this claim to "truth" since such systematic discrimination on the grounds of race does not occur. Instead, the truth claim here is that of representing the empirically defensible claim that indigenous Australians — both in the past and in the present — have been incarcerated and poorly treated by people of Anglo-Saxon descent. This is not a claim which *reproduces* inequality, although it depicts inequality suffered by the speaker.

It may illuminate the discussion to compare this mural with a hypothetical situation, in which a group of people of Anglo-Saxon background created their own banner with the same picture on it, and held the banner up in a street march in support of a white power movement. In that instance, the picture of the Aboriginal arm in a manacle would not simply depict inequality suffered by indigenous Australians, but would also be seeking to reproduce that inequality. The image of a white soldier carrying a rifle would be interpretable as a call to arms for people of Anglo-Saxon descent, to arm themselves against indigenous people. The meaning and force of the image in this instance would be entirely different. Meaning and force are determined by context, not by pigment or words alone.

What of the norms and values appealed to in this case? Although Case F and

Case P were interpreted as appealing to norms and values which *reinforced* truth claims which reproduced inequality, in this case the norms and values appealed to may be conversely interpreted as those which *challenge* inequality. The mural was placed within a broader account of Australian history, which included changes in social, cultural and political life. In this context, a reminder of past and present maltreatment of indigenous people may be interpreted as a challenge to that maltreatment. The norms and values appealed to are ones which challenge maltreatment on the grounds of race. The third level of validity claim — the truthful representation of the speaker's subjectivities — is again difficult to measure in this instance. But an assessment of the empirically assessable elements of the illocutionary force of Case N within a validity claims framework does provide evidence to support the argument that this expression does *not* represent an instance of a hate-speech-act. Instead, it represents a speech-act which seeks to challenge the inequality and discrimination suffered by indigenous Australians. Although people of Anglo-Saxon descent may feel offended by the expression, the mural does not constitute an act of racist discrimination against them.

Applying an analysis of the validity claims raised by the speaker in making the utterance to examples of alleged instances of hate speech has made the identification of a crude and a sophisticated hate-speech-act possible, both of which constituted acts of racist discrimination. The third case assessed did not appear to be identifiable as a hate-speech-act. From this investigation, it appears possible that a validity claims framework could be operationalised into a policy capable of identifying hate-speech-acts as discursive acts of discrimination. Identifying hate-speech-acts as acts of discrimination is the first step in developing an appropriate policy response to hate-speech-acts. As I argued earlier, a capabilities-oriented hate speech policy would seek to take into account the effects of hate speech on individuals' ability to develop their capabilities. Identifying an act of discrimination in a hate-speech-act does not sufficiently describe the effects of hate speech on its victims, because it only describes the illocutionary force of an utterance. In order to describe the *effects* of hate speech on its victims, it is necessary to turn now to an examination of the perlocutionary effects of hate-speech-acts on the hearers.

The perlocutionary effects of hate-speech-acts

I made the suggestion earlier that hate-speech-acts, in carrying out discrimination against targetted victims, silence them. Is this the case? And if so, how does the silencing occur? A number of scholars have sought to expose the considerable negative effects of discrimination generally on victim groups, and there is no room here to canvass all this work.[85] The works which I will discuss below seek to expose the specific effects of discrimination enacted *via expression*. These include (1) a limiting of victims' personal liberty, (2) the internalisation of discriminatory messages, such that the hearer begins to believe the claims of appropriate inequality, (3) the perpetuation of further acts of subordination, and (4) silencing. The most important of these for the purposes of the discussion here is silencing, since this aspect is readily susceptible to remedy via a capabilities-oriented hate speech policy, as proposed in this book.

One of the means by which discrimination enacted via an expression may affect victim groups is by limiting hearers', and hearers' associates', personal liberty. Mari Matsuda, for example, outlines how racist hate-speech can deny its victims personal security and the liberty to pursue their daily lives because they believe — due to the telling of personal experiences of many others — that violent acts of racial hatred are often preceded by speech-acts of racist hatred (1993:17, 22).[86] Matsuda argues that victims and potential victims may begin to view all dominant group members with suspicion, thus placing limits on their ability to maintain broad support networks, limiting social harmony and circumscribing possibilities to form and maintain personal relationships. Recipients of hate-speech-acts may restrict their personal freedom to avoid recurrence of the hate-speech-act or confrontation with actual or potential hate-speakers. This may involve resigning from a job, leaving an educational institution, moving house and avoiding public places (1993:24–25). Matsuda also details effects on sympathetic non-target group members, whose liberties to associate with those who may be targetted by hate speakers are threatened by racist hate-speech-acts due to a desire to avoid becoming victims of violence themselves (1993:25).

A second factor is the internalisation of discriminatory messages, such that hearers begin to believe that the claims raised by the hate speakers are true. Matsuda cites research claiming that, despite conscious attempts to resist the messages, racist hate-speech-acts are capable of planting the idea in the minds of all hearers that racial inferiority may hold some truth (1993:25).[87] Delgado supports Matsuda's findings on this aspect of the harm of what he terms "racist insults", noting that the individual victim, the perpetrators, and society as a whole subconsciously learn, internalise and institutionalise the messages conveyed in racist hate-speech-acts (1993:90–94). Delgado argues further that speech which communicates inferiority tends to produce in its victim the very characteristics of "inferiority" that the speaker intends to ascribe to them (1993:94–95). This process occurs because the victim internalises and comes to believe, and then perform, the attributes of worthlessness conveyed in the discriminatory hate-speech-act. Lawrence argues that shaming and degrading a group of people by labelling them inferior ("stigmatising") inflicts psychological injury by assaulting self-respect and dignity.[88] Because self-esteem and the respect of others are important for participation in society, racist stigmatising becomes self-perpetuating; it reproduces in its target group those qualities attributed to the target group by the stigmatisers (1987:351). Sunstein argues similarly that racist hate speech can have "corrosive consequences on the self respect" of people of colour (1993a:802). Patricia Williams has called the process of injury to self-esteem and self-worth enacted via racist discrimination "spirit-murder" (1987:151).[89]

A third factor which has been argued to be a perlocutionary effect of hate-speech-acts is the perpetuation of discrete, subsequent acts of subordination and discrimination after, and related to, the utterance of the hate-speech-act. This argument has arisen particularly in relation to pornography, when it is perceived as an expressive act which perpetuates the subordination of women. For example, Catharine MacKinnon defines pornography as a speech-act which is degrading to the equality and dignity of women (1993).[90] MacKinnon's argument may be applicable beyond her case study of pornography. She argues pornographic hate-speech-acts damage social equality by expressive means, because they perpetuate subordination. They do this because the speaker is in a position of relative power over the subjects of the speech-act, who are over-whelmingly women. Pornographic speech-acts both subordinate women and lead to other, discrete acts of subordination. This argument was put forward in a US Court case concerning the constitutionality of an ordinance prohibiting pornography. In judgement, Judge Easterbrook accepted the premise that depictions of subordination can perpetuate subordination in subsequent ways, including by contributing to lower wages for women, harrassment in the workplace, and assault and rape of women.[91] He noted that some speech *is* powerful, in the sense that it is able to achieve changes in attitudes and behaviour. He argued that this is the "power" of speech, and it constitutes an important reason why speech, even speech perceived to be insidious, ought to be protected from restriction by the state.[92] To permit restriction of insidious speech, he argued, would be to allow the government to control the institutions of culture. An argument that insidious speech can be powerful is not limited to the subordination of women. Sunstein, for example, argues that racist hate speech contributes to the maintenance of a "caste system" based on race, in which targetted group members are subject to fears of racially motivated violence, experience fear of ongoing subordination and are made aware of a denial on the part of hate speakers of the premise of political equality (1993a: 814). In the Australian report released by the Royal Commission into Aboriginal Deaths in Custody, it was argued that racial vilification is both a "form of violence" and a promoter of subsequent violence against Aboriginal people (1991:70, 71). Akmeemana and Jones also cite arguments in support of the hypothesis that the assertion of superiority by a speaker in a relative position of power in a hate-speech-act creates ongoing relationships of domination and subordination (1995:151–152).

A fourth perlocutionary effect of hate-speech-acts is the idea that hate speech silences its victims. This argument is upheld by a number of scholars. Delgado, for example, argues that many victims of hate-speech-acts choose not to speak back because such a response may provoke further abuse. Also, in many cases the hate speaker is in a position of authority over his/her victim, which further restricts the victim's belief in his or her ability to respond in a meaningful way (1993:95). Targets may fear victimisation, or lack the confidence to challenge a person in a position of authority over them. Interestingly, this argument is overtly sustained by Cases G and H cited in Chapter 1, in which complaints of racial vilification were withdrawn because the complainants feared direct retribution from the hate speaker. In Australia, the National Inquiry into Racist Violence argued that hate speech can silence its victims by creating fear, intimidation and resignation towards their experience of racial hatred (1991:111). Matsuda also cites evidence that victims of hate-speech-acts tend to curtail their own speech-acts as a protective measure in response to hearing the hate speech of others (1993:24–25). Peggy Davis supports Matsuda's argument, describing the effects of ongoing negative, stereotypical perceptions of African Americans as "incessant and cumulative assaults on black self-esteem" (1989:1585). The "microaggression" enacted via racism also produces "deference" in the victim persona (1989:1567); that is to say, conformity to the expectations is placed on the victim group. Post acknowledges that the premise that racist speech may exclude victim group members from the dominant public discourse, devalue their speech and render them unable to iterate a response, may be true. This may limit their ability to participate in deliberative self-governance, an essential component of democratic government (1991:305–307).[93] MacKinnon argues similarly that hate speech damages the ability of both its actual and potential victims to engage in speech by silencing them. Dominant group members "get a lot more speech than others", and hate-speech-acts discriminate against relatively less powerful groups within the community (1993:72).

Rae Langton has synthesised MacKinnon's analysis with Austin's definition of an illocutionary act, to elaborate on the ways in which hate speech can silence (1993).[94] She argues that an important effect of hate-speech-acts is to silence, "make unspeakable", a potential response on the part of an individual victim or the victim group, because in any illocutionary act the speaker speaks with the authority to perform that illocution (Langton 1993:311). This argument accords with the analysis of the validity claims raised by the speakers in Case F and Case P. In both these cases, the power asymmetry *in favour of the speaker* represented in the claims made in the utterance rendered that utterance vulnerable to interpretation as a hate-speech-act. Langton argues further that a response to the authority of the speaker is rendered unspeakable in the uttering of a hate-speech-act via three mechanisms: 1) actual and potential victims fail to speak due to intimidation or a belief that no-one will take them seriously; 2) actual and potential victims do speak, but their speech-act does not achieve its desired effect (and this failure is directly related to their position of relative powerlessness as hearer); and/or 3) actual and potential victims do not possess the authority in the relevant domain, vis a vis the speaker of the hate-speech-act, to be able to utter a meaningful response (1993:314–316). This argument appears to support the argument I have presented here regarding the reinforcement of inequality, and appeal to norms and values which support discrimination, embodied in a hate-speech-act.

It seems, then, that the perlocutionary effects of a hate-speech-act can be identified as inflicting significant harm on individuals and groups. Furthermore, hate-speech-acts enact substantive impediments to the ability of actual and potential victims to respond with speech-acts of their own. This directly contradicts Rauch's proposed panacea to vilification: "Too bad, but you'll live" (1993:27). It also challenges the more common liberal response to harmful speech, which is that speech one abhors can best be dealt with by minimising restraint on speech to allow for a response. Minimal restraint on speech does more than just allow vilification to occur. By not recognising the need to provide assistance to those whose ability to speak is harmed by the speech of others, liberal speech policies which minimise intervention in the speech liberty indirectly contribute to the silencing of victims of hate speech. Hate speech impairs the quality of life of actual and potential hearers of hate-speech-acts. Hate-speech-acts impede the maintenance of conditions within which all individuals' central human capabilities are able to develop and flourish. They do this by constituting acts of discrimination, and by thereby preventing the elucidation of a response (as one of the effects of that discrimination). Since participation in speech is centrally important to the development of many human capabilities, hate-speech-acts can be seen to impair this development.

One more potential pitfall needs to be discussed. That is the question of whether it would be possible to claim that the perlocutionary effects of hate-speech-acts identified here could manifest following the utterance of a speech-act that was simply offensive, rather than only following the utterance of a hate-speech-act, discursive act of discrimination? Some hearers of speech-acts who are personally offended by the utterance may choose not to associate any longer with the speaker, they may feel physically unwell following a confrontation, they may wonder whether the insult contained any "truths" about their personality, and they may feel unable to answer back. But a crucial element missing from these kinds of exchanges is evidence of a systemic power asymmetry between the speaker and the hearer, and in favour of the speaker. In hate-speech-acts this power asymmetry is not contingent or coincidental, but rather a systemic feature of the lifeworld-context within which the speech-act takes place. This allows an interpretation of hate-speech-acts as discursive acts of *discrimination*. When a systemic power asymmetry is absent, the speech-act cannot carry the same illocutionary force. Thus, in implementing a hate speech policy designed to provide assistance to victims to respond, a complaint lodged in relation to an insulting or offensive — but not discriminatory — speech-act would not warrant the provision of a policy response.

A new hate speech policy

I have argued that the harms carried out in the utterance of a hate-speech-act occur because hate-speech-acts do more than simply offend people or hurt their feelings. Racist hate-speech-acts constitute discursive acts of racial discrimination against a target group, acts which reproduce and reinforce inequality on the grounds of race, and which simultaneously appeal to norms and values which legitimate such inequality. A number of effects flow from the enactment of racial discrimination against perceived members of a target group. The effects are related to hearers' and potential hearers' perceived membership of the target group, rather than occurring coincidentally. These effects include a limiting of personal liberty, psychological injury, the internalisation of messages of discrimination, the creation of opportunities to enact further acts of subordination, and silencing. Hate-speech-acts constrain the ability of their targets, and other potential targets, to speak back, to challenge the claims raised in the racist utterance.

How does this analysis provide assistance in answering the questions posed in the first chapter? In the study described in Chapter 1 I outlined three empirical problems related to whether it is possible to implement a hate speech policy capable of achieving the aims cited when the legislation was introduced. The first was the question of understanding why the legislation had been framed in the way that it had. This problem was answered earlier, when it was suggested the legislation's attempt to "balance" free speech concerns (by instituting broad categories of exemption) and hate speech concerns (by providing a resolution process for individual victims of hate speech) arises from an underlying (albeit perhaps unconscious) conception of free speech and speech policy. The dominant theories in defence of free speech emphasise the maximisation of speech *per se* as a central policy goal. This means any attempt to ameliorate the harms of hate speech is counterposed to the goal of maximising speech opportunities. Because the two policy goals are counterposed, speech policy is constructed in such a way as to search for an elusive "balance" between two counterposed interests. In the NSW legislation, this "balance" is perceived as necessary because the legislation is essentially punitive. Conceiving of the goal of speech policy in such a way as to take into account what speech might be capable of doing in and for people's lives, however (a capabilities-oriented approach), enables the two goals to be conceived of as mutually collaborative. If ameliorating the harms of hate speech simultaneously serves the goal of maximising speech opportunities, a goal that has tended to be considered the preserve of "free speech" policy, the two goals may be achieved concurrently. I argue that a capabilities-oriented approach to conceiving of speech policy provides a framework within which it is possible to achieve both these goals. Furthermore, because the hate speech policy proposed here is not punitive there is less need to institute broad-ranging exemptions to preserve speech from over-regulation.

I have also tried to provide answers to the second problem raised in Chapter 1; the question of explaining apparent weaknesses and inconsistencies in the application of the NSW legislation. The empirical study raised a number of procedural limitations in the application of the NSW hate speech policy. I suggested these procedural limitations might arise from the conceptual under-pinnings of the legislation. In three cases (A, B and C), no action was taken against a person known to be committed to racist ideas because it was felt to do so would be of little use. Any harms suffered by members of the Jewish and indigenous communities subjected to the respondent's comments were unable to be ameliorated. Also, in cases D, E and F complaints were unable to be acted on because of the legislation's reliance on individual complainants' willingness and/or ability to carry a complaint to resolution. In cases G and H complaints were withdrawn because the individual complainant feared violent reprisals from the respondent. In cases I, J, K and L, the individual complainant was not a member of the victim group, so the complaint could not be acted on. In all these examples, the legislation's reliance on an individualised complaints and resolution procedure resulted in the ADB being unable to take action against hate-speech-acts.[95] Any harms carried out in these utterances remained immune from response.

The individualised and private resolution process relied upon in the policy studied seems questionable in light of the examination of the phenomenology of hate-speech-acts I have undertaken here. To be unable to respond to the harms of discrimination due to procedural limitations in the policy studied would seem to demonstrate that there are weaknesses in the legislation's approach. To be reliant on a direct and private intervention between individual complainants and individual respondents would seem to suggest that the legislation is insufficiently appreciative of the harms of acts of racial discrimination. The policy's reliance on a private and individualised resolution process renders a significant number of complaints (approximately one quarter of complaints lodged in the study period (Gelber 2000a: 17, 18)) inactionable, achieving nothing to ameliorate the harms of the hate-speech-acts uttered.

If hate speech policy were to be designed in a different way, unreliant on a direct and private intervention between individual complainants and individual respondents, these problems could be overcome. I have argued that an alternative approach to hate speech policy, a capabilities-oriented approach, could be designed in such a way as to provide targets and their supporters with the material, institutional and educational support to enable them to respond to hate-speech-acts. This would allow victims to challenge (by participation in the exercise of the speech liberty) the "silencing" effect of hate-speech-acts, and to contradict (with their own speech) the claims raised by hate speakers.[96] A hate speech policy designed along these lines would not be reliant on a private resolution between an individual complainant and an individual respondent. A complainant would not need to be identified to a hate speaker. A respondent need not even be involved in the resolution process. Instead, the response would be a public act, commensurate with the public act constituted by the vilification which engendered the need for a response. This kind of policy appears able to incorporate an understanding of the harms of hate-speech-acts — both in the validity claims raised and in the perlocutionary effects — into its aims. It would be designed to respond directly to those harms, and thus be more able to ameliorate the harms enacted. Contrasting this proposed policy approach with the policy in place in NSW suggests that the deficiencies in the NSW legislation appear related to its insufficient incorporation of an understanding of the specific harms of hate speech into the complaints resolution process.

This argument answers a related problem. If it can be demonstrated that hate-speech-acts are harmful, the question arises of whether punitive or restrictive sanctions ought to be enforced. For example, why would criminal sanctions not be an appropriate response to particularly virulent instances of hate speech? Criminal sanctions would enable hate speakers to be imprisoned. Such an approach may prevent the hate speaker from enacting discrimination in the broader community, at least during the period of incarceration; however, it would also do very little to ameliorate the harms of hate speech. Unlike the policy proposed in this book, incarceration of a hate speaker would not provide direct assistance to the victims of hate speech to enable them to speak. It would not directly empower the victims of hate speech to challenge the discrimination they suffer. Other punitive approaches, such as the imposition of fines or extraction of private apologies, are also private resolutions to an essentially social problem, and do not provide for a response to the specific harms enacted by hate-speech-acts. Within theories of justice, some scholars argue that punitive sanctions need not be the pre-eminent means of responding to offences. Braithwaite and Pettit argue that retributive theories of justice experienced a resurgence in the 1990s because criminological evidence showed that punishment acted as neither an effective deterrent, nor an effective means of incapacitating offenders, nor a prevention against recidivism,[97] and an alternative theoretical justification for meting out punishment was required. They argue strongly that a social response to offences is more effective, because it fosters a greater enjoyment of "dominion", freedom in the social sense of full citizenship, by offenders, victims and the community at large (1990:2, 4–5, viii).[98] Applied to hate speech policy, this argument implies that punitive sanctions would be unlikely to change the behaviour or attitudes of hate speakers, or prevent them from uttering recurring hate-speech-acts. This critique applies even to complaints "successfully" settled under the policy studied,[99] because in most of these cases the outcome included the facilitation of a private apology or agreement to desist, or the payment of a fine. Instead, a capabilities-oriented policy designed specifically to include the victim community in engendering a response to the hate speech is more likely to achieve the desired outcome of ameliorating the harms of hate speech and preventing its recurrence.

The third problem raised by the study is the question of establishing a workable statutory definition of hate speech. My argument has detailed an approach which is capable of being operationalised into a statutory hate speech model. An examination of the validity claims raised by an alleged hate speaker, including the lifeworld-context within which they are raised, would seem to provide a model for understanding and therefore identifying hate-speech-acts, a model which is reliant on an assessment of whether *discrimination* has been enacted in the utterance. By relying on a determinant of discrimination, this model overcomes the problem of differentiating hate-speech-acts from mere insult. It also is not reliant on an implicit differentiation between crude and "sanitised" racist utterances, but has the potential to render a greater variety of utterances vulnerable to a policy response. Because that response is designed to provide assistance to victims to speak, this does not threaten speech with over-regulation.

Providing an answer to the problems raised by the empirical study described in Chapter 1 is useful, because it helps to explain apparent weaknesses in the policy's application. But it would be more useful to take the analysis further and to expand the remit of the argument. First, it is useful to question whether the problems in hate speech policy identified here are limited to the particular policy selected for the study. A comparative analysis of other policies is warranted and will be undertaken in the next chapter. A second task which has been implicitly mooted, but as yet has not been carried out, is developing greater clarity on the question of what kind of a response might be generated by the hate speech policy proposed in this book. In the final chapter, I will enter tentatively into an analysis of the kind of response which would be commensurate with the aims of a capabilities-oriented hate speech policy.

CHAPTER 5

Australia, the UK and the USA compared

Applying a comparative method at this point in the book expands the argument. First, it allows a questioning of whether the problems in hate speech policy identified in the NSW case study may be applicable in other jurisdictions. Secondly, if the answer to the first question is in the affirmative, it allows for a wider application of the proposed remedy: the institution of a capabilities-oriented hate speech policy, implemented via an "institutionalised argumentation" resolution model. The purpose of this chapter is to illuminate cross-jurisdictional similarities in policy approaches to hate speech, despite the presence of numerous variables. I will examine and compare hate speech policies in Australia, the United Kingdom and the United States. The results will suggest that, despite variables in these countries' structural approach to protecting free speech in law and to responding to hate speech, policy weaknesses remain. These include: a reliance on a policy approach which counterposes the goals of free speech and the necessity of responding to hate speech; a reliance on a conception of hate speech policy as necessarily restrictive or punitive; and a demonstration of some practical difficulties in translating these conceptual parameters into workable and effective statutes. These common weaknesses suggest that the three jurisdictions studied, and possibly others which share the broad characteristics common to these three, may benefit from adopting a capabilities-oriented approach to hate speech policy. Any theoretical proposition becomes more "fruitful" if it can be applied to a variety of systems (Dogan and Pelassy 1990: 115; Mackie and Marsh 1995: 179), and this chapter demonstrates that the theoretical propositions of this book can be applied within a variety of liberal democratic orders.

Similarities in the nations studied

Australia, the United Kingdom and the United States of America can be broadly defined as Western liberal democracies, nations within which concepts of individual freedom and the rule of law are combined with a measure of popular participation in and majority control of political decision-making processes (Kukathas, Lovell and Maley 1990:9–10). These three nations share other common features relevant to speech policy. These include ratification of international treaties providing both for the protection of free speech and for a response to hate speech, and a commitment to the eradication of racial discrimination as evidenced in domestic law.

The three nations participated in the United Nations' General Assembly's unanimous adoption in 1948 of the Universal Declaration of Human Rights (UDHR).[100] In order to implement the UDHR, the United Nations adopted the International Covenant on Economic, Social and Cultural Rights (ICESCR) and the International Covenant on Civil and Political Rights (ICCPR), both in 1966 (Rengger 1995:66–67). The ICCPR upholds a general right to freedom of expression, prohibits arbitrary interference with privacy and "unlawful attacks" on a person's "honour and reputation", and prohibits the propagation of racial hatred when it constitutes an "incitement to discrimination, hostility or violence" (Articles 19, 17(1) and 20(2)). The ICCPR came into force in Australia in 1980, in the UK in 1976 and in the USA in 1992.[101] Below, I will discuss the three nations' reservations and actions in terms of implementing Article 20 of the ICCPR.

The International Convention on the Elimination of All Forms of Racial Discrimination (ICERD) was adopted by the United Nations in 1966 (Rengger 1995:99). This Convention provides for the condemnation by signatory nations of all "propaganda", and organisations based on ideas, of racial superiority, or which attempt to "justify or promote racial hatred or discrimination" and enjoins State Parties[102] to "declare an offence punishable by law" the dissemination of ideas of racial superiority or racial hatred, as well as incitement to racial discrimination (Article 4). The Article also enjoins signatory States to "declare illegal" all propaganda activities which promote and incite racial discrimination. The ICERD also contains a provision for the right to freedom of opinion and expression in Article 5(viii). Debate exists as to the scope of Article 4, specifically the extent to which it permits State Parties to prohibit expressions of racial hatred. This debate appears to turn on the interpretation of the term "racial hatred", and particularly its apposition in the ICERD to the term "racial discrimination". For example, during UNHRC deliberations on the draft of the ICERD, a reference to prohibition of "incitement to racial hatred" was rejected on the grounds that "hatred" could not be quantified (Korengold 1993:726). As it stands, the introductory paragraph to Article 4 acknowledges that State Parties "condemn" the promotion of both "racial hatred" and "racial discrimination", and that they will undertake to adopt measures designed to eradicate "incitement to, or acts of, such discrimination". Article 4(a) refers only to the punishment by law of "incitement to racial discrimination", and Article 4(b) refers to the prohibition of propaganda which "promote[s] and incite[s] racial discrimination". Thus, the specific prohibition of racial hatred was omitted. Some commentators argue this omission specifically neutralises the capacity of the ICERD to allow for the prohibition of racial vilification (e.g. Twomey 1994c: 2; Korengold 1993). However, in the context of the discussion presented in this book, it appears possible that Article 4(a) of the ICERD can be interpreted as allowing for the provision of a legal response to racist hate-speech-acts, insofar as and because racist hate-speech-acts may be considered to be discursive acts of racial discrimination, which enact discrimination on the grounds of race. This interpretation of the scope of Article 4(a) is, however, by no means universal. The ICERD came into force in Australia in 1975, in the UK in 1969 and in the USA in 1994. All three nations registered "reservations" against Article 4 at the time of ratification.[103] Below, I will discuss the three nations' reservations and actions in terms of implementing Article 4 of the ICERD.

Australia, the UK and the USA share a commitment to eradicating racial discrimination, as evidenced in law. In Australia, for example, the federal government has implemented the *Racial Discrimination Act 1975* and the *Racial Hatred Act 1995*. Most of the individual states, which also carry responsibility for anti-discrimination law, have enacted similar statutes prohibiting racial discrimination.[104] In the United Kingdom the passage of the *Human Rights Act 1998* incorporated provisions of the *Race Relations Act 1976*, which had created civil remedies for acts of racial discrimination, and the *Crime and Disorder Act 1988* which had created an offence of "harassment" or "putting people in fear of violence" on the grounds of race. In the United States, the federal *Civil Rights Act* of 1964 provides for equal protection under the law, and protection against discrimination on the grounds of race in the provision of public accommodation and employment. It also prohibits racially discriminatory institutions from benefiting from federally assisted programs.[105] The responsibility for most anti-discrimination policy in the United States rest with the states.

Broadly speaking, then, the three nations under examination share an identification as a liberal democracy, ratification of international treaties designed to preserve the right to free speech and provide a framework for addressing racist hate speech, and a commitment to addressing racial discrimination as evidenced in the enactment of domestic policy.

Differences in the nations studied

It is in the detail, however, that strong differences emerge between these three nations. Despite overarching similarities, important differences exist in terms of these nations' means of implementing international treaty obligations, the specific mechanisms by and extent to which free speech is protected in law, and the nature of attempts that have been made to respond to the problem of racist hate speech.

Means of implementing international treaty obligations

The three nations in question possess different means of implementing international treaty obligations in domestic law. In Australia, ratification of international treaties does not translate directly into domestic legislative implementation of a treaty's provisions. This requires the passage of domestic — federal and/or state[106]–legislation (Gelber 1999: 334). Within the Australian federal system, the Commonwealth has exclusive constitutionally-derived executive power to ratify treaties (Section 61), and when this occurs both the federal and state government become bound by international law to comply with its terms, regardless of the federal division of powers (Twomey 1994b). The bulk of responsibility for human rights law, including the implementation of the terms of international treaties to which Australia is signatory, rests with the states (Gelber 1999: 336; Rose 1992: 39). However, the federal government is playing an increasingly significant role in the implementation of international treaty provisions and the protection of human rights via its constitutional external affairs power (Section 51 xxix),[107] a role which has been validated by the High Court.[108]

In the United Kingdom, the power to negotiate and conclude treaties rests exclusively with the executive branch of government under its prerogative powers, the powers formerly inherent in the Crown and which can be exercised without the consent of parliament (Templeman 1994: 154). Although a treaty requiring ratification is presented to parliament in the form of a White Paper for a period of 21 days,[109] the parliament is not bound to discuss it during this period. Treaties are not self-executing, which means their domestic implementation requires the passage of legislation through the UK Parliament (Templeman 1994: 153). Such legislation, however, may enact only a part of a treaty, may include the treaty as a Schedule to the legislation or may not refer to the treaty at all (Templeman 1994: 172). The treaty enactment process rests with the executive government, and the treaty implementation process rests with the UK Parliament. Because the United Kingdom is a unitary state, no sub-national levels of government are involved.

In the United States, the treaty-enactment and treaty-implementation processes are much more closely linked. Article VI of the Constitution provides that treaties shall be the "supreme Law of the Land" (Damrosch 1994: 205). This means that treaties which either expressly provide to be "self-executing", or which are self-executing by implication due to their terms and context (Riesenfeld and Abbott 1994: 263), become automatically incorporated into US federal law, once ratified. Self-executing treaties do not require municipal implementing legislation, and create individual rights which are recognisable by the courts. Treaties normally considered to be non-self-executing are those which require a substantial expenditure of public funds, or passage of budgetary legislation (Riesenfeld and Abbott 1994: 263). The distinction between self-executing and non-self-executing treaties has been upheld by the Supreme Court since as early as 1829 (Damrosch 1994: 205).

Ratification of a treaty requires two-thirds approval of the Senate, under Article II of the Constitution (Damrosch 1994: 206). In practice, however, the Senate has rendered many otherwise self-executing treaties non-self-executing by adopting a "non-self-executing declaration" at the time of ratification (Damrosch 1994: 206). The inclusion of such declarations appears to stem both from concerns to protect US sovereignty over its law-making procedures, and from Senators, acting as representatives of their states, opposing federal involvement in areas which would otherwise be considered under state jurisdiction. In the arena of human rights treaties, such opposition has been effective. In 1977, the Carter administration asked the Senate to approve the ICCPR, the ICESCR and the ICERD, with a non-self-executing declaration. The suggestion to include the declaration was designed to overcome opposition within the Senate to the idea of self-executing human rights treaties. The Senate did not act during Carter's term, and it was not until 1992 that the Senate was asked to reconsider the ICCPR (Damrosch 1994: 207–210). Ratification of the ICCPR occurred in 1992, with a non-self-executing declaration attached. Ratification also included a reservation on Article 20 which, it was argued, required criminalisation of certain forms of expression which were protected under the First Amendment (Damrosch 1994: 220).[110] The Senate's role in treaty implementation, combined with the Senators' role as guardians of state prerogatives, explain the delay between Australia's and the UK's ratification of the ICCPR and the ICERD, and the United States'. Furthermore, although under constitutional law, treaties prevail over previously enacted state and federal US law, the US Supreme Court has also adopted a "last-in-time" rule. This rule allows for federal law enacted subsequently to ratification of an international treaty to prevail (Damrosch 1994: 216, 215).

The treaty-making process in the US, then, is complex. Although many treaties are considered to be self-executing, importantly the human rights treaties which are relevant to the discussion here have been ratified with a non-self-executing declaration attached. Perceived inconsistencies between the provisions of the First Amendment and international treaty clauses enjoining State Parties to address hate speech have led to the US placing reservations on those articles which could have otherwise provided a justification in international law for the passage of domestic hate speech legislation.

Mechanisms for the protection of free speech

Although the three nations under discussion share a general historical commitment to free speech, the specific mechanisms by which free speech has been protected in law differ markedly.

Although Australia does not possess either a constitutional or statutory Bill of Rights, the High Court has taken an interpretive approach to the Constitution which has important implications for the right to free speech. In two landmark decisions in 1992, the High Court held that because the Australian Constitution enshrined a system of representative government, this implied the right to freedom of communication on "political" matters (Kirby 1993: 1778–1779). The cases involved a finding that two federal statutes were unconstitutional. In *Nationwide News Pty Ltd v. Wills*[111] the High Court found a federal statute[112] invalid which restricted public criticism of a government institution, the federal Industrial Relations Commission, which might bring it or its members into disrepute. In *Australian Capital Television v. The Commonwealth*,[113] the High Court found a Commonwealth statute[114] invalid which restricted access to political broadcasts on radio and television during referenda and election campaigns for both the Commonwealth and the states (Kirk 1995: 38). The justifications for enacting the legislation had included the reduction of financial pressure on political parties, the facilitation of equal access to electronic broadcasting, and the extension of political communication by encouraging longer broadcasts rather than brief advertisements (Kirk 1995: 39).[115]

The judges held that the Constitution establishes and entrenches the Australian system of government as a system of "representative government"

(Kirk 1995:40).[116] This means those who exercise legislative and executive power are directly chosen by and accountable to the people, and exercise their powers as representatives of the people (McDonald 1994:176–177). The judges extrapolated from this that freedom of communication on "political" matters was an "essential", "necessary", "indispensable", "presupposed" or "inherent" element of representative democracy (Kirk 1995:40). In this context, "political" communication was interpreted primarily to mean discussions of issues of public affairs, expressions critical of government policies and institutions, and criticism of candidates for election.[117] They therefore concluded that the Constitution implies a protection of freedom of "political" communication, and held the two statutes under examination invalid. Since these two landmark cases, the High Court has maintained the implied constitutional right to political communication in further cases.[118] With the exception of the constitutional right to communication on political matters, free speech in Australia is a residual right, an "immunity consequent on a limitation of legislative power".[119] Speech that is free is that which is not restricted by laws of limited scope such as, for example, defamation, libel, sedition, obscenity, commercial confidentiality or privacy laws. However, the common law protection of free speech has always been relatively secure.[120] In *Australian Capital Television*, the court referred to Australia's free speech obligations under Article 19(2) of the ICCPR, to earlier cases which had recognised the importance of the freedom to criticise government action,[121] and also cited US First Amendment cases in support of its findings (Barendt 1994:149).

In the United Kingdom, free speech has until recently also been regarded as a residual right, existing where the speech right has not yet been curtailed under other laws such as the law of libel or obscenity. It is from this tradition that Australia derives its own history on free speech policy. UK common law has historically acted as a strong protection on the free speech right. For example, in *Derbyshire County Council v. Times Newspapers Ltd*,[122] Lord Keith noted that the right to free expression is an "essential feature of citizenship and of representative democracy", and that it is a "basic principle of the unwritten British Constitution, protected by the common law".[123] More recent involvement by the United Kingdom in international bodies, and especially the enactment of the *Human Rights Act 1998*, implementing most of the provisions of the European Convention on Human Rights in UK law, demonstrate a renewed interest in delineating the scope of the speech liberty (Barendt 1994:150). The *Human Rights Act 1998* came fully into force on 4 October 2000. The *Act* protects freedom of expression in Schedule I, Article 10. The Convention, like the ICCPR, permits qualification of the exercise of these rights in a lawful manner and in order to protect public safety or order, public health or morals, and the rights of others. Interpretation of the new statutory protection of free speech will take place in the context of the developed common law principle of free speech (Barendt 1994: 150).

The United States, in contrast to the other two countries examined, possesses a strong constitutional protection of the free speech right. The first of the ten amendments added to the Constitution in 1791 guarantees freedom of speech and the press. The history of First Amendment jurisprudence in the USA has been documented at length elsewhere and need not be repeated in detail here.[124] Suffice it to recognise the scope of the constitutional free speech protection embodied in the First Amendment. For example, the First Amendment does not differentiate between "political" and "non-political" speech, but is written in such a manner as to protect a wide range of speech activities. Although the Supreme Court has not interpreted the First Amendment as an absolute protection, it remains a strong constitutional guarantor of freedom of expression in the United States. Furthermore, North American free speech jurisprudence has exerted considerable influence on free speech policy in other jurisdictions.[125] I will undertake below an analysis of the US Supreme Court's interpretation of the extent of the free speech right as it relates to hate speech.

Policy responses to hate speech

Australia
When Australia ratified the ICERD in 1975, it attached a reservation to Article 4 which stated it was "not at present in a position" to implement Article 4(a), but that it would seek to do so "at the first suitable moment" (Twomey 1994c: 2; Akmeemana and Jones 1995: 131, Joint Standing Committee on Foreign Affairs, Defence and Trade (JSCFADT) 1994: 26). When Australia ratified the ICCPR[126] in 1980, a similar reservation was attached to Article 20. Therefore, when the federal government enacted the *Racial Discrimination Act 1975 (Cth)*, it contained no provisions against racial vilification. It took 20 years for such legislation to be enacted federally.

In 1982 the federal Human Rights Commission[127] held a Conference on Freedom of Expression and Racist Propaganda, in response to the finding that one quarter of complaints received by their office related to incidences of racial vilification (HRC 1983: 1). The conference, which was organised to canvass opinion on the subject, noted that a draft Commonwealth Racial Discrimination Bill had contained clauses prohibiting racial vilification, but that these clauses were removed from the *Racial Discrimination Act* 1975 (Cth) before it was passed, due to free speech considerations (HRC 1983: 2–3, 56; Akmeemana and Jones 1995: 131). These clauses had created offences of incitement of racial disharmony and dissemination of ideas based on racial superiority or hatred (Jones 1995: 14). In 1983 the federal Human Rights Commission (HRC) proposed the creation of a civil offence of racial vilification (HRC 1983). In 1987, the Constitutional Commission recommended the introduction of a new section in the Australian Constitution which would prevent the Commonwealth from restricting free speech on political matters, but would permit regulation of other matters such as obscenity or racial hatred (Constitutional Commission 1987).

During this period there also emerged a considerable body of work noting both the scale of expressions of racial hatred in Australia and the lack of a legislative response to curb its incidence and effects. In 1991, the renamed federal Human Rights and Equal Opportunity Commission conducted an investigation into racist violence. The report which emerged from that investigation noted high levels of hatred-induced violence and recommended the instigation of civil penalties for racial hatred, and criminal penalties for racist violence and intimidation (HREOC 1991: 299–301). The same year the report of the Royal Commission into Aboriginal Deaths in Custody (1991: 38, 116) recommended[128] that governments, both federal and state, legislate to proscribe racial vilification with a view to providing civil conciliation mechanisms. This report recommended against the use of criminal sanctions, which were considered inappropriate (Royal Commission into Aboriginal Deaths in Custody 1991: 38, 116). A report completed in 1992 by the Australian Law Reform Commission into *Multiculturalism and the Law* also recommended the creation of a civil offence of racial hatred, to be dealt with by conciliation. It rejected the creation of a criminal offence of racial vilification on the grounds that it would unduly limit freedom of speech (Twomey 1994a: 4). In December 1992 amendments to the *Racial Discrimination Act* 1975 (Cth) were proposed,[129] including the introduction of racial vilification provisions, but when an election was called in early 1993 the legislation lapsed (Jones 1995: 15; Twomey 1994a: 5). In its ninth periodic report to the United Nations concerning implementation of the ICERD, the federal government noted its intention to enact racial vilification legislation, and remove its reservations to Article 4(a) of the ICERD and Article 20 of the ICCPR (United Nations Committee on the Elimination of Racial Discrimination (UNCERD) 1993). In 1994, the

Commonwealth Parliament noted that the previous Bill, "outlawing racial vilification as described in Article 20 of the ICCPR and Article 4(a) of the ICERD", had lapsed and it was noted that debate continued within Australia as to the appropriateness of enacting state and/or Commonwealth racial vilification legislation, and in relation to limiting any such legislation so as not to "proscribe opinions or inhibit free speech as it is understood in a democracy, especially as it involves humour or satire" (JSCFADT 1994:24–25). The report recommended the implementation of Commonwealth racial vilification legislation in areas "not yet subject to legislation under Article 4(a) of the Convention" (JSCFADT 1994:26). When the new *Racial Hatred Bill* was introduced in 1994, it included both criminal and civil offences. None of the criminal provisions were retained when the *Racial Hatred Act 1995* (Cth) was passed. The Act instituted civil penalties for the offence of racial vilification, effectively remedying Australia's reservations on both Article 20(2) of the ICCPR and Article 4(a) of the ICERD.[130]

In 1989 the first state-based racial anti-vilification legislation was passed in New South Wales.[131] Western Australia,[132] the Australian Capital Territory,[133] South Australia,[134] Tasmania,[135] Queensland[136] and Victoria[137] later followed suit (see Appendix B). In the context of only a limited constitutional free speech right, the implementation of anti-vilification laws in Australia has not been challenged by constitutional free speech provisions.

The analysis undertaken in the book thus far has examined the NSW racial anti-vilification legislation in depth. The other civil anti-vilification provisions in force around Australia (federally, and in the ACT, South Australia, Tasmania, Queensland and Victoria) very closely resemble the NSW law, in terms of the statutory definitions used, the provision of wide-ranging free speech exemptions, and the resolution model. The NSW study in this sense is representative of other Australian statutes, and the conclusions drawn are relevant to the other jurisdictions. In order to provide a framework for comparing the Australian experience with that of the UK and the USA, the relevant conclusions drawn from my study of the NSW legislation will be briefly summarised here. This summary clarifies that for the purposes of the comparative study, the emphasis in this chapter is on those findings which related to drawbacks in existing policy arrangements. I have argued thus far that:

1. The NSW legislation was framed in the way it was (i.e. with broad-ranging exemptions) in an attempt to "balance" free speech concerns with a concern to ameliorate the harms of hate speech.

2. This policy approach directly reflects a reliance on a conception of the aim of speech policy as designed to maximise free speech *per se*. This means that (a) any attempt to ameliorate the harms of hate speech is counterposed to the goal of maximising speech opportunities, and (b) a policy response to hate speech is conceived of in restrictive or punitive terms.

3. A capabilities-oriented approach provides a framework within which the two goals — of maximising free speech and ameliorating the harms of hate speech — may be seen as mutually collaborative. This is possible where hate speech policy is conceived not in punitive or restrictive terms, but instead as a policy designed to provide material, educational and institutional support to victims of hate speech, to allow them to respond. This would allow victims to challenge (by participating in the exercise of the speech liberty) the "silencing" effect of hate-speech-acts, and to contradict (with their own speech) the claims raised by hate speakers.

These theoretical conclusions enabled explanations to be offered for apparent inadequacies and weaknesses in the implementation of the NSW legislation in practice. These included that:

4. Problems in application of the NSW racial anti-vilification policy arose due to a reliance on an individualised and private complaints and resolution procedure. These problems in application rendered many harms constituted in the uttering of hate-speech-acts immune from response. The individualised and private nature of the policy approach does not incorporate an understanding of the phenomenology of hate speech as a public speech-act which enacts discrimination into the resolution process.

5. The NSW legislation in practice demonstrates the difficulty of achieving a workable statutory definition of hate speech. It tends to be unable to respond to "sophisticated" or "sanitised" instances of hate speech, because these types of hate speech are more likely to fall under an exemption or to fail to qualify for the statutory definition of hate speech. Yet such types of hate speech may also be capable of constituting harmful discrimination. It has been suggested a difficult-to-enforce statutory definition may arise as a result of a conceptualisation of speech policy in punitive and restrictive terms.

The limitations in NSW hate speech policy have been explained by linking the policy's design with underlying assumptions about the aim of speech policy. Below, I will investigate hate speech policy in the UK and the USA. I will argue that hate speech policy in both these jurisdictions suffers from the same weaknesses as exposed in the NSW example, and for the same underlying reasons.

United Kingdom

The United Kingdom also placed a reservation on Article 20 of the ICCPR at ratification in 1976, and a "declaration" (to similar effect) on Article 4 of the ICERD at ratification in 1969. As noted above, at the time of ratification the UK government rejected the prohibition of the "dissemination of ideas" on the basis that it represented too great an interference in freedom of speech (Twomey 1994a: 241). The laws that have been enacted to respond to racial vilification in the United Kingdom, by contrast with those in Australia, are exclusively criminal provisions. As a result of relying solely on criminal provisions, the laws demand a high standard of proof.

In 1965 the UK government enacted the *Race Relations Act,* which contained Section 6 declaring an offence the incitement of racial hatred, which was defined statutorily as the use of words or the publication or distribution of written material, which was "threatening, abusive or insulting", in a manner which intended to, or was likely to, stir up racial hatred (Bindman 1982: 299). Prosecution required the consent of the Attorney-General, and possible punishment included a fine of £200 or £1000, and 6 months' to 2 years' imprisonment (Bindman 1982: 299). The use of the term "threatening, abusive or insulting" was derived from criminal public order provisions, which already created an offence of using such words or behaviour with the intent to, or in a manner likely to, breach the peace (*Public Order Act 1936*) (Lester and Bindman 1972: 350). The type of criminal offence created under this legislation was designed to respond to racial vilification likely to stir up racial hatred. In this sense it was not designed to respond to expressions of racial hatred *per se.*

In 1976, this provision was removed from the *Race Relations Act* and inserted in the *Public Order Act* (as Section 5A).[138] When this change occurred, the requirement of demonstrating intent to stir up racial hatred was removed, leaving only the requirement to demonstrate objective likelihood that racial hatred would be stirred up (Twomey 1994a: 238–239; Bindman 1982: 300). This change was justified on two grounds. First, it was claimed that the incidence of racial vilification was increasing, rather than decreasing (Bindman 1982: 301). Secondly, it was claimed incidences of vilification appeared to be becoming more sophisticated, in the sense that alleged hate speakers claimed the views they were expressing were part of public debate or designed to elicit sympathy, not hatred, for its victims (Twomey 1994a: 242–243), and that they denied an intention to incite racial hatred. For example, in 1968 four members of the Racial Preservation Society were prosecuted[139] for the publication of a newsletter which referred to the dangers of racial contact and "race mixing", and speculated about genetic differences between races. The newsletter openly denied the authors' intention to stir up racial hatred, declaring their purpose was to effect the return of non-Anglo-Saxon people to "their own countries" from "this overcrowded island" (Bindman 1982: 299). The newsletter's authors judiciously avoided the use of extreme language which could be characterised as "threatening, abusive or insulting", utilising instead more moderate prose. The four defendants were acquitted (Bindman 1982: 299). In 1967, a leader of the National Socialist Movement, was also prosecuted for the distribution of a leaflet entitled "The Colonial Invasion". In the leaflet it was argued that "the presence of this coloured million in our midst is a menace to our nation" (Lester and Bindman 1972: 368). Although the defendant claimed his intent had been to inform people of potential problems arising from immigration, he was convicted and imprisoned for 18 months (Bindman 1982: 299). It is interesting that in late 1967 a member of the Black Power Movement, Michael Abdul Malik (known as Michael X) was convicted and sentenced to 12 months' imprisonment for incitement of racial hatred against white people. At a public meeting, Malik had said, "the white man has no soul" and "you get to know a lot in prison, a lot that can terrify the white man".[140] The legislation was put in place with the aim of preventing racist expressions against people of colour, yet in this case a person of colour was imprisoned under the same law.

In 1985, a review of the *Public Order Act* recommended further amendments to criminalise the expression of racial hatred *per se*, but the government rejected this option, arguing that the "reasonable exercise of freedom of expression" should be protected, even where the views expressed were "unpleasant" (Twomey 1994a: 238). The government's rejection of this option concurred with its continued reservation to Article 4 of the ICERD on free speech grounds. Other recommendations, however, were enacted in the form of the *Public Order Act 1986* which, in Section 18, reintroduced the requirement of intent to demonstrate an offence had been committed, but allowed for *either* the demonstration of intent *or* the demonstration of an objective likelihood that racial hatred would be stirred up (Twomey 1994a: 238–239).[141] The offence was further qualified by allowing that if a person did not intend, and was not aware, that their actions could stir up racial hatred, objective likelihood could not be demonstrated (Section 23). Reasons cited at the time for the reintroduction of the intent requirement were that sometimes the material in question intended to stir up racial hatred, but did not succeed because the target audience was not susceptible, for example members of the clergy (Twomey 1994a: 239).

Despite the vacillation on the question of whether intent and/or objective likelihood should be interpreted as requirements for the constitution of an offence, the difficulty noted above, of the statute's reliance on the term "threatening, abusive or insulting", remains unresolved. While the use of this term is a logical corollary to enacting provisions resting on disturbances to public order, the term does not allow for the prosecution of restrained expression (Lester and Bindman 1972:361–362). In their report in 1994 to the United Nations concerning implementation of the ICCPR, the UK government noted that it had no plans to extend the scope of its laws in response to racial vilification, because it regarded the public order provisions as sufficient (United Nations Human Rights Committee (UNHRC) 1994). In their reports concerning implementation of the ICERD, the UK government noted that its interpretation of Article 4 at the time of ratification remained valid (UNCERD 1996), and that no additional legislation was necessary (UNCERD 1995). More recently, criminal provisions against racially motivated offences, including offences against "public order" and "harassment", have been supplemented by the introduction of the *Crime and Disorder Act 1998* (Sections 31 and 32).

A comparison of the UK provisions with those in Australia raises three points for discussion. The UK provisions are exclusively criminal whereas Australia's are primarily civil. The UK policy relies on provisions related to the maintenance of public order, and not to the harms which may be caused by hate speech itself. The government's express interpretation of Article 4 of the ICERD is that it allows for undue restriction on freedom of expression. The UK government's reluctance to introduce civil provisions capable of responding to racial vilification, their reaffirmation of a reluctance to implement such provisions on free speech grounds, and their use of the term "unpleasant" to describe expressions of racial hatred imply a particular understanding of hate speech. They imply an understanding of hate speech as an expression of ideas rather than as a discursive act, constituting significant harm. The UK government implies, via the legislation it has enacted and the legislation it refuses to enact, that the best mechanism by which free speech might be maintained is the minimising of government restriction on expression. This implies a reliance in UK policy-making on both a speech-conduct dichotomy, and a conception of speech policy as able to be operationalised via the maximisation of free speech. In other words, despite the significant differences which exist between UK and Australian hate speech policy, an analysis of the UK legislation in practice allows similar conclusions to be drawn as those drawn from a critical analysis of the NSW laws. These are:

1. The UK legislation has been framed in the manner it has (exclusively criminal provisions, with a high standard of proof), in an attempt to "balance" free speech concerns with a concern to ameliorate the harms of hate speech.

Indeed, in a report to the United Nations, the UK government expressed its policy goal in precisely these terms: "The United Kingdom Government firmly believes that it strikes the right balance between maintaining the country's long traditions of freedom of speech and protecting its citizens from abuse and insult" (UNCERD 1996).

2. This policy approach directly reflects a reliance on a conception of the aim of speech policy as designed to maximise free speech *per se*. This means that (a) any attempt to ameliorate the harms of hate speech is counterposed to the goal of maximising speech opportunities, and (b) the policy response to hate speech is conceived of in restrictive or punitive terms.

This implies that the utilisation of a capabilities-oriented approach, which both maximises free speech and ameliorates the harms of hate speech, could improve hate speech policy outcomes in the UK, as well as in Australia.

There is a third area of comparison to be made between UK and Australian hate speech policy. This is a comparison of the statutory definition of hate speech. Again, despite significant differences in the detail of the two policies in terms of the definitions used, both the UK and the Australian legislation demonstrate the difficulty of achieving a workable statutory definition of hate speech. Not only do both policies demonstrate this difficulty, they also share the feature of finding it difficult to respond to "sophisticated" or "sanitised" instances of hate speech. In the UK case, this difficulty is exacerbated by the high standard of proof required to prove criminal behaviour. Nevertheless, in both cases types of hate speech which may be capable of enacting harmful discrimination with significant perlocutionary effects[142] appear immune from a policy response.

United States

The United States' implementation of hate speech policy is unique. The USA ratified the ICCPR in 1992, with a reservation to Article 20 which, it was claimed, would have required the criminalisation of forms of expression protected under the First Amendment. Furthermore, the ICCPR was adopted with a non-self-executing declaration. A reservation was also lodged against Article 4 of the ICERD at its ratification in 1994. In a 1994 report to the United Nations regarding implementation of the ICCPR, the US government referred to the "strength of the First Amendment's protection of freedom of speech" which justified its reservation on Article 20 (UNHRC 1994c). In so doing, the government referred to recent Supreme Court decisions which had sought to clarify the scope of the First Amendment right. In order to understand the impact of free speech jurisprudence on hate speech policy, I will briefly outline some of these decisions.

The First Amendment guarantees freedom of religion, freedom of speech and the press, the right of assembly and the right of petition. In interpreting free speech doctrine, the courts have consistently upheld the doctrine of content-neutrality, the idea that the state may not discriminate on the grounds of the content of speech. A number of statutes seeking to impose content-based restrictions on speech have been declared invalid by the Supreme Court. For example, in 1992 under a Minnesota law a youth was convicted of using words "producing anger or resentment on the basis of race". He had erected and then burnt a crude cross on the lawn of a black family living across the street from his home. On appeal, the law was found to be constitutionally invalid[143] because it discriminated on the grounds of subject matter. In 1978, a street parade by the National Socialist Party was banned under an ordinance which had been enacted in the village of Skokie, Illinois. The ordinance prohibited the dissemination of materials which would promote hatred towards people on the basis of heritage. The parade included the wearing of Nazi uniforms and bearing of swastikas. The ordinance was declared unconstitutional,[144] because it turned on content. On the same content-neutrality basis, in 1937 the Supreme Court declared communists had the right to speak freely and run for office.[145] The US courts consistently uphold the constitutional principle that

> the right to engage in propaganda of war is as protected as the right to advocate pacifism, and the advocacy of hatred as protected as the advocacy of fellowship (UNHRC 1994c).

Some limited restrictions on speech have been upheld as constitutionally valid. Some obscenity, for example, has been held to be speech that is not protected by the First Amendment on the basis that it does not constitute "speech" designed to be so protected.[146] The "clear and present danger" doctrine[147] provides for constitutionally permissible restrictions on some speech where that speech can be demonstrated to cause danger that is both grave and imminent, strictly interpreted. An example of the limited interpretation of this doctrine is that it was not able to be used to punish someone who, wearing a hood at a Ku Klux Klan rally, stated that "the nigger should be returned to Africa, the Jew returned to Israel".[148] In this case, the Court held that the clear and present danger doctrine only allowed for the restriction of speech which incited imminent lawlessness. In a finding related to the march by Nazis in the village of Skokie, Illinois, the federal court noted that government may proscribe content on the basis only of "imminent danger of grave substantial evil",[149] a qualification they felt the march did not fulfil. Words which are considered to cause an immediate breach of the peace and grave danger of violence are regarded as "fighting words" and are not protected by the First Amendment. The definition of "fighting words" has been considerably narrowed since it was used in 1942 when a man was convicted for declaring: "You are a God damned racketeer" and "a damned Fascist and the whole government of Rochester are Fascists or agents of Fascists" on a sidewalk in New Hampshire.[150] Subsequent court cases which have updated and severely delimited the *Chaplinsky* decision include *Terminiello v. Chicago*,[151] which recognised and took into account that the exercise of free speech normally invites dispute. Then *Cohen v. California*[152] qualified the doctrine by cautioning that a state's fear of disturbance was not considered sufficient to define "fighting words", because capable citizens must make their own decisions as to the effect of language. This case involved a man wearing a jacket emblazoned with the words "Fuck the Draft" in protest at conscription policies during the Vietnam War. The same case further qualified the fighting words doctrine by adding the requirement that a target audience must have no reasonable means of escaping the receipt of the communication. Finally, *Gooding v. Wilson*[153] further narrowed the fighting words definition to language causing immediate acts of violence by the individual to whom the remark is addressed (Hentoff 1980: 306–310). In a separate finding it has been held that when a public official complains of libel, they must demonstrate that the statement was made with "actual malice" in order to uphold a claim for damages.[154] This severely restricts the ability of public officials to recover damages under defamation laws.

The fighting words and clear and present danger doctrines define the limited kinds of "harm" that are held by the courts to be sufficient to warrant legal intervention, within the context of First Amendment free speech protections. They define this harm as a discrete act of grave violence, immediately subsequent and attributable to a remark. In light of the earlier discussion, this appears to be a narrow and somewhat Millian definition of harm which does not recognise that a hate-speech-act may, in itself, constitute a harmful act of discrimination. Relying on this narrow definition of the harm requisite to warrant legal intervention suggests one of two possibilities. The first is that free speech jurisprudence in the United States is informed by a speech-conduct dichotomy, where this strict delineation of subsequent harm conforms to "acts" which are regulable and all other speech is protected expressive activity. It is important to note that the suggestion that First Amendment jurisprudence upholds a speech-conduct dichotomy is not intended to imply that the Supreme Court delineates "speech" as only words. The Supreme Court has made many decisions in which an engagement in an expressive activity, such as burning the flag or burning a cross, has been held to be "speech" and therefore subject to First Amendment protections. What is meant here is that Supreme Court decisions uphold a delineation between protected expressive activity on the one hand ("speech" which includes most words and some actions), and sufficiently harmful expressive activity ("acts" which include only some strictly delineated actions) on the other.[155]

If this is the case, US First Amendment jurisprudence is rendered vulnerable to charges of an unwillingness to incorporate significant scholarly developments in the understanding of what it is one does when one speaks, into the interpretation and application of law. This is a searching criticism. The Supreme Court appears reluctant to permit speech-acts to be regulated unless they invoke a discrete, immediate, grave and violent act. Speech-acts are thus held not to constitute harmful acts in and of themselves. This reasoning implies an unwillingness to recognise the potential harms of hate-speech-acts as severe enough to warrant regulation of some kind. But the harms of hate-speech-acts, according to the phenomenology and argument outlined in this book, need not be related to the identification of a discrete, immediate, grave and violent act. Hate-speech-acts can be harmful in and of themselves. First Amendment jurisprudence appears unwilling to recognise this.

The second possibility is that free speech jurisprudence in the United States recognises that speech may be a kind of conduct, but severely delineates the kind of conduct which might warrant intervention. This would imply that speech, like other types of conduct, is not automatically immune from regulation but ought to be regulated according to criteria such as the degree of harm it causes. Actions which harm others, and which injure others' ability to live a life of quality, are generally regulable. Murder, kidnapping and assault are obvious examples. Other actions, which exhibit a less direct measure of harm, are nevertheless also regulable on the basis of the harm they cause. For example, discrimination is prohibited, as is sexual harassment. This would tend to imply that the delineation of harm for acts which warrant regulation is not necessarily an "immediate" or "grave" danger of a discrete act of violence. Yet First

Amendment jurisprudence has demonstrated that speech-acts may only be regulated where the harm that occurs is "immediate" and "grave" and causally related to the utterance of the speech-act. So speech, or expressive activity, *has* been treated differently from other acts. This implies that if speech has been treated differently from other acts, the suggestion that First Amendment jurisprudence treats speech as a kind of conduct may be questioned, because it appears potentially contradictory. To hold this view would be to argue at one and the same time that speech is a kind of conduct, and therefore subject to similar tests of regulation as other conduct, and that speech only deserves regulation when it is conduct which presents an imminent and grave danger of violence. Since this view appears contradictory, it is logical to deduce that First Amendment jurisprudence relies on the upholding of a potentially unviable speech-conduct dichotomy.

Another area in which restrictions on hate speech have been challenged is the implementation of speech codes on university campuses in North America. Public universities are bound by constitutional law. Private universities can in principle impose restrictions on speech because (as private institutions) they are not bound by constitutional law, although their conduct tends to be informed by constitutional law (Sunstein 1993a: 197). The rationale for the introduction of such codes is that universities are charged with an educational mission, and therefore are responsible for maintaining an environment within which the realisation of that mission is possible and equally accessible. Also, campus students can be defined (unlike the public at large) as a "captive audience" (Lawrence 1993: 71; Matsuda 1993: 44–45).[156]

An example of a campus behaviour code is that which has been implemented at Stanford University, a private institution which chooses to comply with First Amendment interpretations of the scope of the speech liberty (Sunstein 1993a: 203). The Stanford code prohibits threats of violence, and also harassment by "personal vilification". This is defined as the use of "fighting words" or symbols, in a manner intended to stigmatise, and addressed directly at intended victims. "Fighting words" are defined as those which convey "direct and visceral hatred or contempt for human beings" (Lawrence 1993: 67). This definition of "fighting words" is wider than that adopted by the Supreme Court in the cases cited above, but this may be explained by the fact that students may be regarded as a captive audience. Furthermore, this definition is directed at the prohibition of words under specific circumstances, that is when they are directed at another individual or group of individuals. A broader hate speech code enacted at the University of Michigan has, by contrast, been held to be invalid on First

Amendment grounds. This code sought to prohibit "any verbal or physical behavior which stigmatizes or victimizes" an individual, and which "creates an intimidating, hostile or demeaning environment for educational pursuits" (Sunstein 1993a: 198). This code, reliant upon terms like "demeaning" and not restricted to face to face encounters, was considered too broad by the courts. Despite the nominal greater licence permitted private universities, which are not bound to adhere to constitutional law and the First Amendment, the Stanford example demonstrates an interconnection with First Amendment jurisprudence that tends to concur with the argument that a speech-conduct dichotomy informs the design of campus speech codes.

It appears, then, that US hate speech policy influenced by First Amendment jurisprudence exhibits a similar theoretical problem to one unearthed in the Australian and UK examples. This is the idea that speech policy tends to be conceived as designed to maximise free speech *per se*. This means that: (a) any attempt to ameliorate the harms of hate speech is counterposed to the goal of maximising speech opportunities, and (b) the policy response to hate speech is conceived of in restrictive or punitive terms. As the *R. A. V.* and *Skokie* decisions demonstrate, policies enacted with the intention of preventing racial hatred have been overridden in favour of free speech concerns. Even in the case of campus speech codes, the speech identified as warranting a response is narrowly defined so as not to impinge too greatly on the speech liberty, and the policy response created is a prohibitive one. The two goals have quite clearly been counterposed, and where policies have been restrictive or punitive they have been rejected in favour of free speech concerns.

What possibilities exist, then, for a non-punitive approach towards speech policy, which might not conflict with the First Amendment? Barendt argues the US Supreme Court has in the past demonstrated a hostility to the idea that the free speech right embodied in the First Amendment entails equal rights or access to the means of expression (1994: 153). He cites their rejection of a claim that the First Amendment entailed a right to access the broadcasting media,[157] a claim that the First Amendment entailed the right to place unstamped mail in letterboxes,[158] a claim that enforced provision of the right of reply was consistent with First Amendment principles,[159] and a claim that the First Amendment entailed the right to paste notices on lamp posts[160] as evidence for this (1994: 152–154). In an earlier, and instructive, case[161] the Supreme Court had upheld the idea that some individuals, under some circumstances, did have the right of reply to personal attacks in the broadcast media. In this instance, the decision turned on the policy-making powers of the Federal Communications Commission

(FCC), a body established to coordinate legitimate government regulation of the broadcast media. Communications media in the United States are statutorily obliged to ensure the "public interest" is served by their coverage.[162] Until 1987, the FCC enforced the public interest provision in part via a "fairness doctrine", which worked on the principle that coverage of important issues must be adequate and must fairly reflect different points of view. As a corollary to this doctrine, the FCC implemented two other rules: the "personal attack" rule and the "political editorial" rule.[163] The personal attack rule provides that when, during the presentation of views on controversial issues of public importance, a personal attack is made upon the integrity of an identified person, the aggrieved person must be notified of the broadcast and given the opportunity to respond (FCC 1998).[164] The rationale for upholding this rule in the *Red Lion* decision was that the broadcaster themselves would be unable to do this adequately.[165] The Supreme Court's decision in this case was that an FCC policy which provided that an individual be given the opportunity to respond to a personal attack was within the authority of the FCC because they were legitimately implementing congressional policy. This decision, then, turned on the constitutionality of an FCC policy designed to "enhance" rather than abridge freedom of speech.[166]

Some later decisions appear to challenge the premise that government policies aimed at providing speech for some individuals are an enhancement of freedom of speech, and therefore compatible with the First Amendment. For example in the 1973 case regarding access to the broadcast media, the Supreme Court held that the First Amendment did not oblige broadcasters to accept all paid advertisements, and that broadcasters were entitled to refuse an absolute right of access. This was on the grounds that obliging broadcasters to accept paid advertisements, even where they would otherwise choose not to, could allow for the monopolisation of their airwaves by those who could afford to pay. Furthermore, implementation of an absolute right of access to broadcasting media would involve the FCC to an unacceptable degree in mediating access to, and therefore unduly regulating, broadcasting operations.[167] In a similar case, the Supreme Court upheld the idea that a media outlet could not be compelled to print something it otherwise would not, something which "reason" tells them they should not publish.[168] Government enforcement of an automatic right of access *to all* could dampen debate, as media outlets sought to avoid controversy rather than generate situations in which they could be obliged to provide a response.

These cases tend to support Barendt's argument that the Supreme Court has been generally hostile to the notion of free speech as a positive liberty, when this is interpreted as a liberty which enjoins the provision of access to speech by some media. The more recent cases tend to turn on the inappropriateness of government intervening in the editorial decisions of privately-owned media outlets. Barendt notes that in these cases the claims to equal access and to promotion of speech opportunities were made against institutions whose commercial interests would in some way be affected — media "oligopolies" (1994:154).

However, where the regulation under question was derived from congressional policy, the outcome was different. In 1987 the FCC repealed the fairness doctrine. The rationale for repeal was that the public interest the doctrine was designed to serve was henceforth able to be served by a marketplace of media, ensured by an increase in the number of media outlets. The repeal of the doctrine, therefore, did not serve to repeal the public interest rationale, but instead to enforce it by other means (FCC 1998). A later petition filed by numerous media outlets to effect repeal of the political editorial and personal attack rules failed. In June 1998 the FCC found that these two rules continued to serve public interest by ensuring a "right of access" to the media under specific circumstances, in a manner which served the public interest (FCC 1998). In particular, the FCC emphasised that these rules ensured a right of reply under circumstances which ensured the *same audience* that had heard the political endorsement or personal attack would be given the opportunity to hear the reply (FCC 1998).

It appears possible, then, that a speech policy approach based on a concept of making provision for the exercise of the speech right as a right of reply may, subject to narrow conditions, not raise the same First Amendment problems as punitive or restrictive measures. This means a capabilities-oriented speech policy such as suggested in this book may be able to be implemented in the context of the strict First Amendment protections of free speech that exist in the US. If the assisted response were framed in such a way as to provide a group of individuals with enhanced use of some kind of public fora, within or around a neighbourhood or street or community centre for example, such a response could avoid coming into direct conflict with the speech opportunities of media "oligopolies". Furthermore, in relevant instances, an assisted response could be framed in such a way as to provide the same audience which was subject to the hate-speech-act with the opportunity to hear the assisted response from the victim group. This approach may avoid tackling the Supreme Court's hostility to the idea of a positive speech right, where the provision of that positive speech right might be perceived to enjoin the government to overbroad involvement in the regulation of private media interests and decision-making. This is an interesting possibility.

As current policy stands, then, the US example demonstrates some commonalities with the Australian and UK cases. In spite of considerable differences, especially regarding the strong constitutional free speech protection, US policy-makers tend to conceive of the aim of speech policy as the maximisation of speech. Attempts that have been made thus far to ameliorate the harms of hate speech have been perceived by the courts as directly counterposed to the goal of maximising speech opportunities, and have been conceived by the hate speech policy-makers as restrictive or punitive in nature. A capabilities-oriented approach may be capable of integrating the two policy goals — of maximising free speech and ameliorating the harms of hate speech — in a mutually collaborative manner and therefore may be applied to improve hate speech policy outcomes in the USA, as well as Australia and the UK. The specific policy weaknesses identified in Australia and the UK, especially the difficulty of devising a workable statutory definition of hate speech, do not apply in practice[169] in the US in the absence of a federal hate speech policy.[170]

In conclusion, the theoretical difficulties and problems of implementation identified in the NSW legislation appear to exist in the other jurisdictions studied, despite the presence of significant differences in their means of implementing international treaty obligations and their mechanisms for protecting free speech. This implies two things. First, the kind of critical analysis of the application of speech theory to speech policy presented in this book is applicable in other jurisdictions sharing the commonalities evidenced by these three nations: an identification as liberal democracies, a commitment to upholding free speech in law, and a commitment to the eradication of racial discrimination. Secondly, this conclusion implies that the capabilities-oriented approach to hate speech policy advocated in this book may be applicable in other similar jurisdictions also. This considerably expands the potential applications and usefulness of the study. It also raises the question, mooted earlier, of more precisely outlining what a capabilities-oriented speech policy might look like. I will begin this task in the next chapter.

CHAPTER 6

A policy of 'speaking back'

In this chapter I will begin to explore the ways in which a capabilities-oriented hate speech policy, a policy of "speaking back", might be operationalised. Although it has been suggested that the identification of a hate-speech-act allows for the recognition of *who* might be able to make use of such a policy, the question of *how* such individuals might utilise the policy has not yet been explored. I will clarify this question here, by elucidating an alternative framework for a hate speech policy. I will not prescribe the formal details of such a policy, as to do so would require a degree of detail which would obscure the argument. However, I will try to answer potential objections to the hate speech policy proposed and I will canvass other proposals that have been made to deal with hate speech, in order to expose any weaknesses and to clarify the differences between already-existing policy proposals and the proposals I make in this book. Finally, I will consider the potential application of the hate speech policy I propose to some well-known "hard cases".

Implementing a "speaking back" policy

I have argued thus far that the integration of capabilities theory into speech policy incorporates considerations of what speech might be capable of doing in and for people's lives. Insofar as the argument can be sustained that some people are prevented from engaging in speech by the hate speech of others, I have suggested it is appropriate to respond to that silencing by providing the educational, material and institutional support which would enable the victims of hate speech to speak back, a capabilities-oriented approach. Thus, the goal of maximising participation in the speech liberty and the goal of ameliorating the harms of hate speech are able to be achieved collaboratively and simultaneously. To recapitulate briefly, I have argued that the hate-speech-acts of hate speakers are capable of inhibiting the ability to speak of its victims. This occurs when an utterance is made which raises "truth" claims of an objective world characterised by inequality, and where the hate speaker is in a position of power relative to the hearer. These claims can be assessed on empirical grounds. A hate-speech-act simultaneously raises claims of the "rightness" of norms and values which enact and support discrimination. These claims can be challenged in terms of their "rightness", both in terms of whether the norms and values exist in the community which is being appealed to, and in terms of the appropriateness of those norms and values within the lifeworld-context in which the appeal is made. A hate-speech-act simultaneously raises claims of the "sincerity" with which the speaker raises claims of hatred and a belief in the appropriateness of enacting discrimination against the hearer. This claim provides some guidance as to the intent of the speaker, but is much more difficult to assess. Thus, the claims raised by the speaker in a hate-speech-act have been summarised in Figure 1.

> Assessable validity claims embodied in
> HATE SPEECH:
> 1. Objective world - inequality
> 2. Norms and values - support and
>   enact discrimination
> 3. Subjectivities - hatred
> [Habermas]

Figure 1.

The perlocutionary force of a hate-speech-act embodies a range of negative effects on the human persona. I have argued that hate-speech-acts directly counteract an individual's ability to pursue the architectonic and ubiquitous functionings of practical reason and affiliation, that is to say the functionings that are central to living a fully human life. Practical reason and affiliation are essential attributes required by each individual in order to plan and manage his/her own life, in cooperation with others. Hate-speech-acts have the illocutionary force of a harmful act of discrimination, with identifiable perlocutionary effects including rendering its victims silent; unable to speak back. This is an effect of hate speech which requires amelioration, and which at the same time directly contradicts the participation objective of the speech policy envisaged. Viewed within the context of a capabilities-oriented hate speech policy, the identification of silencing as a perlocutionary effect of hate speech justifies and warrants a policy response. The argument thus far has been summarised in Figure 2.

What kind of a response would be warranted within this framework? As I outlined earlier, the validity claims framework derived from Habermas' theory

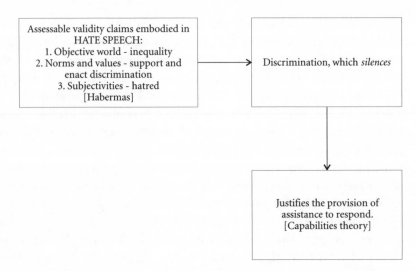

Figure 2.

of communicative action can be used both as a model for understanding the meaning of an expression, and as a model for identifying the appropriate communicative response to hate-speech-acts. I will focus on the second of these tasks here. Within a capabilities framework, the primary task of social policy is support-oriented (as opposed to punishment- or restriction-oriented). This means a capabilities-oriented speech policy would invoke institutional, material and educational support to overcome the impact of hate speech. This means providing an assisted response to those who would seek to contradict and counter the effects of hate-speech-acts.[171] This means that citizens would be empowered to respond to, and to seek to contradict, the impact of and the discrimination embodied in the utterance. The kind of communicative action which would be likely to be effective in response to hate-speech-acts would be that which sought to raise an alternative set of validity claims which contested the validity claims made by the hate speaker. Utilising the same method as was used to identify hate-speech-acts, then, it seems possible to develop a model response to hate-speech-acts. The speakers who might choose to engage in a communicative response would be trying to do two things: firstly, seeking to contradict the validity claims contained within the speech-act, and secondly, seeking to "undo" or counteract the perlocutionary effects of the hate-speech-act via active participation in the development and formation of a response. In this sense, the development and formation of a response could directly empower those seeking to be involved in it.

The first validity claim to be raised by responders to hate speech utterances would be the claim of establishing an objective state of affairs in the world. The objective standard or "truth" which could be claimed by responders would be a state of affairs within which "equality", as opposed to inequality embodied by the power asymmetry in favour of the hate speaker, was a paramount goal.[172] The responders' claim, therefore, would seek to contradict the hate speakers' claims of inequality by engaging and participating directly in the very process of speaking, thus overcoming the silencing effect of subordination. At the same time, the responders' claim would constitute an appeal to the lifeworld to whom the utterance was addressed. This appeal would raise the claim that equality is possible, that power asymmetries are amendable to correction, and that the specific charges levelled against the responders in previous hate-speech-acts are incorrect. The kinds of claims made in the racist hate-speech-acts identified in the NSW study included that people of colour are undeserving of protection by the law, that they deserve to be shot or physically harmed, that they are inferior or animal-like, that they engender social instability, that they are criminals, that they abuse welfare privileges, and that they are dirty. These claims, resting in stereotypes, could be directly contradicted via the use of empirical evidence in the counter speech response. The "truth" claims made by responders would appeal to an entirely different kind of objective world than that appealed to by the hate speakers.

The second validity claim, that of the norms and values which would be appealed to by responders in such a hate speech policy, would be norms and values which support anti-discrimination measures. The "rightness", both in the sense of these norms and values existing in the lifeworld being appealed to, and in the sense of the appropriateness of anti-discrimination measures in the lifeworld being appealed to, can be supported with reference to anti-discrimination standards and norms developed around the world. The appeal by counter speakers to norms and values supporting anti-discrimination measures would seek to contradict the claims of norms and values raised by the hate speakers.

What of the third validity claim, the subjectivities expressed by the counter speakers within such a hate speech policy framework? As discussed, the "sincerity" with which a speaker represents their own subjectivities is extraordinarily difficult to measure. However, within the context of a policy-led response by counter speakers, one element of the counter speakers' subjectivities is identifiable. Engaging in a counter speech response would empower the victims of hate speech to speak back. The discernible benefit to individuals' subjectivities of engaging in counter speech to respond to hate-speech-acts is their empowerment to speak.

The utterances made by those involved in counter speech supported by a hate speech policy, then, seek to challenge (by participating in speaking) and contradict (via raising new validity claims) the meaning, the force and the effects of hate-speech-acts. This implies a process of engagement with the meaning of the claims, a process of argumentation. Indeed, Habermas suggests that argumentation around the meaning of validity claims raised by speakers allows the participants in such argumentation to test meaning, to raise their own validity claims in response, and allows the speakers to modify their own validity claims (Habermas 1984:25). So argumentation provides a framework within which participants can enter into a "discourse", an ongoing discussion within which it should become possible to achieve agreement on the validity claims raised, "if only the argumentation could be conducted openly enough, and continued long enough" (Habermas 1984:42). A capabilities-oriented hate speech policy seems to be a policy which promotes argumentation. The aim of enabling victims to speak back is both to provide them with the support to enable them to be capable of engaging in the speech liberty, and to enable them to counter directly the validity claims raised previously by the hate speakers. The policy, then, can be described as one of "institutionalised argumentation", and would allow for the development of a *counter speech* response. Such a response could directly challenge the validity claims raised by the hate speaker, by raising counter validity claims. It could also help to create the conditions of an "ideal speech situation" envisaged by Habermas — a situation characterised by an absence of constraints on the practising of speech-acts.

The idea that a community's counter speech may be capable over the longer term of achieving changes in behaviour is not new. Jon Elster, for example, argues that the system of public discussion will encourage people to speak in terms acceptable to the community they are appealing to. Elster calls the "civilising force of hypocrisy", the idea that at the very least a public discussion of ideas forces or induces speakers to hide "base motives" (1998:111). My argument proposes that counter speech might, over the longer term, change the behaviour and even the attitudes of hate speakers whose validity claims are challenged. It might be possible that the knowledge that hate speech could lead to providing funding to dignify the target audience in the eyes of the community could deter hate speakers from engaging in hate speech, since such a program would counteract their intentions.[173] It might also be possible that the model of institutionalised argumentation here could achieve a "civilising force", a moderation of the claims raised by previous hate speakers, such that they would cease to discursively enact discrimination. This would be no small feat. Even if the "sincerity" with which this were to occur were subject to question, if the validity claims raised by previous hate speakers no longer represented an objective world suffused with inequality on the grounds of race, and no longer appealed to norms and values which supported and saw the enactment of such discrimination as appropriate, much would have been achieved. The cycle of communicative action engaged in by hate speech utterances and counter speech responses is summarised in Figure 3.

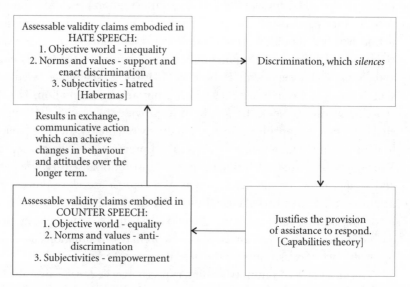

Figure 3. Institutionalised argumentation: The cylce of communicative action in hate speech utterances and counter speech responses.

Types of responses

Questions of which hate-speech-acts to respond to, and in what manner, would require assessment in relation to the actual circumstances of a hate-speech-act. Although it has already been noted that speech-acts which can be assessed as hate-speech-acts allow for a policy-led response, the question of the concrete circumstances within which a counter speech response might be generated has not yet been clarified. This is an important consideration, because it goes to the issue of the appropriate scope of a counter speech response. It would seem appropriate, for instance, that counter speakers are able to appeal to the same community to which the hate speakers appealed. For example, if a hate-speech-act occurred randomly on the street, the victim and/or victim groups might choose to respond by producing a local newsletter for distribution within that neighbourhood. It is important to note that the hate-speaker need not be identified or identifiable, nor need the hate-speaker be individually the subject of a response to the hate-speech-act. Accordingly, this kind of policy need not suffer the procedural limitations involved in an individualised resolution process, such as when the hate-speaker cannot be identified, when the hate-speaker is not willing to comply with requests for information or apologies, when the complainant feels intimidated or threatened by the hate-speaker, or when the complainant withdraws from a complaint because s/he does not wish to be personally identified to the hate-speaker. These are important limitations on an individualised resolution process, which are not present in a capabilities-oriented hate speech policy. If a hate-speech-act occurred in a more public forum, such as the workplace, would-be responders could assist in the development of an anti-racism program within that workplace. If the hate-speech-act occurred in the media, responders may wish to request a right of reply in the same medium, to reach the same audience. Under the current NSW racial anti-vilification legislation, provisions exist to respond to hate-speech-acts that occur in a workplace by developing and conducting an anti-racism program within that workplace. This is a beneficial provision. The difference between the NSW provision and the proposal I make here is that in a capabilities-oriented hate speech policy, the involvement and participation of members of the victim group in implementing and developing a response is crucial. Unless members of the victim group are involved in generating their own response, the response cannot achieve the goal of ameliorating the silencing effects of hate-speech-acts by empowering victim communities to speak back. Under United States constitutional free speech protections, given the *Red Lion* decision and recent deliberations of the Federal Communications Commission (see Chapter 5), it may even be possible to institute a right of reply response to hate-speech-acts within the media. Alternatively, a more general and long-term media-focussed approach might be developed. The Australian Broadcasting Corporation, a government-owned broadcaster, used to air a weekly 15-minute program called "Media Watch". The program scans the electronic and print news and current affairs of the previous week and highlights anomalies or errors in coverage, or evidence of bias. It could conceivably be possible for would-be responders to develop a kind of "Racism Watch" public television program, which would seek to communicate the alternative validity claims outlined above.

Institutions

What institutions might be capable of overseeing, or assisting in the implementation of, such a policy? This is a question of particular import since it has been raised as an objection to the feasibility of the kind of policy proposed here. Sunstein argues that although the idea of a kind of "affirmative action" on speech "makes some sense", such an idea would be difficult to implement (1993b:263). Two of the most important barriers to implementation of an affirmative speech policy (and a capabilities-oriented hate speech policy as described here might be described in this manner, although Sunstein has not specified exactly what is meant by the term) include the difficulty of judging "good" speech which could warrant affirmative action, and the absence of "trustworthy" institutions to implement such a judgement (Sunstein 1993b: 263). Sunstein's first objection has already been answered. It has been argued here that a judgement on whose speech, and what kind of speech, might warrant the provision of assistance may be made within the framework of a validity claims analysis of hate-speech-acts as provided in this book. Once a hate-speech-act has been identified, capabilities theory provides a framework within which it is possible to justify the provision of assistance to would-be responders.

Sunstein's second objection, however, is cogent. Sunstein refers to the absence of institutions which are "trustworthy" enough to make good decisions about affirmative action on speech. In the context of the argument presented here, one might ask whether institutions exist, or could be developed, which are "trustworthy" enough to be able to utilise the methodological and analytical framework presented here, both for identifying hate-speech-acts and for developing a response. Many Western liberal democratic states have passed a variety of anti-discrimination statutes, and have put in place structural mechanisms for implementing their terms. In Australia, for example, the federal Human Rights and Equal Opportunity Commission and the New South Wales Anti-Discrimination Board are responsible for implementing the terms of anti-discrimination statutes. Furthermore, the institutions required to implement anti-discrimination measures reach beyond government structures and include human resources departments in private sector companies, and programs developed and implemented by departments within the public sector. Under

Australia's *Affirmative Action (Equal Opportunity for Women) Act 1986* (Cth), for example, employers with more than 100 employees in sectors including private companies, higher education, voluntary bodies, trade unions and group training schemes are required to develop, implement and report to the Affirmative Action Agency on the progress of affirmative action programs for women. In Australia, implementation of affirmative action does not require the application of a quota system, but rather a more general application of principles of equal opportunity to employment and promotion opportunities. (Affirmative Action Review Secretariat 1998:6–7).[174] With already-existing structures and mechanisms in place to implement a variety of forms of anti-discrimination statutes, it seems likely that, given sufficient attention is paid to training those responsible for implementing the policy and working with target groups, a hate speech policy designed along the lines proposed here would be operable. The question of these institutions' ability to make "good" decisions on what speech might require assistance would be greatly assisted by the use of the methodological framework suggested here. This policy could be used as an adjunct to already-existing hate speech policy, rather than as a replacement, especially in the initial phasing-in period. As institutions and communities likely to take advantage of such a policy became more aware of its scope and provisions, the need for ongoing reliance on the former policy could be reassessed.

Possible objections

Designing a hate speech policy in this manner allows some important objections to be overcome. I will now elaborate on five objections that might be raised: the concern that such a policy might be misused; the concern that it may be overused; the lack of specific exemptions; the question of resource implications in the policy's implementation; and the suggestion that already-existing hate speech policies have an important educative function despite any weaknesses in their application. First, the concern might be raised that developing a hate speech policy designed to provide people with support to enable them to speak could be used by some groups who were not envisaged by the policy-makers as warranting such support. For example, would the policy proposed here be able to be used by neo-Nazi groups to claim assistance to speak? Such groups could claim, for example, that their efforts to raise issues in public debate concerning immigration and unemployment were "silenced" by their opponents. The answer to this problem lies in maintaining an understanding of the proposed hate speech policy in its entirety. While it may be true that neo-Nazi groups and others could claim to have been "silenced" by opponents more numerous, more articulate, better financed or more vocal, the other elements involved in identifying those eligible to make use of the policy would be absent. In order to make use of the hate speech policy proposed, an individual or group must be able to identify the use of a hate speech utterance against them. This would involve a clear demonstration of an utterance which raised a claim of an objective world characterised by inequality, and to norms and values which enact and support discrimination. These claims require assessment in the lifeworld-context within which they are raised. The identification of such claims is essential to identifying the hate-speech-act, and locating it as a discursive act capable of inhibiting the development and exercise of capabilities in hearers. While some people may vigorously and vocally oppose neo-Nazi groups, and even try to silence them, neo-Nazi groups cannot make a legitimate claim to systemic discrimination. Speech-acts which seek to oppose neo-Nazis' beliefs do not perpetrate, perpetuate and maintain racist systemic discrimination against them, however vehemently opponents may condemn neo-Nazis' beliefs and practices. Empirical investigation determines this. Furthermore, in order to benefit from this policy, it has been assessed that counter speakers would raise the kinds of validity claims which would support an objective world character-ised by *equality*, and imbued with norms and values which support anti-discrimination measures. The speech of neo-Nazis does not fit this definition of "counter speech". Because speech against neo-Nazis does not enact racist discrimination (even if it silences them), and because the speech of neo-Nazis cannot be defined as counter speech, the policy would be unable to be used by neo-Nazis and racists to claim assistance to speak.

A second concern which might be raised against the hate speech policy proposed in this book is its potential for overuse, by individuals or groups who claim "insult" to be "vilification". I sought to clarify this problem above, in the context of defining the phenomenology of hate-speech-acts. Because the policy I propose relies on the identification of the discursive enactment of discrimina-tion, this allows insults to be differentiated from hate-speech-acts. Where the discursive enactment of racial discrimination can be identified, a policy response is warranted in order to ensure that the hearers are provided with the appropriate material, educational and institutional support to move them across the threshold of capabilities. Because discrimination has been defined in the sense of systemic power asymmetries and historical marginalisation, its identification is empirically assessable.

A third objection which may be raised in response to the hate speech policy proposed here is that it makes no provision for exemptions. In the NSW legislation studied, fair reporting of remarks made by others and discussions undertaken for academic or scientific research purposes are exempt from the legislation's provisions. These exemptions appeared to arise from a desire to protect speech from excessive government regulation, and to allow speech to occur which is considered an essential part of public debate. A capabilities-oriented hate speech policy designed along the lines proposed here would be unlikely to require statutory exemption provisions, for a number of reasons. Firstly, a response to hate-speech-acts generated under this policy would be designed to enable victims to speak back. This speaking back would be carried out in a public forum of some kind, but would not require the presence of the hate speaker/s who provided the motivation for the response. If, therefore, a hate-speech-act was uttered, and then in the reporting of the event repeated, the response generated to counteract the effects of that hate-speech-act would be a single, united response. Neither the original hate speaker, nor a reporter, would necessarily be required to be present at the generation of the response, which might occur via a separate news article, a community meeting, or the distribution of a leaflet within a community. Because the focus of the policy is not on punishing individuals, exemptions are less necessary. Secondly, if a hate-speech-act were to be uttered in the context of academic or scientific research a response would be even more important. Because the purpose of academic and scientific research is the accumulation of specialised knowledge, an ability to hear and assess competing arguments regarding objective claims to "truth" appears an essential component of the process. Such utterances not only do not require exemption, they (even more than general public debate) require an active engagement in response. Because the policy proposed here is designed to *encourage* and make more speech possible, it is likely to *enhance* the discovery and accumulation of both specialised and general knowledge. It is therefore likely to enhance academic and scientific research and debate.

A fourth objection may be added to a consideration of the plausibility of a capabilities-oriented hate speech policy: the question of resource implications. A policy designed along the lines suggested here would have considerable resource implications. Its implementation would require the training of staff, and possibly also the appointment of new staff, within whatever agency was selected to oversee the policy. However, many institutions and practices in liberal democratic orders which achieve outcomes beneficial to the development of individuals' capabilities are expensive. The benefits of the policy may mean the cost is worthwhile.

A fifth objection that could be raised to the hate speech policy proposed here is that despite any shortcomings which occur in already-existing hate speech policies in the jurisdictions studied, the existence of a hate speech policy itself serves an educative function. It sends a message to the community as a whole that vilification is not to be tolerated. Such claims were made, for example, in parliamentary discussion prior to enactment of the NSW legislation studied (NSWPDLA 4 May 1989: 7491, 7922, 7924; NSWPDLA 10 May 1989: 7812, 7814). There is merit to this claim, since the enactment of legislation such as this does set a legal standard on behaviour. The importance of anti-discrimination measures which both provide recourse to victims and play an educative role by their presence has been widely accepted within Western liberal democratic orders. However, the educative role of such legislation is only one aspect. Current hate speech policy appears vulnerable to a range of criticisms, including that it inadequately responds to the harms of hate speech (especially to the silencing effects), that it unnecessarily counterposes the two goals of maximising speech opportunities and responding to hate speech, and that it renders much hate speech immune from regulation by adopting an unviable statutory definition of hate speech. This implies there is considerable room for improvement. The educative function of such a law ought not remove or override an expectation of effectiveness from hate speech policy.

The hate speech policy proposed in this book assists in the development of individual capabilities among those who most require the provision of institutional, material and educational support to cross the capabilities threshold, thereby responding directly to the phenomenology of hate speech which inhibits the development and exercise of their capabilities. It provides the responders with the authority to carry out a speech-act with the illocutionary force of promoting equality. This policy also recognises the important and distinctive role that participating in speech can play generally in developing individual capabilities, and in assisting in the overall planning, management and development of a society of free and equal citizens. Such a policy seems capable of truly reconciling the importance of speech to human and social development in numerous ways (an understanding which implicitly rests at the "core" of any free speech principle), and the harms of hate speech.

Other hate speech policy proposals

In order to expose any weaknesses and to clarify the differences between already-existing policy proposals and the proposals made in this book, I will also canvass policy proposals put forward by other scholars in the field of speech policy. Other studies which have recognised the harms of hate speech, have argued in favour of a regulatory response to hate speech. A range of options has been proposed, many of which are oriented towards the imposition of punitive or restrictive provisions on individual hate-speakers after the utterance of a hate-speech act. These include:

1. allowing for the classification of a *sui generis* category of "low value" hate-speech-act which may be regulable while leaving speech important to, especially political, public discussion free from restriction (Matsuda 1993; MacKinnon and Dworkin in *American Booksellers Ass'n. Inc. v. Hudnut*, 771 F. 2d 323 (1985));

2. advocating an "accommodationist" approach where face-to-face encounters may be regulated via libel laws, but group libel may not (Flahvin 1995);

3. allowing tort claims (civil suits for damages) by individual victims of hate speech (Delgado 1993);

4. issuing an admonition to recipients of hate-speech-acts to counter its harmful effects by "restaging and resignifying" the language of the hate-speaker (Butler 1997:13);

5. instigating content-neutral restrictions on speech, which are focussed not on the content of the utterance but on an assessment of harm. This can be justified by the neutral claim of reducing inequality ("caste-like features") (Sunstein 1993a);

6. allowing for a one-way, content-based hate speech law which punishes hate-speech acts directed at historically disadvantaged groups (Matsuda 1989:2357);

7. permitting group defamation claims against vilifiers, subject to a strict interpretation of the "harm" the speech invokes (Sadurski 1992; MacKinnon 1993; Scutt 1993).

The first proposal is difficult to operationalise, because as I have discussed above the possibility of hate-speech as "low value" speech can be significantly challenged on more than one ground. An assessment of hate-speech-acts according to Habermas' validity claims lends further weight to this rejection, because it clarifies the difficulty of delineating "low-value" and "high-value" speech. Instead, a communicative action approach suggests an embedded, multi-layered analysis of speech-acts to determine which expressions may be justifiably subject to an assisted response on the basis of whether an act of discrimination occurred in the utterance. This approach is not reliant on a delineation between "political" and "non-political" or "low value" and "high value" speech. Instead, within this framework both crude and sophisticated speech-acts are assessed in terms of the validity claims raised, and their impact on the hearer. The second proposal reflects some examples of regulation of hate-speech on US university campuses (Grey 1990; Strossen 1990). Flahvin argues that the strength of focussing on face-to-face encounters only is that such an approach would be aimed only at speech which intimidates the victim, rather than at speech which conveys a message about the whole group to which a victim is perceived to belong (1995:337–338). This approach would render many speech-acts immune from regulation, a consequence which appears to be motivated by a desire to provide for the protection of speech from excessive government regulation. On this ground, this policy appears to be vulnerable to the criticism that it overlooks the phenomenology of hate-speech-acts. As argued above, hate-speech-acts have a negative impact on individual hearers, on the group to which they are perceived to belong, and on others in association with the victims. According to the model developed above, Habermas' validity claims are raised simultaneously, and the perlocutionary effects of the hate-speech-act occur immediately the illocution is uttered. The accommodationist approach, therefore, is open to criticism of failure to take proper account of the phenomenology of hate speech. Hate speech policy drafted along these lines may justifiably be criticised for having very little impact on the amelioration of hate-speech-acts because it could leave all but one partial effect (the effect on an individual in a face-to-face encounter) of the utterance immune from regulation. Another criticism of this approach also can be made of the third proposal and regards the usefulness of the policy in ameliorating the silencing effects of a hate-speech-act. The third proposal places the emphasis for proceeding on a hate-speech complaint on the determination and resolution of the individual victim to pursue a claim for damages incurred when subjected to a hate-speech-act. Even if considerable numbers of cases resulted in good publicity and the winning of significant damages claims, this proposal provides no support to an individual to pursue a complaint in the courts. It also does not provide for direct involvement in the formation of a response by those subjected to the hate-speech-acts, and therefore does not ameliorate the silencing effects of hate speech.

In light of the same discussion regarding the phenomenology of hate-speech, the fourth proposal may also be criticised. This proposal stands out from the others in the sense that it does not advocate restriction or punishment of hate-speech-acts. Instead, the proposal argues for hate-speech-acts to be responded to by "restaging and resignifying" the hate speakers' language. Butler draws on the agency of language, arguing that in recognising themselves as targets of injurious language, those targets are constituted within the terms of that language and therefore and thereby are granted the possibility of responding and countering the injurious language in a meaningful way. Thus, a hate-speech-act risks "inaugurating a subject in speech" who can counter the injurious utterance (1997:1–3). Indeed, Butler argues this resignifying of injurious language is already taking place in rap music and political parody (1997:14). However, there is an important flaw in this approach. That is that possessing the knowledge that the language of the abuser may be appropriated and reconstructed does not necessarily equate with the possession of the *ability* to do so. Butler's emphasis on a linguistically-constituted agency overlooks other effects of language use. Her proposal does not take the "silencing" and disempowering effects of hate speech sufficiently into account, and therefore appears to falls down in the transition from a concept to implementation in policy terms.

The last three proposals (5, 6 and 7) appear to rest on a broader appreciation of the harms of hate-speech-acts, and as such do go a significant way towards recognising the harm constituted by hate-speech-acts. However, despite recognising the harms of hate-speech-acts, these proposals display a reliance on restrictive or punitive policy provisions in response to hate speech. Indeed, all the proposals outlined, except that of Butler, share this reliance. This reliance on restriction (proposal 5) or punishment (proposals 6 and 7) has been explained elsewhere in this book as arising from a concern to "balance" free speech goals with an amelioration of the harms of hate speech. This results in conceptions of hate speech policy as a policy which is necessarily counterposed to the goal of maximising speech opportunities. To that extent, these proposals are vulnerable to the criticism that the two goals need not be counterposed. Furthermore, it can be argued that to counterpose these two goals is likely to limit the effectiveness of a hate speech policy, because it is likely to result in a reliance on a statutory definition of hate speech which is difficult to operationalise. For example, Matsuda uses the term "persecutory, hateful and degrading" (1993:36) to describe racist hate-speech-acts. Delgado argues that a "reasonable person would recognise" when a "racial insult" is "intended to demean" (1993:109). These definitions appear difficult to assess, which implies that they would be difficult to implement in policy, and that policy-makers could continue to face the problem of finding it difficult to achieve a workable statutory definition of hate speech. By contrast, utilising the framework proposed in this book allows for hate speech policy to relinquish the search for an elusive "balance" between two competing policy goals, and provides for their pursuit in mutual collaboration.

Potential applications — the "hard cases"

In order to assess the hate speech policy proposed here in the light of actual events, I will now explore the viability of applying this policy to some well known "hard cases", cases where a capabilities-oriented hate speech policy may have been of assistance. In R. A. V.,[175] for example, referred to in Chapter 5, an ordinance which prohibited the display of symbols which arouse anger, alarm or resentment on the basis of race was found unconstitutional on the grounds that it was a viewpoint-based regulation. The case involved the prosecution of Robert Viktora, a minor at the time of the offence, who constructed a crude cross from wooden chair legs, and then erected and burned it inside the yard of the Jones family's home, an African-American family. The perpetrator lived across the street from his targets. The act could have been, and was eventually, prosecuted under other criminal statutes including the prohibition of arson and criminal damage to property. An instance such as this seems to offer a good candidate for a capabilities-oriented response. The event occurred within a neighbourhood area, so it is likely that assisted community involvement in the generation of a response might be capable of having some impact on race relations in the area, and on empowering African-Americans and their support-ers to respond to such racist taunts and attacks. The production and local distribution of a newsletter, or the holding of neighbourhood community meetings to seek to counter the racist content of the attack may have been warranted. If the local African American community were provided with the appropriate support to engage in such activities, the message of the racist hate-speaker may have been able to be more effectively thwarted or minimised than an individualised outcome under ordinary criminal law was able to provide.

In the Skokie case,[176] a village ordinance prohibiting the dissemination of materials which would promote hatred towards persons on the basis of their heritage was struck down as unconstitutional. The ordinance had been used to prohibit a march by the National Socialist Party of America, on the grounds that violations of its terms were anticipated. The ordinance was held to be unconstitutional because its use in this manner represented prior restraint, and the holding of the march did not meet the test of posing sufficient danger to public order that it warranted prohibition (a "clear and present danger" test). The potential audience was not a captive one.[177] The march was allowed to proceed. During deliberations on the case, it was noted that in the same time period a four-part documentary about the Holocaust had been screened on US television. It would have been interesting to apply a capabilities-oriented hate speech policy to this event. The case generated an enormous amount of publicity, probably a great deal more than would ordinarily have been promoted by the neo-Nazi party themselves if the march had not initially been prohibited. Under normal circumstances, if a neo-Nazi party were to organise a march, what kinds of responses could be generated? The most effective responses might be generated not by directly confronting the neo-Nazi party, whose members would be likely to be committed racists and anti-Semites,[178] but by facilitating the raising of awareness within the community generally about twentieth century history, and the means by which discriminatory attitudes might be recruited to devastatingly unequal ends.

There are less complex examples which might also benefit from a capabilities-oriented hate speech policy. In Case M in the NSW study, for example, a capabilities oriented hate speech policy could allow for more to have been done to ameliorate the effects of an expression which stereotyped Arab men as violent, irrational child abusers. Most obviously, community involvement could have been made possible in resolution of the complaint. In Case I, a complaint was lodged about poems which vilified people of Asian descent. Although the ADB found the poems to be vilifying, they could take no action because the complaint was not lodged by a person of Asian descent. Under an alternative hate speech policy as proposed here, it might have been possible to involve Asian community members in the area of the relevant club in generating a response to the hate speech. In another complaint, Case L, a community organisation distributed a booklet to legal studies students critical of immigration by people of Asian descent and of Aboriginal land rights. In this instance, an alternative policy could have allowed for the generation of an alternative booklet to the same students, perhaps supplemented with information on the same topics from the Australian Human Rights and Equal Opportunity Commission.

It also might be possible in the future to develop the model proposed here to speech-acts which perpetrate, perpetuate and maintain systemic discrimination on grounds other than race. To the extent that it can be established that systemic discrimination exists on other grounds, and that validity claims can be made which seek to perpetrate, perpetuate and maintain that discrimination, it seems plausible. The investigation of this question, however, would involve considerable attention and there is no room to investigate this here. Nevertheless, such an extension of the policy would be intellectually coherent subject to the satisfaction of the conditions cited above, and possible if reliant upon the same framework and method proposed here.

In conclusion, this chapter has explored the operationalisation of a capabilities-oriented hate speech policy, via the provision of support to encourage and enable a process of "institutionalised argumentation". This model allows for the validity claims of hate speakers to be answered, in a manner which challenges the validity claims raised. This opens up the possibility for an exchange of ideas. In this manner, it might over the longer term be possible to achieve changes in behaviour and even attitudes. This policy attempts to achieve change discursively, by collectively constructing desired goals (Habermas 1987: 271). The process of institutionalised argumentation would constitute a discursive construction of the goal of eliminating racist discrimination. The kind of policy proposed in this book provides an answer to those who declare that speech one doesn't like ought not to be banned, but ought to be answered, by allowing for the first time for public policy to assist in the generation of that response. This policy thus seems capable of recognising and responding to the importance of speech to individual development, the importance of speech to the discursive, collective, social construction of debate and goals (an understanding which implicitly rests at the "core" of any free speech principle), and the harms of hate speech.

Conclusion

> "Would you tell me please, which way I
> ought to go from here?"
> "That depends a good deal on where you
> want to get to", said the Cat.
> Lewis Carroll, *Alice in Wonderland*

I have argued in favour of a capabilities theory approach to speech policy because it provides a framework within which it becomes possible to view the two goals of securing free speech and ameliorating the harms of hate speech as mutually collaborative and simultaneously facilitated. Such a hate speech policy would be designed not to punish hate speakers or to restrict aberrant speech, but to provide assistance to speak to victim communities. This would allow victim communities to respond to, contradict and counteract hate-speech-acts. This policy would encourage and make it possible for the victims of hate speech to "speak back". Victims' *counter speech* response would contradict the claims made by hate speakers, and enable victims to overcome the silencing effects of hate speech. A policy designed to make counter speech possible therefore maximises participation in the exercise of the speech liberty, and simultaneously serves to overcome the debilitating, marginalising, disempowering and silencing effects of harmful, discursive acts of discrimination constituted by hate-speech-acts. By allowing for a hate speech policy centered on the provision of assistance to generate a response to hate speech utterances, this policy enhances participation in speech.

This novel and imaginative approach to hate speech policy is necessary because the "balance" sought by policy makers between maintaining free speech conditions and ameliorating the harms of hate speech arises from a normative assumption that the aim of speech policy ought to be to minimise restraint on the exercise of the speech liberty. Such an assumption limits potential policy approaches to free speech and hate speech. It assumes that the goal of ameliorating harmful speech can and should be integrated into speech policy as a *residual* policy goal. In other words, only the speech that is left after that speech considered necessarily immune from government restraint is removed, is considered actionable, harmful speech.

These conclusions explain the three central problems raised in the empirical study conducted for this book. These were the problem of understanding why the NSW policy was framed in terms which rendered much hate speech immune from regulatory response, explaining apparent inconsistencies in the policy's application, and whether it was possible to devise a workable statutory definition of hate speech. The first problem has been explained by identifying that the NSW legislation seeks to maintain a "balance" between the competing interests of securing free speech and ameliorating the harms of hate speech. This "balance" directly counterposes the two goals, by providing on the one hand for broad exemptions to categories of actionable speech, and on the other hand facilitating a predominantly punitive (albeit via civil provisions) resolution process. This "balance" arises from the theoretical assumptions underlying the design of the NSW policy. The second problem has been explained by demonstrating that the reliance on a private and individualised resolution process in individual complaints means that the legislation is incapable of responding directly to the identified harms of hate speech — including the silencing of victims. By contrast, a "speaking back" approach to hate speech policy could provide for an inclusive resolution process, one which could involve the generation of a public response to hate speech, in a manner conducive to developing the human capabilities of its victims. The third problem has been solved by proposing a speech-act theory analysis as a way of understanding that expressions may be acts, and by proposing a validity claims analysis as a way of understanding and identifying which expressions constitute hate-speech-acts. By locating an analysis of what hate-speech-acts are capable of doing within the framework of Habermas' theory of communicative action, I have demonstrated how hate-speech-acts are capable of discursively enacting discrimination. This discrimination is able to prevent the victims of hate speech from developing their individual capabilities, and from living a fully human life. One of the most important ways this occurs is by silencing, by rendering a response to the hate-speech-act "unspeakable". Within the context of capabilities theory, this effect of hate-speech-acts allows for the provision of a policy response designed to overcome this inequitable and unjust burden.

I have described my policy proposal as a policy of "institutionalised argumentation". This model allows for the provision of support to enable the generation of a counter speech response. This response would directly challenge the claims made by the hate speaker in uttering the hate-speech-act, and would also empower the victims of hate speech to speak back, thus overcoming the disarming and disempowering silencing effects of hate-speech-acts. Over time, the institutionalisation of this discourse creates openings for the challenging of hate speakers' validity claims, and thus perhaps for achieving changes in behaviour. By providing for institutional support to make such counter speech possible, the proposed policy directly confronts the challenge of ensuring participation in speech that is absent, or underemphasised in many speech policy arguments.

The idea that speech policy could mean not just minimising restraint on the speech liberty, but also taking active steps to ensure participation in speech, has been raised elsewhere. In Norway, for example, in 1999 a Governmental Commission on Freedom of Expression proposed amendments to Article 100 of the Norwegian Constitution which would enshrine the right to free speech. At the same time, the Article provided that it is "the responsibility of the authorities of the State to create conditions enabling an open and enlightened public debate". In explaining the inclusion of this clause in the Article, the Commission noted that the obligation to create such conditions included an obligation to "help underprivileged groups to be heard by providing them with the necessary means of addressing a wider audience" (Norwegian Governmental Commission on Freedom of Expression 1999). Although this provision has not been designed specifically as a response to hate speech, its significance and purpose are very closely related to the proposal made in this book, because the Norwegian policy is designed to provide conditions under which marginalised groups may be empowered to speak. The inclusion of this clause in the Norwegian Constitution may provide evidence of the beginnings of an acceptance within Western liberal democratic states that free speech policy may require more than the absence of restraint on the part of governments.

A hate speech policy designed along these lines has the potential to shift the parameters of debates around speech policy. It allows policy makers to consider how to enhance participation in the exercise of the speech liberty. This includes recognising who might, under current circumstances, be excluded from exercising the speech liberty. It also includes considering the concrete ways in which putting a capabilities-oriented hate speech policy into practice might improve people's lives.

Notes

1. The terms "speech" and "expression" will be used interchangeably throughout the book. Debate over the use of these terms is clarified in Chapter 3. For the purposes of the recommendations made here, the terms are intended to mean expressive activity. They include the use of symbols or insignia when the use of these things can be understood as expressive. To this extent, the terms are also used interchangeably with the concept of "language" in the sense of an idea communicated via expression, including but not limited to both sound-based and written means of expression.

2. The discussion in this book will be limited to liberal-democratic jurisdictions.

3. The discussion in the book centres on the phenomenon of "hate speech". Some commentators regard "hate speech" as a type of "hate crime" (Knoll 1994). For the purposes of this book, the discussion will center on the phenomenon of "hate speech", integrated with an analysis of speech as a kind of conduct. The perpetration of a hate crime may or may not include the utterance of a hate-speech-act, but the perpetration of a hate crime is identified primarily not via any utterance but via the carrying out of expressive, *and* physically violent conduct. A discussion of hate crimes remains beyond the scope of this book, although the issue is a related one, which is being pursued in research elsewhere (see Gelber 2000b).

4. The terms "liberty" and "freedom" will be used interchangeably.

5. The term "race" is intended to be used broadly in this book. It is intended to include notions of race, heritage, nationality, colour, ethnicity, ethno-religious status and national origin. "Racism" is defined as an asymmetrical power relationship between diverse racially or ethnically-defined members of society, a relationship within which powerful groups circumscribe less powerful groups in order to limit the way they can define knowledge and gain access to resources (HRC 1982: 19). The theoretical and methodological framework utilised in this book justifies this definition of racist hate-speech-acts — linked with systemic discrimination, rather than, for example, individual pathology.

6. I am grateful to the NSW Anti-Discrimination Board, which made racial vilification case files available to me for the purposes of this study, and to the Ethics Committee, University of Sydney, which granted permission for me to gain access to the case files. Some aspects of this investigation have been dealt with elsewhere in Gelber 2000a. At the time of conducting this research, Queensland and Victoria did not have anti-vilification statutes. Western Australian racial anti-vilification legislation, enacted in 1990, applies only to narrowly-defined criminal offence and to date no prosecutions have taken place under its terms. The Australian Capital Territory possesses racial anti-vilification legislation which mirrors that of NSW, so independent examination of complaints would be unlikely to reveal any evidence not forthcoming from a study of the NSW legislation in practice. South Australia passed racial anti-vilification legislation in 1996, with both civil and criminal provisions. The recent

enactment of this legislation limits the undertaking of a comprehensive analysis of its implementation. Tasmanian anti-vilification legislation, enacted in December 1998, is subject to the same exemptions and utilises the same statutory definitions of vilification as the NSW legislation, and demonstrates some minor procedural differences from the NSW legislation. Its recent enactment also means insufficient evidence is available to examine the legislation's implementation in practice. Commonwealth legislation was introduced in 1995, allowing NSW residents to choose whether to lodge complaints under NSW or Commonwealth legislation. Since neither the number, nor substance, of complaints lodged under the NSW legislation altered subsequent to 1995, as revealed in Annual Reports of the ADB, it is unlikely an independent review of the Commonwealth legislation in practice would be necessary to augment the qualitative data revealed by the NSW study. (See Appendix B)

7. *Anti-Discrimination Act* (NSW) 1977, ss 20C and 20D.

8.   The empirical study into 568 complaints lodged under the NSW racial anti-vilification law was undertaken with the permission of the Ethics Committee, University of Sydney, and following completion by the researcher of a Confidentiality Agreement with the NSW Anti-Discrimination Board. Since undertaking this study, NSW statutory requirements have changed and privacy statutes currently prohibit the granting of access to detailed case file material for research purposes. The only material currently available to members of the public for research purposes is pre-anonymised data from the NSW Anti-Discrimination Board's complaints database.

9.   The Administrative Decisions Tribunal (Equal Opportunity Division) was so named in October 1998. Prior to this it was called the Equal Opportunity Tribunal. In this paper the term "Tribunal" is intended to mean both.

10.   Subsequent amendments to the Anti-Discrimination Act 1977 (NSW) prohibit transgender vilification (ss 38S, 38T, passed in 1996), homosexual vilification (ss 49ZT, 49ZTA, passed in 1994), and vilification on grounds of HIV/AIDS (s 49ZXB, passed in 1994). John Dowd noted in interview (1998) that it would have been possible to set up an alternative framework for vilification, such as for example was the case with the setting up of the Privacy Committee. Dowd claimed this option was rejected by the government at the time for pragmatic reasons (it was logistically easier to use a framework already set up, and already publicly understood as providing redress for perceived acts of discrimination) and because opponents of a privacy committee-type model claimed it lacked enforcement power.

11.   The criminal offence of "serious racial vilification" involves the making of public threats to person or property on the ground of race, and requires referrals to the Attorney-General for prosecution. In practice, it is the Office of the Director of Public Prosecutions which assesses the merits of the case. Despite several referrals, no case has yet been considered to provide sufficient grounds for pursuing prosecution.

12.   The definition of a representative organisation within the legislation is limited and applies only to organisations which have a "genuine concern" with the promotion or mediation of issues related specifically to that ethnic or ethno-religious group.

13.   Amendment to the legislation in 1994 (*Anti-Discrimination Amendment Act* 1994, No. 9 of 1994) which allowed the lodging of complaints by a representative body on behalf of an

individual was carried out following a report on the practice of the law (Parliament of New South Wales Legislative Council 1992).

14.   The maximum penalty under the criminal provisions is a fine of $5000 for individuals or 6 months' imprisonment; or a $10,000 fine for corporations (Twomey 1994c: 3).

15.   *Phillips v Aboriginal Legal Service* Equal Opportunity Tribunal Complaint No 23 of 1992.

16.   This amendment followed discussion in Samios' parliamentary report and other criticisms of the NSW legislation (e.g. McNamara 1997, Solomon 1994) that this particular aspect of the legislation was weak. There were many reasons why vilified individuals may not wish to make complaints, including their status as a member of a victimised group with all the attendant confidence problems, their fear of retribution, their lack of understanding of the law which may be related to English language difficulties, and so on. Recommendations were made that the law allow for representative complaints to be lodged. When this was implemented in the 1994 amendment, representative complaints were permitted, but they still had to be lodged on behalf of a named individual who was a member of the allegedly vilified group.

17.   Terminiello v. Chicago, 337 U.S. 1 (1949).

18.   *Byous v. State*, 175 S.E. 2d 106, 107.

19.   The 1989 NSW legislation preceded the later High Court "free speech" decisions in *Australian Capital Television Pty Ltd v Commonwealth (1992)* 177 CLR 106 and *Nationwide News Pty Ltd v Wills (1992)* 177 CLR 1 which found an implied constitutional right to "political" communication in Australia.

20.   *R v D and E Marinkovic 1996,* Equal Opportunity Tribunal Complaint No 124 of 1995.

21.   The research method is qualitative. The qualitative method provides an in-depth examination of specific case study outcomes in order to provide an accurate and sensitive picture of the legislation in practice. Using this qualitative method, even single cases can provide evidence to substantiate the arguments presented (Marsh and Stoker eds. 1995: 137–172; King, Keohane and Verba 1994: 1–33). The qualitative method is helpful in this context, because in conducting the study it was important to be able to be attentive to the tone and quality of legislative responses to instances of hate speech. A quantitative method would have been unable to demonstrate these attributes of the legislation's operation.

22.   This complainant originally wanted the complaint prosecuted under criminal provisions. However, the ADB felt the remarks would not survive the strict definition warranted for criminal prosecution, and recommended a Tribunal hearing under civil provisions.

23.   Research included perusal of ABC program sales information on broadcasts concerning Aboriginal culture, an interview with the President of the ADB at the time the complaint was acted on (Mark, 1999), and perusal of the complaint file itself where no notations existed linking the complaint to subsequent media representations of Aboriginal culture.

24.   The driver of the vehicle from which the comments were uttered was identified.

25.   A later request from the complainant to re-open the file had to be declined due to statutory limitations.

26. These amount to approximately 21% of cases in the 1989–1994 period and 16.5% of cases in the 1995–1998 period (Gelber 2000a: 17, 18).

27. This figure was derived from calculations of demographic change in the population.

28. The author regrets that this letter cannot be identified, due to statutory provisions protecting the complainant's and respondent's anonymity.

29. The term "truth" is highly controvertible, as will be discussed below. Notwithstanding the epistemological difficulties of the term, Mill intends it to mean the most reasonable, or "rational", interpretation of events. I should like to make clear I am not making any truth claims here; the term is Mill's.

30. *On Liberty*, first published in 1859, has become a central text in debates examining the tensions between individual liberty and the social order. Mill was particularly concerned to establish a theory of individual liberty incorporating protection from both oppressive popular opinion, which he called the "tyranny of the majority", and government authority (Riley 1998: 42). Mill's arguments were developed in four major works: *Considerations on Representative Government* (1861); *The Subjection of Women* (written in 1861 but published in 1869); *Utilitarianism* (1861) (which clarified Mill's notion of happiness, the scope and content of the sphere of morality and developed a theory of justice); and *On Liberty* (1859) which sought to justify a sphere of non-interference in which individuals are able to make the autonomous choices necessary for them to be able to enjoy individuality and pursue happiness (Gray in Mill 1991) Gray disagrees with theorists who argued that the last two works represent different lines of argument in Mill's work, citing consistencies between the utilitarian theory of justice developed in *Utilitarianism* and the personal liberty necessary for the pursuit of individuality in *On Liberty*. Mill's work has informed liberal deontology and the philosophy of law around the question of the speech liberty.

31. This analogy was used by Justice Holmes, dissenting, in *Abrams vs U.S.*, 250 U.S. 616, (1919) at 630–1. Justice Frankfurter concurred in *Dennis v. United States*, 341 U.S. 494 (1951) at 546–53.

32. Rauch defines "liberal science" as the liberal intellectual system which produces knowledge. The terms stands in contradistinction to the liberal political system ("democracy") and the liberal economic system ("capitalism") (1993: 4).

33. The idea that "truths" are contestable must be entertained as an ontological possibility. Dworkin, for example, critiques claims that it is possible to deny objective truth from a standpoint of some external vantage point, immune from influence by the evaluative framework the truth-questioners seek to condemn (1996). Jackson, Oppy and Smith (1994), on the other hand, argue via an integration of theories of non-cognitivism in ethics into a theory of truth, that ethical sentences are not "truth apt", i.e. true or false.

34. Sunstein, for example, describes the difference between "content-based" speech regulations, which turn on the question of the issue under discussion, and "viewpoint-based" speech regulations, which turn on the question of the point of view expressed by the speaker (1993b: 8–14).

35. For a discussion of the differences between negative and positive liberties, see in particular Berlin 1969, Skinner 1984. It is noted that the terms are not entirely mutually exclusive and considerable debate exists as to the viability of the differentiation. Nevertheless, to the extent that it helps to differentiate policy approaches on speech, the distinction is useful here. I am grateful to Lisa Hill for her assistance in developing this point.

36. This is the distinction Barendt (1985) fails to make when he includes rights-based arguments within the argument from democracy.

37. See *Taking Rights Seriously* (1977a); *The Philosophy of Law (ed.)* (1977b); *A Matter of Principle* (1985).

38. Furthermore, because liberty is derivative from equality, Dworkin argues that it is not inconsistent with the practice of reverse discrimination (1977a: 223–239). The significance of the affirmative action argument will be discussed later in this chapter.

39. See especially Dworkin (1977a), Chapter 12 "What Rights Do We Have?": 266–278.

40. The use of case studies here is not intended to imply the findings relied solely or even primarily on the argument from rights. They demonstrate that free speech arguments can be viewed as absolutist. I have sought to establish elsewhere that this is particularly the case for the argument from rights.

41. These dimensions of speech will be examined in detail in later chapters.

42. For example, *Whitney v. California*, 274 U.S. 357 (1927).

43. See the discussion of the Australian High Court's "free speech" cases in Chapter 5.

44. I have drawn this analogy from Jane Elliott's "Blue Eyes, Brown Eyes" exercise. See for example *Blue-eyes [videorecording]*. Director of photography, Waldemar Hauschild, writen and directed by Bertram Verhaag in cooperation with Jane Elliott. Denkmal Filmproduktion, Munich, 1997.

45. Sadurski also supports this argument (1994: 178–179).

46. Furthermore, Schauer argues that the incorporation of equal participation into a justification for free speech policy renders the argument from democracy unable to provide an independent argument for a free speech principle at all, because it contradicts the principle of popular sovereignty (1982: 41–42). Schauer's objection here appears rooted in a premise that the "argument from democracy" is synonymous with an "argument from majoritarian democracy". In my argument, the notion of equality (in terms of equal access to participation in the speech liberty) is incorporated within the framework of capabilities theory. I critique the argument from democracy here both in terms of its application as an argument from majoritarian democracy, and as an argument from participatory democracy. I share Schauer's general suspicions that it is difficult to provide a sustainable defence of a free speech principle within the argument from democracy, but on different grounds. Schauer equates the argument from democracy with majoritarianism. I discuss the argument from democracy's inability to provide a justification or mechanism to ensure equal participation in the exercise of the speech liberty.

47. Berlin acknowledges the potential for overlap between the two categories (1969: 121).

48. Sen also criticises the absence of restraint as only a "procedural fulfillment of libertarian rights" which is all that negative freedom demands (1993a: 30).

49.   Furthermore, good decisions are context-sensitive, in the sense that they take the context of one's experience into account. But this does not render them context-bound (i.e. relativist) because it remains right anywhere in the world to attend to context, and to attend to context is to make the humanly correct decisions (Nussbaum 1993a: 257). Contextual responsiveness and "getting it right" are therefore mutually supportive values.

50.   Although this extension of the critique is of course not a necessary one. In the passages that follow, I will suggest other reasons for the superiority of a capabilities approach to the development of speech policy.

51.   Nussbaum notes, of course, that the capabilities also involve limits. For example, it is human to prefer recurrent hunger plus eating to a life with neither hunger nor eating. A humanly "good" way of ensuring each of the capabilities would be unlikely to include the absolute removal of the need, but rather a careful evaluation of the ways in which the need might be satisfied in a human way (1990: 224).

52.   Nussbaum notes the interaction and overlapping between the categories (1990: 225). Nevertheless, they provide useful guidance to the discussion.

53.   However, the argument from self-development discussed earlier in this chapter does not provide a framework within which to justify ensuring the means of participation to those who wish to speak.

54.   Nussbaum notes she chooses to define external capabilites in this way because not all the functionings are made available at every time. However, external capabilites must still be realised in order for a person to become fully capable at some point in time (1988: 164).

55.   Speech-act theory in general is aimed at establishing ways of determining the meaning of utterances within the context in which they are uttered (see for example Searle 1980) and is not limited to Austin and Habermas.

56.   The terms "act", "actions", "activities" and "conduct" will be used interchangeably in this chapter, except where it is made clear in the text that something else is intended. The terms are intended to be synonymous with a broad notion of human activities.

57.   The focus of this chapter, and this book, is on hate speech, not the broader and altogether different problem of hate crimes (See Gelber 2000b, Williams 1998). It is interesting to note, however, that in a discussion of both hate speech and hate crimes the charge has been raised that a restriction could mean punishment of people's thoughts. Mill conceived of expression as simply the externalisation of thought, and therefore to be considered as sacrosanct and necessarily free from intervention as thought. But the expression of ideas may be differentiated from simply holding those ideas because communicative activity is, by definition, interactive. The holding of an idea in a wholly non-communicative manner (i.e. a thought) need not have any impact on others at all. A differentiation is therefore maintained here between thought and expression. The question under discussion here is the viability of a differentiation between "speech" and "acts", as defined in the body of the book.

58.   Habermas also notes the dominance of a Cartesian model of human nature in 20th Century thought (1984: viii).

59.   This is the "clear and present danger" test, derived from *Schenk v. United States*, 249 U.S. 47 (1919). United States First Amendment jurisprudence will be discussed in greater detail in Chapter 5.

60.   In *Cohen v. California*, 403 U.S. 15 (1971).

61.   The discussion here, as were Austin's (1975) and Searle's (1973), is confined to "serious" utterances, not for example an actor performing a play (Austin 1975:22).

62.   Jennifer Lopez in *Out of Sight*, released in Australia 1998.

63.   Although this proposition may not alarm policy-makers themselves, it is nevertheless cause for concern in the context of this book, where the purpose of uncovering philosophical assumptions underlying policy is to expose their translation into weaknesses in the policy's implementation and outcomes.

64.   This applies whether those responsible for drafting and implementing legislative restrictions on speech were aware of this philosophical problem or not. I am uncovering the philosophical assumptions of speech policy here; whether they have been articulated by policy-makers is largely immaterial.

65.   Austin acknowledged that to say anything at all is to act in the most basic sense that to speak is to act. To say anything includes three components: the phonetic, the phatic and the rhetic. A "phonetic" act is the act of uttering noises. A "phatic" act is the act of uttering words or vocables. A "rhetic" act is the act of using words with a "sense" and "reference" (which together are equivalent to "meaning") (1975:92–93; Searle 1973:146). When someone makes an utterance in the sense of saying words or sentences, these three elements are combined. Since the discussion here is confined to complete utterances, this level of detail is not directly relevant.

66.   For acknowledgement of this debate, see for example Davis 1989.

67.   Habermas acknowledges that the speech-act component of this theoretical approach was developed from the work of Austin (1979:7).

68.   The use of the term "pragmatics" is contested. In linguistics, pragmatics is an established sub-field. For a historical overview of this debate, see Levinson 1983, especially 1–53.

69.   Some authors refer to Habermas' delineation of a fourth validity claim in his earlier work (Habermas 1970), the claim in an explicative utterance of the comprehensibility of speakers addressing each other (e.g. Wodak 1996:30). The idea of validity claims is revisited and clarified in Habermas' later work (1984; 1987). Both explicative and evaluative utterances are considered and critiqued (1984:39, 42 ff). The notion of the "well formedness" of symbolic/explicative expressions (against which their comprehensibility may be examined) is later "left aside" (1984:99), and evaluatives are assimilated with expressives, i.e. utterances which can be assessed on the basis of the sincerity of their subjectivities. Habermas' argument overall rests on the tripartite delineation I use in this book, between the criticisable validity claims of truth, rightness and sincerity (e.g. 1984:75, 137, 278, 302–9, 329–330).

70.   Habermas devotes considerable time to developing a further differentiation between illocutionary acts. He identifies three types of illocutions, which conform to his three levels of validity claims. Habermas identifies "constatives" as speech-acts which represent states of affairs, can be rejected on "truth" grounds, and are related to the objective world. "Regulat-

ives" are speech-acts which establish interpersonal relations, can be rejected on "rightness" grounds, and are related to the social world. "Expressives" are speech-acts which are self-representative, can be rejected on "truthful" grounds, and are related to the subjective world (Habermas 1984:329). This differentiation is reflected in the discussion below concerning the three levels of validity claims.

71.   Habermas notes, of course, the contestability of his proposals (see esp. 1984:310–319) and considerable debate within speech-act theory as to the distinctions between locutionary, illocutionary and perlocutionary speech-acts (1984:292).

72.   Thus, Habermas' theory of communicative rationality supports his broader emancipatory project of developing the means by which humans may successfully engage in communicative action, in order to develop new institutions which respond to discursively agreed upon decisions (1984:xxxvii).

73.   Habermas calls this "rationally motivated" agreement. An excursus on the meaning of "rationality" is central to Habermas' whole project (see esp. 1984, Part I;1987). An in-depth examination of this question is too broad to be contained in an aside here. Habermas is concerned to develop a concept of rationality not limited by subjective and individualist premises. For the purposes of this discussion "rationally motivated agreement" is intended to mean agreement on the intent and meaning of communicative action reached discursively between subjects who share common bases of understanding. The "practice of argumentation" acts as a court of appeal to resolve disagreement, as opposed to the use of force, for example (Habermas 1984:17–18).

74.   Habermas defines the "lifeworld" as the intersubjectively shared traditions of a community. Each member of a community finds the lifeworld already interpreted, and adopts a reflective attitude towards it during their lifetime (1984:82–83).

75.   Because communicative action connects with social and cultural institutions, it confronts cultural and historical diversity. This raises a relativist challenge to Habermas' claims of universalism. Habermas responds to these claims by arguing the case for relativism is not conclusive, and furthermore the universalist claims of communicative rationality may be tested against empirical and theoretical research (1984; 1987).

76.   Habermas argues that some speech-acts are not connected with criticisable validity claims, such as imperatives (orders). Rejection by a hearer of an imperative necessitates rejecting the speaker's power, not a validity claim (1984:305).

77.   Of course, saying all speech is conduct and it therefore no longer qualified for the automatic "special immunity" from government intervention accorded to speech does not mean that conduct absorbs the "special immunity" provision. To argue this would be nonsensical, because not all conduct warrants the same response.

78.   "Racism" was defined for the purposes of this book in the introduction.

79.   Singular and plural will be used interchangeably. It is the view of the author that the phenomenology of a hate-speech-act is not affected by whether the speaker/s and listener/s are one individual or many.

80.   Following publication of the articles, the newspaper in question printed several letters to the editor criticising its tone. The ADB declined to pursue the matter as, on balance, the

article was not found to pass the legislative hatred threshold required to be defined as vilification. The ADB noted that if it had been considered to pass the hatred threshold, it was likely the article would have fallen under a 'public debate' exemption in the legislation.

81.   The ADB declined this complaint as it was found not to constitute vilification.

82.   Australia has ratified the Universal Declaration of Human Rights and the International Covenant on Civil and Political Rights, as will be discussed in the next chapter.

83.   The "White Australia Policy" was established in 1901 as a defensive measure against Asian immigration and indentured Pacific Islander labour. In practice, following World War II it was slowly liberalised, and finally abolished by Whitlam's federal ALP government (Jayasuriya 1999: 16–21).

84.   The United Kingdom example of legislative responses to racist hate speech, including the specific example of "moderate" hate speech referred to, will be dealt with in Chapter 5.

85.   For a comprehensive literature review concerning the effects of racial prejudice and discrimination, see Simpson and Yinger (1985). For an overview of literature alleging the harms of hate speech, see Akmeemana and Jones (1995).

86.   It is not necessary to demonstrate a causal or linear relationship between hate-speech-acts and overtly violent crimes of hate here; it is sufficient to recognise the fear among actual victims, potential victims and the community at large that such a relationship exists. Arguments in support of the hypothesis that hate speech may promote violence against victim groups appear in Lederer and Delgado (eds.) (1995).

87.   See also Allport (1954) on how the holder of prejudice de-individualises the victim.

88.   It has been argued that the "psychic injury" that can be caused by racist hate speech which implicates the group identity of a hearer (Sadurski 1992: 185–188) can invoke symptoms including rapid pulse rate, difficulty breathing, nightmares, post traumatic stress disorder, suicide and psychosis (Matsuda 1993: 24).

89.   Williams defines "spirit-murder" as disregard for others whose lives qualitatively depend on our regard, noting it can manifest in many ways including racist discrimination, cultural obliteration and genocide (1987: 151). Spirit-murder, she argues, is as "devastating", "costly" and "psychically obliterating" as assault (1987: 129).

90.   I regard the example of pornography as more complex than racist hate-speech-acts, because gender subordination is more complex. For example, is pornography more discriminatory than advertisements which depict women happily responsible for cleaning bathrooms? If these two examples are regarded as equally harmful depictions of women's subordination, this raises obstacles to regulation. Furthermore, erotic material simultaneously raises questions of women's subordination and questions of eroticisation. Sunstein regards the issues raised by pornography as different from those raised by racist hate speech because the latter is often "part and parcel of public debate", whereas the former is not (1993a: 813).

91.   *American Booksellers Association Inc. v. Hudnut,* 771 F. 2d 323 (1985), at 329. The case found the ordinance prohibiting pornography to be unconstitutional on the basis that it was overbroad and unduly restricted freedom of speech, and that it therefore violated the First Amendment.

92.   *American Booksellers Ass'n. Inc. v. Hudnut,* 771 F. 2d 323 (1985), at 329–330.

93. Post details a range of harms of hate speech, including psychological injury, deontic harm (because it is "wrong" and goes against the principle of equality), subordination and silencing (1991). He argues the truth of this premise does not justify the restriction of racist speech because restraints on racist speech would only impair public discourse, and not repair the silencing of victim group members (1991:309). It is precisely this challenge — of repairing the silencing — which is the focus of the proposal in this book for a new hate speech policy.

94. Both Langton's and MacKinnon's arguments turn on two linked premises. The first is that the unequal gender pattern of sexual violence means sexual violence is an epistemological representation of discrimination against women. The second is that pornography legitimates sexual violence (sexually explicit work which does not do this is not defined as "pornography"). Both of these premises are problematic. Nevertheless, as will be revealed, Langton's argument is useful here in so far as it establishes that where a speech-act can be interpreted to discriminate, one of the effects of that speech-act is to silence its actual and potential victims.

95. In total, these cases amounted to approximately 23% of finalised complaints in the period 1989–1994, and 21.5% of finalised complaints in the period 1995–1998 (Gelber 2000a: 17, 18).

96. The ways in which this could occur will be discussed in detail in Chapter 6.

97. For evidence supporting this contention, see for example Johnson 1997.

98. Braithwaite and Pettit's argument (1990) builds on an earlier explanatory theory of crime provided by Braithwaite (1989), in which he argues in favour of prioritising moralising social control over punitive social control in responding to, and lowering the incidence of, crime.

99. These amount to approximately 21% of cases in the 1989–1994 period and 16.5% of cases in the 1995–1998 period (Gelber 2000a: 17, 18).

100. Interestingly, Article 19 of the UDHR provides for the right to education directed at the "full development of the human personality", a clause which could be interpreted as providing justification for the introduction of a capabilities-oriented hate speech policy.

101. The ICCPR was adopted by the UN in 1966, and came into force for the UN in 1976, 3 months after its ratification by 35 governments. A nation "ratifies" a treaty if it becomes an initial signatory. Later signature means a nation "accedes" to a treaty. However, nations in which multilateral treaties come into force often use the term "ratify", regardless of the date at which this occurred. Throughout the rest of this chapter, therefore, the term "ratify" will be used to mean the time at which the treaty entered into force for that nation. Also, the instrument need not immediately come into force for a nation after ratification or accession. This may require further action on the part of the signatory nation, as will be described below.

102. "State Party" is the term used to describe a nation which has ratified or acceded to a United Nations treaty or convention.

103. For details of the ratification status of a range of UN conventions, see www.unhchr.ch/tbs/doc.nsf.

104. *Anti-Discrimination Act 1977* (NSW), *Equal Opportunity Act 1984* (SA), *Discrimination Act 1991* (ACT), *Anti-Discrimination Act 1991* (Queensland), *Racial and Religious Tolerance Act 2001* (Victoria), *Anti-Discrimination Act* 1996 (Northern Territory), *Anti-Discrimination Act 1998* (Tasmania).

105. The 14th Amendment to the Constitution provides for equal protection of the law to all citizens, and the 5th Amendment ensures the right to due process of the law for all citizens, although they do not apply specifically to race.

106. The term "state" here denotes a sub-national, regional government, and is not to be confused with the term "State Party" which is defined above. The terms "federal government" and "Commonwealth" are coterminous and are intended to mean the central government.

107. For discussion of the limits of the external affairs power see for example Galligan 1983; Gelber 1999; Howard 1988.

108. In decisions including *Koowarta v Bjelke Petersen* (1982) 153 CLR 168, and the *Tasmanian Dams* case (*Commonwealth v Tasmania* (1983) 156 CLR 1.

109. This is referred to as the "Ponsonby rule" and was introduced in 1924. The Ponsonby rule was modified in 1981 so that it did not apply to bilateral double taxation agreements (Templeman 1994: 158–159).

110. A reservation means the signatory nation does not agree to be bound by international law to the particular article under dispute. The implications of this reservation will be discussed below.

111. *Nationwide News Pty Ltd v. Wills* (1992) 177 CLR 1.

112. Section 299 (1)(d)(ii) of the *Industrial Relations Act* 1988 (Cth).

113. *Australian Capital Television v. The Commonwealth* (1992) 177 CLR 106.

114. Part IIID of the *Broadcasting Act* 1942 (Cth). The legislation also mandated the provision of free time to candidates by broadcasters during election campaigns (Kirk 1995: 38). This free time favoured political parties which already held parliamentary seats. Non-candidates were completely excluded.

115. The findings in these cases have attracted criticisms that the High Court overstepped its role as interpreter of constitutional law, that the decisions were poorly made, and that the decisions marked a shift in Constitutional interpretation of sovereignty (see discussion in Blackshield 1994; McDonald 1994: 160–1; Glass 1995: 29; Kirk 1995: 37).

116. This was not the first time the High Court had made this particular finding. See for example *Attorney-General (Cth); Ex rel McKinlay v. Commonwealth* (1975) 135 CLR 1.

117. A distinction between "political" and "non-political" speech is maintained by Sunstein (1993a: 796) in support of his argument that speech which is not intended as part of the exchange of ideas may not be protected expressive activity under the First Amendment. The limits of what constitutes "political communication" in the Australian context remain to be determined in future High Court judgements (Barendt 1994: 161–164). A distinction between "political" and "non-political" speech may be difficult to make (Coper 1994: 188). For the purposes of the comparison in this chapter, it is not necessary to clarify the concept further than has already occurred, since it is sufficient to note the limitations of protection of free speech in Australian constitutional law, in contrast to United States' constitutional law. The distinction also becomes less important in the context of a hate speech policy designed not to silence or punish hate speech, but to provide assistance in order that it may be answered. The kinds of speech which would warrant a policy-assisted response have been identified earlier, and do not revolve around their delineation as "political" or "non-political".

118.   *Theophanous v. Herald and Weekly Times Ltd* (1994) 182 CLR 104 and *Stephens v. West Australian Newspapers Ltd* (1994) 182 CLR 211, which involved defamation cases brought under state law by public figures against defendants who countered by citing their right to free speech on political matters; *Cunliffe v. Commonwealth* (1994) 182 CLR 272.

119.   *Australian Capital Television Pty. Ltd. v. Commonwealth of Australia* (1992) 177 CLR 106.

120.   For example, in *Davis v. Commonwealth* (1988) CLR 79, legislation passed by the federal government to grant the Australian Bicentennial Authority exclusive commercial use of some common expressions was regarded as an "extraordinary intrusion into freedom of expression" (at 100) and overridden.

121.   For example, *Commonwealth of Australia v. John Fairfax and Sons Ltd* (1980) 147 CLR 39, at 52.

122.   *Derbyshire County Council v. Times Newspapers Ltd* (1993) AC 534 declared that for public officials to be able to recover damages under libel laws, they must demonstrate malice on the part of the speaker. This higher libel threshold for public figures is derived from the well-known US Supreme Court case, *New York Times Co. v. Sullivan*, 376 U.S. 254 (1964). *Sullivan* also informed the reasoning behind the Australian High Court free speech cases, reinforcing the idea that public figures ought to be open to scrutiny and criticism (Barendt 1994: 149–150). Thus, a close (but not identical) jurisprudential link between the three nations exists, one which appears to rest in their liberal democratic traditions and be expressed at least in part in their decisions on speech policy.

123.   *Derbyshire County Council v. Times Newspapers Ltd* (1993) AC 534, at 540.

124.   See for example Hentoff 1980; Murphy 1972; Dworkin R 1992; Knoll 1994; Smolla 1992.

125.   Indeed, Barendt suggests that "exporting" the First Amendment "may well be the most significant contribution the United States makes to international legal culture towards the end of the twentieth century" (1994: 149).

126.   Except Article 41 which entered into force for Australia on 28 January 1993 and allows the United Nations Human Rights Committee (UNHRC) to hear complaints lodged by one State Party against another State Party. This followed on from Australia's ratification of the First Optional Protocol of the ICCPR, which entered into force on 25 December 1991 and allows individuals to lodge complaints with the UNHRC of ICCPR violations in Australia.

127.   The Human Rights Commission was first established in 1981. In 1986 it was reconstituted as the Human Rights and Equal Opportunity Commission.

128.   Recommendation No. 213.

129.   *Racial Discrimination Amendment Bill* 1992 (Cth).

130.   An official reservation remains on Article 4(a) of the ICERD because the federal legislation did not include criminal sanctions.

131.   *Anti-Discrimination Act 1977* (NSW), ss 20C and 20D.

132.   *Criminal Code Amendment (Racist Harassment and Incitement to Racial Hatred) Act 1990* (WA), which amends the *Criminal Code 1913* (WA), ss 77–80.

133.   *Discrimination Act 1991* (ACT), ss 66 and 67.

134.   *Racial Vilification Act 1996* (SA).

135.   *Anti-Discrimination Act 1998* (Tas), s19.

136.   *Anti-Discrimination Amendment Act 2001* (Qld), ss 124A and 131A.

137.   *Racial and Religious Tolerance Act 2001* (Vic).

138.   This resulted in the amended *Race Relations Act 1976*.

139.   *R. v. Hancock.*

140.   *R. v. Malik* (1968) 1 WLR 353, at 355.

141.   Section 23 of the *Public Order Act 1986* also created an offence of possessing written material which is threatening, abusive or insulting if the possessor intended to publish or distribute the material, *and* they intended to stir up racial hatred, or it was likely racial hatred would be stirred up by their so doing.

142.   Indeed, the members of the Racial Preservation Society cited earlier declared their intent to achieve the perlocutionary effect of securing the expulsion of non-whites from Britain, thereby recognising the perlocutionary potential of their speech-acts.

143.   *R.A.V. v. City of St. Paul*, 505 U.S. 377 (1992).

144.   *Skokie v. National Socialist Party*, 373 NE 2d. 21 (1978); *Smith v. Collin*, 439 U.S. 916 (1978).

145.   *DeJonge v. Oregon*, 299 U.S. 353 (1937).

146.   *Miller v. California*, 413 U.S. 15 (1973).

147.   Initially developed in *Schenk v. United States*, 249 U.S. 47 (1919).

148.   *Brandenburg v. Ohio*, 395 U.S. 444 (1969).

149.   *Smith v. Collin*, 439 U.S. 916 (1978).

150.   *Chaplinsky v. New Hampshire*, 315 U.S. 568 (1942).

151.   *Terminiello v. Chicago*, 337 U.S. 1 (1949).

152.   *Cohen v. California*, 403 U.S. 15 (1971).

153.   *Gooding v. Wilson*, 405 U.S. 518 (1972)

154.   *New York Times Co. v. Sullivan*, 376 U.S. 254 (1964).

155.   I am grateful to Helen Pringle for her assistance in developing this point.

156.   In contrast, for example, to *Cohen v. California*, 403 U.S. 15 (1971) cited above.

157.   *CBS v. Democratic National Committee*, 412 U.S. 94 (1973).

158.   *US Postal Service v. Council of Greenburgh Civic Association*, 453 U.S. 114 (1981). This decision turned on whether the United States Postal Service had a right to exclusive use of

mailboxes designated for their commercial interests. The decision was therefore "content-neutral". The Supreme Court found the Postal Service did have this exclusive right, and a statute banning the unauthorised and unpaid placing of notices in designated mail boxes was upheld.

159. *Miami Herald v. Tornillo* 418 U.S. 241 (1974).

160. *City Council for Los Angeles v Vincent,* 104 S. Ct. 2118 (1984). This decision turned on whether a municipal authority had the right to regulate on the basis of aesthetics, and was regarded as "content-neutral". A statute banning the placing of posters on some areas including lamp posts and hydrants was not considered overly broad, because these areas were not considered "public fora" subject to free speech protections. The statute was upheld.

161. *Red Lion Broadcasting Co., Inc., et al v. Federal Communications Commission,* 395 U.S. 367 (1969).

162. *Communications Act 1934.*

163. These rules were codified by the FCC in 1967: *Personal Attack and Political Editorials,* 8 FCC 2d 721, 722 (1967).

164. The political editorial rule provides that when a licensee endorses or opposes a political candidate in an election, they must notify the candidate's opponent and offer them an opportunity to respond (FCC 1998). It is therefore directly concerned with ensuring fair coverage in elections.

165. *Red Lion op cit* at 378–379.

166. *Red Lion op cit* : 375. The justices further argued that the First Amendment was designed to protect the rights of the viewing and listening public, not the rights of broadcasters (p 368).

167. *CBS v. Democratic National Committee,* 412 U.S. 94 (1973) at pp 95–98.

168. *Miami Herald v. Tornillo,* 418 U.S. 241 (1974) at pp 256–257. This finding is consistent with an earlier finding in *Associated Press v. United States,* 326 U.S. 1 (1945).

169. Many states in the United States, as well as the federal government, have enacted hate crime laws. These usually have the effect of either monitoring or providing for harsher penalties for crimes which are demonstrated to be motivated by racial hatred. Because these statutes rely on enhancing penalties for already-existing criminal acts, and the US government has consistently declined to enact legislation regarding expressions of racial hatred, a discussion of hate crimes legislation is not directly relevant to the discussion here. For further information, see Gelber 2000b, Jacobs and Potter 1998.

170. Although, of course, many US scholars have contributed to the discussion around defining hate speech. Many of these contributions have been recognised elsewhere in this book, and form an important part of the available literature.

171. Here, the identity of potential responders is broadly defined and intended to include those at whom the speech-act is directed, the group(s) to which they are perceived to belong, or anyone in affiliation affected by the hate-speech-act.

172. It would be important here that the notion of "equality" not be over-simplified, stripped of its content. The term "equality" has been integrated into this book in a manner intended to denote substantive, embedded equality, assessable via empirical investigation of the lifeworld circumstances within which groups and individuals find themselves.

173.   I am grateful to John Braithwaite for raising this point.

174.   Failure to report, however, results only in the employer being named in the Commonwealth Parliament. Affirmative action policies in Australia, and worldwide, are currently undergoing review and reconsideration. There is no scope here to enter into this debate. See for example Ireland (1996).

175.   *R.A.V. v. City of St. Paul*, 505 U.S. 377 (1992).

176.   *Skokie v. National Socialist Party*, 373 NE 2d. 21 (1978); *Smith v. Collin*, 439 U.S. 916 (1978).

177.   Although it was noted during deliberations that at the time of the application to march 40,500 of the village's 70,000 residents were Jewish.

178.   In judgement it was noted that the party's beliefs included the inferiority of Black Americans, and a belief that they should be forcibly repatriated to Africa, and that Jews held inordinate power worldwide.

179.   This Act amends the *Criminal Code 1913 (WA)*, ss 77–80.

180.   A major reason for the decline was said to be the arrest and imprisonment of a leader of the ANM on other criminal charges (Jones 1997:222).

181.   At the time of its repeal, no complaints against Section 126 had satisfied the "dual threshold" test of demonstrating both incitement to discriminate and advocacy of hatred (Jones 1997:222; White 1997:4), and the section had therefore never been implemented.

182.   Potential remedies also include the imposition of a fine at the discretion of Hearing Commissioners. No statutory upper or lower limit exists and to date no fines have been imposed under the *Racial Hatred Act 1995*. However, precedent exists in cases heard under the *Racial Discrimination Act 1975* of fines in the region of $2000 to $5000. At the time of writing two racial vilification complaints await judgement under the *Racial Hatred Act 1995*, which could involve the imposition of fines as a remedy.

References

Abel, Richard 1994. *Speech and Respect*. London: Stevens and Sons/Sweet and Maxwell.

Affirmative Action Review Secretariat 1998. *Regulatory Review of the Affirmative Action (Equal Opportunity for Women) Act 1986*. Issues Paper. Canberra: Department of Workplace Relations and Small Business.

Akmeemana, Saku and Jones, Melinda 1995. "Fighting Racial Hatred". In *The Racial Discrimination Act: A Review*, Race Discrimination Commissioner. Canberra: Commonwealth of Australia.

Allport, Gordon 1954. *The Nature of Prejudice*. Massachusetts: Addison-Wesley.

Anti-Discrimination Board NSW 1994. *Balancing the Act: A Submission to the NSW Law Reform Commission's Review of the Anti-Discrimination Act 1977 (NSW)*. May. Sydney: ADB NSW.

Anti-Discrimination Board of New South Wales (ADB) 1994. *Annual Report 1993/1994*. Sydney: ADB NSW.

Anti-Discrimination Board of New South Wales (ADB) 1995. *Annual Report 1994/1995*. Sydney: ADB NSW.

Anti-Discrimination Board of New South Wales (ADB) 1996. *Annual Report 1995/1996*. Sydney: ADB NSW.

Anti-Discrimination Board of New South Wales (ADB) 1997. *Annual Report 1996/1997*. Sydney: ADB NSW.

Anti-Discrimination Board of NSW and EOT 1990. *Annual Report 1989/1990*. Sydney: ADB NSW.

Anti-Discrimination Board of NSW and EOT 1991. *Annual Report 1990/1991*. Sydney: ADB NSW.

Anti-Discrimination Board of NSW and EOT 1992. *Annual Report 1991/1992*. Sydney: ADB NSW.

Austin, J. L. 1975. *How To Do Things With Words*. 2nd edition, edited by J. Urmson and M. Sbisa. Oxford: Clarendon Press.

Australian Law Reform Commission (ALRC) 1992. *Multiculturalism and the Law: Report No. 57*. Sydney: ALRC.

Bailey, P. 1990. *Human Rights: Australia in an International Context*. Sydney: Butterworths.

Baldwin, T. 1984. "MacCallum and the two concepts of freedom". *Ratio* XXVI (2): 125–142.

Barendt, Eric 1985. *Freedom of Speech*. Oxford: Clarendon Press.

Barendt, Eric 1994. "Free Speech in Australia: A Comparative Perspective". *Sydney Law Review* 16 (2): 149–165.

Berlin, Isaiah 1969. *Four Essays on Liberty*. Oxford: Oxford University Press.

Bindman, Geoffrey 1982. "Incitement to Racial Hatred". *New Law Journal*. March 25: 299–302.

Blackshield, A. R. 1994. "Reinterpreting the Constitution". In *Developments in Australian Politics*, Brett, Gillespie and Goot (eds.), 23–59. Melbourne: Macmillan.

Bollinger, Lee 1986. *The Tolerant Society: Free Speech and Extremist Speech in America.* Oxford: Clarendon Press.

Bracken, Harry M. 1994. *Freedom of Speech: Words Are Not Deeds.* Westport, Connecticut: Praeger.

Braithwaite, John 1989. *Crime, Shame and Reintegration.* Cambridge: Cambridge University Press.

Braithwaite, John and Pettit, Philip 1990. *Not Just Deserts: A Republican Theory of Criminal Justice.* Oxford: Clarendon Press.

Butler, Judith 1997. *Excitable Speech.* New York: Routledge.

Campbell, Tom D. 1994. "Democracy, Human Rights and Positive Law". *Sydney Law Review* 16 (195): 195–212.

Caplan, Jan 1986. "Speaking the Right Language: The Nazi Party and the Civil Service Vote in the Weimar Republic". In *The Formation of the Nazi Constituency: 1919–1933,* Thomas Childers (ed.). Sydney: Croom Helm.

Carroll, Lewis 1978. *Alice's Adventures in Wonderland and Through the Looking Glass.* London: Methuen.

Casper, Jonathan and Brereton, David 1984. "Evaluating Criminal Justice Reforms". *Law and Society Review.* 18 (1): 121–144.

Chan, Janet 1992. *Policing in a Multicultural Society — A Study of NSW Police.* Final Report to the NSW Police Service.

Childers, Thomas (ed.) 1986. *The Formation of the Nazi Constituency: 1919–1933.* Sydney: Croom Helm.

Chomsky, Noam 1968. *Language and Mind.* New York: Harcourt, Brace and World.

Cohen, G. A. 1993. "Equality of What? On Welfare, Goods, and Capabilities", In Nussbaum and Sen (eds.). *Quality of Life.* Oxford: Clarendon Press.

Coliver, Sandra (ed.) 1992. *Striking the Balance: Hate Speech, Freedom of Expression and Non-Discrimination.* Human Rights Centre, University of Essex.

Commonwealth of Australia 1995. *Trick or Treaty? Commonwealth Power to Make and Implement Treaties.* Report by the Senate Legal and Constitutional References Committee, November. Canberra: Parliament House.

Commonwealth Parliamentary Debates, House of Representatives (CPDHR) 1994. Weekly Hansard, Thirty-Seventh Parliament, First Session — Fifth Period. Canberra: AGPS.

Commonwealth Parliamentary Debates, House of Representatives (CPDHR) 1996. Weekly Hansard, 38th Parliament, First Session — Second Period. Canberra: AGPS.

Commonwealth Parliamentary Debates, Senate (CPDS) 1994. Weekly Hansard, Thirty-Seventh Parliament, First Session — Fifth Period. Canberra: AGPS.

Constitutional Commission 1987. *Report of the Advisory Committee on Individual and Democratic Rights Under the Constitution.* Canberra: AGPS.

Constitutional Commission 1988. *Final Report.* 2 Vols. Canberra: AGPS.

Cope, B.; Castles, S.; Kalantzis, M. 1991. *Immigration, Ethnic Conflicts and Social Cohesion.* Bureau of Immigration Research, Canberra: AGPS.

Coper, Michael 1994. "The High Court and Free Speech: Visions of Democracy or Delusions of Grandeur?". *Sydney Law Review* 16 (2): 185–194.

Cover, R. 1986. "Violence and the Word". *Yale Law Journal* 95: 1601.

Craig, Gordon 1998. "Destiny in any case". *New York Review of Books*, XLV (19), December 3: 4–6.

Cunneen, Chris; Fraser, David and Tomsen, Stephen (eds.) 1997. *Faces of Hate: Hate Crime in Australia*. Sydney: Hawkins Press.

Cuomo, Glenn R (ed.) 1995. *National Socialist Cultural Police*. New York: St Martin's Press.

Damrosch, Lori 1994. "The Role of the United States Senate Concerning 'Self-Executing' and 'Non-Self-Executing' Treaties". In *Parliamentary Participation in the Making and Operation of Treaties: A Comparative Study*, S. Riesenfeld and F. Abbott (eds.). Dordrecht: Martinus Nijhoff Publishers.

Davis, Peggy 1989. "Law as Microaggression". *Yale Law Journal* 98: 1559–1577.

Davis, Steven 1980. "Perlocutions". In *Speech Act Theory and Pragmatics*, Searle, Kiefer and Bierwisch (eds.). Dordrecht, Holland: D Reidel Publishing Company.

Delgado, Richard 1993. "Words that Wound: A Tort Action for Racial Insults, Epithets and Name Calling". In *Words that Wound: Critical Race Theory, Assaultive Speech, and the First Amendment*, M. Matsuda, C. Larence, R. Delgado and K. Crenshaw (eds.), 89–110. Colorado: Westview Press.

Department of Foreign Affairs, Canberra 1975. *Australian Treaty Series 1975 No 40, International Convention on the Elimination of All Forms of Racial Discrimination*.

Descartes, Rene 1966. *The Meditations and Selections from the Principles of Rene Descartes*. Translated by John Veitch. Illinois: The Open Court Publishing Company.

Dogan, Mattei and Pelassy, Dominique 1990. *How to Compare Nations: Strategies in Comparative Politics*. 2nd edition. Chatham, N. J.: Chatham House Publishers Inc.

Dowd, J. Justice 1998. *Transcript of interview conducted by Katharine Gelber*, Supreme Court Building, Sydney, 18 August.

Dworkin, Ronald 1981. "What is Equality? Part 2: Equality of Resources". *Philosophy and Public Affairs* 10: 283–345.

Dworkin, Ronald 1977a. *Taking Rights Seriously*. London: Duckworth.

Dworkin R. M. (ed.) 1977b. *The Philosophy of Law*. Oxford: Oxford University Press.

Dworkin, Ronald 1985. *A Matter of Principle*. Cambridge, MA: Harvard University Press.

Dworkin, Ronald 1992. "The Coming Battles Over Free Speech". *New York Review of Books*, June 11, 1992: 55–62.

Dworkin, Ronald 1996. "Objectivity and Truth: You'd Better Believe It". *Philosophy and Public Affairs* 25 (2): 87–139.

Eastman, Kate 1994. "Drafting Vilification Laws: Legal and Policy Issues". *Australian Journal of Human Rights* 1 (1): 285–297.

Elster, Jon (ed.) 1998. *Deliberative Democracy*. New York: Cambridge University Press.

Encel, S. 1971. "The Nature of Race Prejudice in Australia". In *Racism: The Australian Experience*, Vol 1, F. Stevens (ed.). Sydney: ANZ Book Company.

Federal Bureau of Investigation (FBI) 1997. *Hate Crime Statistics 1997*. http://www.fbi.gov/ucr/hc97all.pdf.

Federal Communications Commission (FCC) 1998. *Joint Statement of Commissioner Susan Ness and Commissioner Gloria Tristani concerning the Political Editorial and Personal Attack Rules*. Gen. Docket No. 83–484. 22 June.

Fish, Stanley 1994. *There's No Such Thing as Free Speech: And It's a Good Thing Too*. New York: Oxford University Press.

Fiss, Owen 1996. *The Irony of Free Speech*. Cambridge, Ma: Harvard University Press.

Flahvin, Anne 1995. "Can Legislation Prohibiting Hate Speech be Justified in Light of Free Speech Principles?". *UNSW Law Journal* 18 (2): 327–240.

Freckleton, Ian 1994. "Censorship and Vilification Legislation". *Australian Journal of Human Rights* 1 (1): 327–352.

Galligan, Brian 1983. "The *Dams* case: A Political Analysis". In *The South West Dam Dispute: The Legal and Political Issues*, M. Sornarajah (ed.). Hobart: University of Tasmania Press.

Galligan, Brian 1995. *A Federal Republic*. Melbourne: Cambridge University Press.

Gelber, Katharine 1999. "Treaties and Intergovernmental Relations in Australia: Political Implications of the Toonen Case". *Australian Journal of Politics and History* 45 (3): 330–346.

Gelber, Katharine 2000a. "Implementing Racial Anti-Vilification Laws in New South Wales 1989 to 1998: A Study". *Australian Journal of Public Administration* 59 (1): 13–23.

Gelber, Katharine 2000b. "Hate Crimes: Public Policy Implications of the Inclusion of Gender". *Australian Journal of Political Science* 35 (2): 275–289.

Gibbs, Benjamin 1976. *Freedom and Liberation*. Brighton: Sussex University Press.

Glass, Arthur 1995. "Freedom of Speech and the Constitution: Australian Capital Television and the Application of Constitutional Rights". *Sydney Law Review* 17 (1): 29–42.

Gray, John 1983. *Mill On Liberty: A Defence*. London: Routledge and Kegan Paul.

Grey, T. 1990. "Responding to Abusive Speech on Campus: A Model Statute". *Reconstruction*: 50.

Grimm, Eve 1992. "The Victorian Religious and Racial Vilification Bill 1992: An Overview". *Without Prejudice* 5: 20–25.

Habermas, J. 1970. "Towards a Theory of Communicative Competence". *Inquiry* 13: 360–375.

Habermas, J. 1979. *Communication and the Evolution of Society. Translated and with an introduction by Thomas McCarthy*. London: Heinemann.

Habermas, J. 1983. *Moralbewußtsein und kommunikatives Handeln*. Frankfurt am Main: Suhrkamp.

Habermas, J. 1984. *The Theory of Communicative Action, Volume 1: Reason and the Rationalization of Society*. London: Heinemann.

Habermas, J. 1987. *The Theory of Communicative Action, Volume 2: Lifeworld and System: A Critique of Functionalist Reason*. Cambridge: Polity Press.

Harrington, T. 1977. "Oceana". In *The Political Works of James Harrington*, J. Pockock (ed.). Cambridge: Cambridge University Press.

Hennessy, N. and Smith, P. 1994. "Have We Got It Right? NSW Racial Vilification Laws Five Years On.". *Australian Journal of Human Rights* 1 (1): 249–264.

Hentoff, Nat 1980. *The First Freedom: The Tumultuous History of Free Speech in America*. New York: Delacorte Press.

Hill, Lisa 1999. "Homo Economicus, 'Different Voices', and the Liberal Psyche". *International Journal of Applied Philosophy* 13 (1): 21–46.

Hobbes, T. 1958. *Leviathan (first published 1651). With an introduction by H Schneider*. New York: The Liberal Arts Press Inc.

Hornsby, Jennifer 1994. "Illocution and its Significance". In *Foundations of Speech Act Theory: Philosophical and Linguistic Perspectives*, S. Tsohatzidis (ed.). London: Routledge.

Howard, Colin 1988. "The Explosive Implications of the External Affairs Power". *IPA Review*, August-October: 7–11.

Human Rights and Equal Opportunity Commission (HREOC) 1982. *Incitement to Racial Hatred: Issues and Analysis: Occasional Paper No 1*. Sydney: AGPS.

Human Rights and Equal Opportunity Commission (HREOC) 1991. *Racist Violence: Report of the National Inquiry Into Racist Violence in Australia*. Canberra: AGPS

Human Rights and Equal Opportunity Commission (HREOC) 1995. *Racial Discrimination Act*. Sydney: HREOC.

Human Rights and Equal Opportunity Commission (HREOC) 1997a. *Annual Report 1996/97*. Sydney: Sterling Press.

Human Rights and Equal Opportunity Commission (HREOC) 1998a. *Face the Facts: Some Questions and Answers About Immigration, Refugees and Indigenous Affairs*. Sydney: HREOC.

Human Rights and Equal Opportunity Commission (HREOC) 1998b. *Annual Report 1997/98*. Sydney: Sterling Press.

Human Rights Commission (HRC) 1982. *Incitement to Racial Hatred: The International Experience*. Canberra: AGPS.

Human Rights Commission (HRC) 1983. *Words that Wound. Proceedings of the Conference on Freedom of Expression and Racist Propaganda*. Canberra: AGPS.

Hurka, Thomas 1999. "The Three Faces of Flourishing". *Social Philosophy and Policy*. 16 (1): 44–71.

Ireland, Ian 1996. "The Death Throes of Affirmative Action? The Adarand and Kalanke Decisions and Implications for Australia", *Department of the Parliamentary Library Current Issues Brief*, Law and Public Administration Group, Vol. 1, 1996/97, 19 August.

Jackson, Frank; Oppy, Graham; Smith, Michael 1994. "Minimalism and Truth Aptness". *Mind* 103 (411): 287–303.

Jacobs, James and Potter, Kimberley 1998. *Hate Crimes: Criminal Law and Identity Politics*. New York: Oxford University Press.

James, Pierre 1991. "Legislating Against the Racist Right". *Without Prejudice*. No. 4, December 1991: 30–37.

Jayasuriya, Laksiri 1999. *Racism, Immigration and the Law: The Australian Experience*. Nedlands, WA: University of Western Australia.

Johnson, D. 1997. *Proposed Statement of Objective of the 'Organisation for Sensible and Effective Prison Policy'*. Sacramento.

Joint Standing Committee on Foreign Affairs, Defence and Trade (JSCFADT) 1994. *A Review of Australia's Efforts to Promote and Protect Human Rights. The Parliament of the Commonwealth of Australia*. Canberra: Australian Government Publishing Service.

Jones, Jeremy 1994. "Holocaust Denial: 'Clear and Present' Racial Vilification". *Australian Journal of Human Rights* 1 (1): 169–184.

Jones, Melinda 1994a. "Empowering Victims of Racial Hatred by Outlawing Spirit-Murder". *Australian Journal of Human Rights* 1 (1): 299–326.

Jones, Melinda 1994b. "Racial Vilification Laws: A Solution for Australian Racism?" *Australian Journal of Human Rights* 1 (1): 140–148.

Jones, Melinda 1994c. "Using the Law to Combat Hate Speech". *Without Prejudice*, No. 7, April: 14–19.

Jones, Melinda 1995. "Extremist Speech and Australian Democracy". *The Crossexaminer* 3 (1): 10–15.

Kalantzis, M. and Cope, B. 1998. "Why Are We Closing The Door To Migrants?" *Sun Herald*, 15 March: 47, 48.

Kelsen, Hans 1961. *General Theory of Law and State*. New York: Russell and Russell.

King, G.; Keohane, R.; Verba, Sidney 1994. *Designing Social Inquiry: Scientific Inference in Qualitative Research*. Princeton, NJ: Princeton University Press.

Kirby, The Hon. Mr Justice Michael 1993. "Freedom of Expression: Some Recent Australian Developments". *Commonwealth Law Bulletin* 19 (4): 1178–1781.

Kirk, Jeremy 1995. "Constitutional Implications from Representative Democracy". *Federal Law Review* 23 (1): 37–76.

Knoll, David 1994. "Anti-Vilification Laws: Some Recent Developments in the United States and their Implications for Proposed Legislation in the Commonwealth of Australia". *Australian Journal of Human Rights*. 1 (1). http://www. austlii.edu.au/au/other/ahric/ajhr/ajhr1114knoll.html.

Korengold, Michael 1993. "Lessons in Confronting Racist Speech: Good Intentions, Bad Results and Article 4(a) of the Convention on the Elimination of All Forms of Racial Discrimination". *Minnesota Law Review* 77: 719.

Langton, Rae 1993. "Speech Acts and Unspeakable Acts". *Philosophy and Public Affairs* 22 (4): 293–330.

Lawrence, C. 1987. "The Id, the Ego, and Equal Protection: Reckoning with Unconscious Racism". *Stanley Law Review* 39: 317–388.

Lawrence, Charles R. III 1993. "If He Hollers Let Him Go: Regulating Racist Speech on Campus". In *Words That Wound: Critical Race Theory, Assaultive Speech and the First Amendment*, M. Matsuda, C. Lawrence, R.Delgado and K. Crenshaw (eds.), 53–88. Boulder, Colorado: Westview Press.

Lester, Anthony and Bindman, Geoffrey 1972. *Race and Law*. London: Longman.

Levinson, Stephen 1983. *Pragmatics*. Cambridge: Cambridge University Press.

Lewis, David 1997. "Mill and Milqueoast". In *Mill's On Liberty: Critical Essays*, G. Dworkin (ed.). New York:Rowman and Littlefield.

Liberal Party of Australia (NSW) 1988. *Ethnic Affairs: New Directions for NSW. Election* leaflet.

Lieb, Hans-Heinrich 1980. "Syntactic Meanings". In *Speech Act Theory and Pragmatics*, Searle, Kiefer and Bierwisch (eds.). Dordrecht, Holland:D Reidel Publishing Company.

MacCallum, Gerald 1967. "Negative and Positive Freedom". *Philosophical Review*. 76: 312–334.

MacIntyre, A. 1981. *After Virtue*. Notre Dame: Notre Dame University Press.

Mackie, Tom and Marsh, David 1995. "The Comparative Method". In *Theory and Methods in Political Science*, Marsh and Stoker (eds.), 173–188. London: MacMillan.

MacKinnon, Catharine 1993. *Only Words*. Cambridge, Ma: Harvard University Press.

Mahoney, Kathleen 1994. "Hate Vilification Legislation with Freedom of Expression: Where is the Balance?", *Keynote address to Conference presented by Ethnic Affairs Commission NSW and Bureau of Ethnic Affairs, Qld*, in Melbourne, June. Sydney: Ethnic Affairs Commission NSW.

Mahoney, Kathleen 1995. "Combatting Racism and Prejudice". Concluding remarks at the National Conference, Without Prejudice: Racism and Antisemitism in Contemporary Australia. Melbourne, 11/12 June. *Without Prejudice*, No. 8, April 1995: 85–86.

Mark, Steven 1999. *Transcript of interview conducted on 18 February by Katharine Gelber,* by telephone, Sydney.

Matsuda, M. 1989. "Public Response to Hate Speech: Considering the Victim's Story". *Michigan Law Review* 87: 2320.

Matsuda, M. 1993. "Public Response to Racist Speech: Considering the Victim's Story". In *Words that Wound: Critical Race Theory, Assaultive Speech, and the First Amendment,* M. Matsuda, C. Lawrence, R. Delgado and K. Crenshaw (eds.), 17–52. Colorado: Westview Press.

Matsuda, M.; Lawrence, C.; Delgado, R. and Crenshaw, K. 1993. *Words that Wound: Critical Race Theory, Assaultive Speech, and the First Amendment.* Boulder, Colorado: Westview Press.

McDonald, Leighton 1994. "The Denizens of Democracy: The High Court and the 'Free Speech' cases". *Public Law Review* 5 (3): 160–198.

McNamara, Luke 1994. "Criminalising Racial Hatred: Learning from the Canadian Experience". *Australian Journal of Human Rights.* 1 (1): 198–210.

McNamara, Luke 1995a. "Responding to Hate in a Multicultural Society: Forms of Legal Intervention", *Paper presented to 50th Anniversary Conference, Australasian Law Teachers' Association.*

McNamara, Luke 1995b. "Confronting the reality of hate speech". *Alternative Law Journal* 20 (5): 231–234.

McNamara, Luke 1997. "Research Report: A Profile of Racial Vilification Complaints lodged with the New South Wales Anti-Discrimination Board". *International Journal of Discrimination and the Law* 2: 349–378.

Meiklejohn, A 1965. "Free Speech and its Relation to Self Government", *Political Freedom: The Constitutional Powers of the People.* Oxford: Oxford University Press.

Mill, John Stuart 1991. *On Liberty and Other Essays.* With an introduction by John Gray. Oxford: Oxford University Press.

Motsch, Wolfgang 1980. "Situational Context and Illocutionary Force". In *Speech Act Theory and Pragmatics,* Searle, Kiefer and Bierwisch (eds.). Dordrecht, Holland: D Reidel Publishing Company.

Murphy, Paul 1972. *The Meaning of Freedom of Speech: First Amendment Freedoms from Wilson to FDR.* Connecticut: Greenwood Publishing Company.

New South Wales Parliamentary Debates, Legislative Assembly (NSWPDLA) 1989. Hansard (Third Series). Session 1988–89, Second Session of the Forty-Ninth Parliament. Sydney: NSW Government.

New South Wales Parliamentary Debates, Legislative Council (NSWPDLC) 1989. Hansard (Third Series). Session 1988–89, Second Session of the Forty-Ninth Parliament. Sydney: NSW Government.

Norwegian Governmental Commission on Freedom of Expression 1999. *Report of the Norwegian Governmental Commission on Freedom of Expression, appointed on 23 August 1996. English Summary.* September. http://odin.dep.no/html/nofovalt/offpub/nou/1999–27/kap12.htm.

NSW Government 1988. Discussion Paper on Racial Vilification and Proposed Amendments to the Anti-Discrimination Act 1977. Sydney: NSW Government.

Nussbaum, Martha C. and Sen, Amartya (eds.) 1993b. *The Quality of Life.* Oxford: Clarendon Press.

Nussbaum, Martha C. 1986. *The Fragility of Goodness: Luck and Ethics in Greek Tragedy and Philosophy.* Cambridge: Cambridge University Press.

Nussbaum, Martha C. 1988. "Nature, Function and Capability: Aristotle on Political Distribution". *Oxford Studies in Ancient Philosophy* Suppl. Vol.: 145–184.

Nussbaum, Martha C. 1990. "Aristotelian Social Democracy". In *Liberalism and the Good,* R. Douglass and G. Mara (eds.). New York: Routledge.

Nussbaum, Martha C. 1993a. "Non-Relative Virtues: An Aristotelian Approach". In *Quality of Life,* Nussbaum and Sen (eds.). Oxford: Clarendon Press.

Nussbaum, Martha C. 1999. "The Professor of Parody: The Hip Defeatism of Judith Butler". *The New Republic,* 22 February: 37–45.

Office of Ombudsman NSW 1993. *Report on Allegations of Police Bias Against Asian Students.* Special Report to Parliament. Sydney.

Ozolins, Uldis 1994. "Immigration and Immigrants". In *Developments in Australian Politics,* Brett, Gillespie and Goot (eds.), 202–216. Melbourne: MacMillan.

Parkin, Andrew and Hardcastle, Leonie 1997. "Immigration and Ethnic Affairs Policy". In *Government, Politics, Power and Policy in Australia.* 6th edition, Woodward, Parkin and Summers (eds.), 486–509. Melbourne: Longman Cheshire.

Parliament of New South Wales Legislative Council 1992. *Report of the Review by the Hon. James Samios, MBE, MLC, into the Operation of the Racial Vilification Law of New South Wales.* Sydney: NSW Government.

Pateman, Carole 1988. *The Sexual Contract.* Oxford: Polity Press.

Post, R. 1991. "Racist Speech, Democracy, and the First Amendment". *William and Mary Law Review* 32: 267–327.

Pringle, Helen 1999. "What We Have Here is a Failure to Communicate: The Other Larry Flynt and the Problem of Free Speech", *Proceedings of the 1999 Conference of the Australasian Political Studies Association,* September 26–29, University of Sydney.

Rauch, Jonathon 1993. *Kindly Inquisitors.* Chicago: Chicago University Press.

Rawls, John 1971. *A Theory of Justice.* Cambridge, Ma: Harvard University Press.

Raz, Joseph 1994. "Free Expression and Personal Identification". In *Free Expression: Essays in Law and Philosophy,* W. Waluchow (ed.), 1–30. Oxford: Clarendon Press.

Rees, J.C. 1960. "A Re-Reading of Mill on Liberty", *Political Studies, viii.*

Rees, John 1985. *John Stuart Mill's "On Liberty".* Oxford: Clarendon Press.

Rengger, N. 1995. *Treaties and Alliances of the World.* London: Cartermill International Ltd.

Reynolds, Henry 1995. *Fate of a Free People.* Victoria: Penguin.

Richards, David 1988. "Toleration and Free Speech". *Philosophy and Public Affairs* 17: 323–336.

Richards, David 1994. "Free Speech as Toleration". In *Free Expression: Essays in Law and Philosophy,* W. Waluchow (ed.), 31–58. Oxford: Clarendon Press.

Riesenfeld, S. and Abbott, F. (eds.) 1994. *Parliamentary Participation in the Making and Operation of Treaties: A Comparative Study.* Dordrecht: Martinus Nijhoff Publishers.

Riley, Jonathan 1998. *Mill On Liberty.* London: Routledge.

Robertson, G. 1988. "Free Speech: Reaching the Boundaries", Text of Article 19 Lecture, Human Rights Centre, UNSW 12 September 1988, *Australian Society. October 1988: 24–27.*

Ronalds, Chris 1998. *Discrimination: Law and Practice.* Leichhardt, NSW: Federation Press.

Rose, A. 1992. "Commonwealth State Aspects: Implementation of the First Optional Protocol" (Paper delivered at a symposium), *Internationalising Human Rights: Australia's Accession to the First Optional Protocol*. Centre for Comparative Constitutional Studies, University of Melbourne: Melbourne.

Rowse, Tim 1994. "Aborigines: Citizens and Colonial Subjects". In *Developments in Australian Politics*, Brett, Gillespie and Goot (eds.), 182–201. Melbourne: MacMillan.

Royal Commission into Aboriginal Deaths in Custody 1991. *National Report, Volume 5. By Commissioner Elliott Johnston QC*. Canberra: AGPS.

Russell, Bertrand 1996. *The History of Western Philosophy*. London: Routledge.

Sadurski, W. 1994. "Racial Vilification: Psychic Harm and Affirmative Action". In *Freedom of Communication*, T. Campbell and W. Sadurski (eds.). Dartmouth.

Sadurski, Wojciech 1992. "Offending with Impunity: Racial Vilification and Freedom of Speech". *Sydney Law Review* 14 (2): 163–195.

Samios, James M.L.C. 1998. *Transcript of interview conducted on 1 October by Katharine Gelber*, at NSW Parliament House, Macquarie St, Sydney.

Scanlon, Thomas 1977. "A Theory of Freedom of Expression". In *The Philosophy of Law*, R. Dworkin (ed.). Oxford: Oxford University Press.

Schauer, Frederick 1982. *Free Speech: a Philosophical Enquiry*. New York: Cambridge University Press.

Schauer, Frederick 1992. "Uncoupling Speech". *Columbia Law Review* 92: 1321.

Schauer, Frederick 1993. "The Phenomenology of Speech and Harm". *Ethics* 103: 635–653.

Schlesinger, Arthur 1974. "Politics and the American Language". *American Scholar* 43 (4): 553–562.

Scutt, Jocelynne A. 1993. "Group Defamation and the Vilification of Women". *Womanspeak*, June-July: 4–5.

Searle, J.; Kiefer, F. and Bierwisch, M. (eds.) 1980. *Speech Act Theory and Pragmatics*. Dordrecht, Holland: D Reidel Publishing Company.

Searle, John and Vanderveken, Daniel 1985. *Foundations of Illocutionary Logic*. Cambridge: Cambridge University Press.

Searle, John 1973. "Austin on Locutionary and Illocutionary Acts". In *Essays on J. L. Austin*, G. Warnock (ed.). Oxford: Clarendon Press.

Searle, John 1980. "The Background of Meaning". In *Speech Act Theory and Pragmatics*, Searle, Kiefer and Bierwisch (eds.). Dordrecht, Holland: D Reidel Publishing Company.

Sen, Amartya 1980. "Equality of What?". *The Tanner Lectures on Human Values*. Salt Lake City: University of Utah Press.

Sen, Amartya 1990. "Justice: Means versus Freedoms". *Philosophy and Public Affairs* 19 (2): 111–121.

Sen, Amartya 1993a." Capability and Well-Being". In *The Quality of Life*, Nussbaum and Sen (eds.). Oxford: Clarendon Press.

Simpson, G. and Yinger, J. 1985. *Racial and Cultural Minorities: An Analysis of Prejudice and Discrimination*. 5th edition. New York: Harper and Row.

Skinner, Quentin 1984. "The Idea of Negative Liberty: Philosophical and Historical Perspectives". In *Philosophy in History: Essays on the Historiography of Philosophy*, R. Rorty, J. Schneewind and Q. Skinner (eds.). Cambridge: Cambridge University Press.

Skinner, Quentin 1997. *Liberty before Liberalism*. Cambridge: Cambridge University Press.

Smolla, Rodney 1992. *Free Speech in an Open Society.* Oxford: Oxford University Press.

Smyth, Terry 1998. "Floored by a swastika". *Sun Herald,* 22 March: 23.

Solomon, Tamsin 1994. "Problems in Drafting Legislation Against Racist Activities". *Australian Journal of Human Rights* 1 (1): 265–284.

Stone, Adrienne 1998. "Freedom of Political Communication, the Constitution and the Common Law". *Federal Law Review* 26 (2): 219–257.

Strossen, N. 1990. "Regulating Racist Speech on Campus: A Modest Proposal?" *Duke Law Journal* 40: 484.

Sunstein, Cass 1993a. "Words, Conduct, Caste". *The University of Chicago Law Review* 60 (3 and 4): 795–844.

Sunstein, Cass 1993b. *Democracy and the Problem of Free Speech.* New York: The Free Press.

Taylor, Charles 1979. "What's Wrong With Negative Liberty". In *The Idea of Freedom: Essays in Honour of Isaiah Berlin,* Alan Ryan (ed.). Oxford: Oxford University Press.

Templeman, The Right Hon. The Lord 1994. "Treaty-Making and the British Parliament". In *Parliamentary Participation in the Making and Operation of Treaties: A Comparative Study,* S. Riesenfeld and F. Abbott (eds.). Dordrecht: Martinus Nijhoff Publishers.

Ten, C. L. 1980. *Mill On Liberty.* Oxford: Clarendon Press.

Twomey, Anne 1994a. "Laws Against Incitement to Racial Hatred in the United Kingdom". *Australian Journal of Human Rights* 1 (1): 235–247.

Twomey, Anne 1994b. *Strange Bedfellows: The UN Human Rights Committee and the Tasmanian Parliament,* Parliamentary Research Service, Parliament of the Commonwealth of Australia, No. 6, 1994.

Twomey, Anne 1994c. *Racial Hatred Bill: Bill Digest 174/1994,* 10 November. Report prepared by the Parliamentary Research Service. Canberra: Commonwealth of Australia.

United Nations Centre for Human Rights, (UNCHR) Geneva 1991. *Second Decade to Combat Racism and Racial Discrimination: Global Compilation of National Legislation Against Racial Discrimination.* New York: United Nations.

United Nations Committee on the Elimination of Racial Discrimination (UNCERD) 1993. Ninth periodic reports of States parties due in 1992: Australia. 23/09/93. CERD/C.223/Add.1 (State Party Report) 14 September.

United Nations Committee on the Elimination of Racial Discrimination (UNCERD) 1995. Thirteenth periodic reports of States parties due in 1994: United Kingdom of Great Britain and Northern Ireland. 12/05/95. CERD/C/263/ADD.7. (State Party Report). 20 April.

United Nations Committee on the Elimination of Racial Discrimination (UNCERD) 1996. Fourteenth periodic reports of States parties due in 1996: United Kingdom of Great Britain and Northern Ireland. 02/12/96. CERD/C/299/Add.9. (State Party Report). 22 August.

United Nations Human Rights Committee (UNHRC) 1994a. General Comment 16 (Twenty-third session, 1988), Compilation of General Comments and Recommendations Adopted by Human Rights Treaty Bodies, U. N. Doc HRI\GEN\1\Rev.1.

United Nations Human Rights Committee (UNHRC) 1994b. Fourth periodic reports of States parties due in 1994: United Kingdom of Great Britain and Northern Ireland. 19/12/94. CCPR/C/95/Add.3. (State Party Report). 14 October.

United Nations Human Rights Committee (UNHRC) 1994c. Initial reports of States parties due in 1993: United States of America. 24/08/94. CCPR/C/81/Add.4. (State Party Report). 29 July.

van Dijk, Teun A. 1995. "Elite Discourse and the Reproduction of Racism". In *Hate Speech*, R. Whillock and D. Slayden (eds.). Thousand Oaks, CA: Sage Publications.

Vass, Nathan 1997. "Pressure on Carr to act over race law". *Sydney Morning Herald*, 2 February: 3.

Victoria Parliamentary Debates, Legislative Assembly (VPDLA) 1996. Hansard. Fifty-Third Parliament, First Session. Melbourne.

Walzer, Michael 1997. *On Toleration: The Castle Lectures in Ethics, Politics and Economics.* New York: Yale University Press.

Welch, David (ed.) 1983. *Nazi Propaganda: The Power and the Limitations.* London: Croom Helm.

Western Australian (WA) Law Reform Commission 1989. *Incitement to Racial Hatred, Project No. 86, Issues Paper.* Perth.

Whillock R. and Slayden D. (eds.) 1995. *Hate Speech.* Thousand Oaks, CA: Sage Publications.

White, Ben 1997. "Racial Vilification and the Freedom of Speech: Reality not Rhetoric". *National Law Review* No. 3. http://www.nlr.com.au/ARTICLES/ 003/003RACIA.HTM.

Williams, Kevin 1999. *Transcript of interview conducted by Katharine Gelber on 15 January with Senior Education Officer, Aboriginal and Torres Strait Islander Team, Anti-Discrimination Board of NSW.*

Williams, Patricia 1987. "Spirit-Murdering the Messenger: The Discourse of Fingerpointing as the Law's Response to Racism". *University of Miami Review* 42: 127–157.

Williams, Patricia 1998. "Canon To The Ordinary". *The Nation* 267 (15): 9.

Zeman, Z A B 1964. *Nazi Propaganda.* London: Oxford University Press.

Australian court cases cited

Australian Capital Television Pty Ltd and others v. The Commonwealth (1992) 177 CLR 106.

Commonwealth v Tasmania (1983) 156 CLR 1.

Commonwealth of Australia v. John Fairfax and Sons Ltd (1980) 147 CLR 39.

Cunliffe v. Commonwealth (1994) 182 CLR 272.

Davis v. Commonwealth (1988) 166 CLR 79.

Koowarta v Bjelke Petersen (1982) 153 CLR 168.

Nationwide News Pty Ltd v. Wills (1992) 177 CLR 1.

Stephens v. West Australian Newspapers Ltd (1994) 182 CLR 211.

Theophanous v. Herald and Weekly Times Ltd (1994) 182 CLR 104.

NSW Equal Opportunity Tribunal Cases (Australia)

Davis v. Nunn, Complaint No. 107 of 1997, *Judgement made on 6 March 1998, Equal Opportunity Tribunal NSW.*

Harou-Sourdon v. TCN Channel Nine Pty Ltd, Complaint No 2 of 1992, Judgement made on 23 June 1994, Equal Opportunity Tribunal NSW.

Patten v. State of New South Wales, Complaint Nos 91 and 92 of 1995, Judgement made on 21 January 1997, Equal Opportunity Tribunal NSW.

R v D and E Marinkovic, Complaint No 124 of 1995, *Judgement made on 19 September 1996, Equal Opportunity Tribunal NSW.*

Wagga Wagga Aboriginal Action Group and Ors v. Eldridge, Complaint Nos 74, 78 and 79 of 1994, Judgement made on 19 May 1995, Equal Opportunity Tribunal NSW.

United States legal cases cited

Abrams v. U.S., 250 U.S. 616 (1919).

American Booksellers Ass'n. Inc. v. Hudnut, 771 F.2d 323 (1985).

Associated Press v. United States, 326 U.S. 1 (1945).

Brandenburg v. Ohio, 395 U.S. 444 (1969).

CBS v. Democratic National Committee, 412 U.S. 94 (1973).

Chaplinsky v. New Hampshire, 315 U.S. 568 (1942).

City Council for Los Angeles v. Vincent, 104 S. Ct. 2118 (1984).

Cohen v. California, 403 U.S. 15 (1971).

DeFunis v. Odegard, 416 U.S. 312 (1974).

DeJonge v. Oregon, 299 U.S. 353 (1937).

Dennis v. United States, 341 U.S. 494 (1951).

Gooding v. Wilson, 405 U.S. 518 (1972).

Miami Herald v. Tornillo, 418 U.S. 241 (1974).

Miller v. California, 413 U.S. 15 (1973).

New York Times Co. v. Sullivan, 376 U.S. 254 (1964).

R.A.V. v. City of St Paul, 505 U.S. 377 (1992).

Red Lion Broadcasting Co., Inc., et al v. Federal Communications Commission, 395 U.S. 367 (1969).

Schenk v. United States, 249 U.S. 47 (1919).

Skokie v. National Socialist Party, 373 NE 2d. 21 (1978).

Smith v. Collin, 439 U.S. 916 (1978).

Terminiello v. Chicago, 337 U.S. 1 (1949).

U.S. Postal Service v. Council of Greenburgh Civic Association, 453 U.S. 114 (1981).

Whitney v. Califonia, 274 U.S. 357 (1927).

United Kingdom legal cases cited

Derbyshire County Council v. Times Newspapers Ltd (1993) AC 534.

R. v. Malik (1968) 1 WLR 353.

Appendix

Appendix A. A summary of cases referred to in the book, and derived from an empirical study into the operation of the NSW racial anti-vilification statute, 1989–1998.

Case Name	Complaint details	Outcome
Case A	Anti-Semitic vilification in an amateur radio broadcast. Comments included "I'm not racist, I just hate Jews", "Hitler had the right idea ... the trouble is he missed a few", and a reference to "diseased Jews".	Complainant felt the legislation was unable to provide assistance because the respondent was a committed anti-Semite, and withdrew the complaint.
Case B	Vilification of Aborigines and Torres Strait Islanders by a well-known public figure with a history of comments prejudicial to indigenous people. The respondent described Aboriginal religion as "bizarre", "primitive" and "animalistic", adding that "lots and lots of Aboriginal people are educated enough to understand that".	Complainant felt there was little point engaging in protracted debate with a person known for making such comments, and no further action was taken.
Case C	A flyer distributed in a neighbourhood vilified Asian residents.	Complainant was not of Asian descent, so complaint inactionable. Also, ADB noted the respondent was a committed anti-Asian community group.
Case D	A pamphlet blamed "ethnics" for crime and advocated reduced immigration.	Complainant withdrew due to lack of time to pursue the complaint.

Case Name	Complaint details	Outcome
Case E	Comments made on a radio talkback program criticising Islamic practices and Muslim people. The ADB found that, on balance, the comments did constitute vilification.	Contact was lost with the complainant and the file was closed.
Case F	An indigenous woman was targetted with the comments, "you black slut", "you're nothing but a coon", "I've shot worse coons than you".	Complainant moved residence and was uncontactable, so file closed.
Case G	A service station proprietor racially vilified a customer.	Due to fear of violent reprisals, the complainant withdrew the complaint.
Case H	A person of Chinese descent was told to "go back to China", "we let you into this country and you destroy it".	After receiving threatening phone calls, the complainant withdrew the complaint.
Case I	Poems in a club newsletter vilified Asian people.	The complainant was not of Asian descent so no action could be taken.
Case J	A cartoon in an industry magazine vilified Aborigines.	The complainant was not indigenous so no action could be taken.
Case K	An erotic magazine described pictures of people of Asian descent as a "Dirty Orientals Value Pack".	The complainant was not of Asian descent so no action could be taken.
Case L	A booklet was distributed to legal studies students criticising immigration by people of Asian descent and Aboriginal land rights.	No people of Asian descent of indigenous people could be found to fulfil the "representative complaint" requirement, so no action could be taken.
Case M	A fundamentalist religious organisation distributed pamphlets portraying people of Arab descent as violent, irrational child abusers.	The distributors denied knowledge the pamphlet was vilifying, and no action could be taken.

Case Name	Complaint details	Outcome
Case N	A mural was painted on the wall of a school in an area characterised by high ethnic mix and with a high population of indigenous residents. The mural depicted an armed soldier of Anglo-Saxon descent standing in front of a Union Jack flag. In the foreground, the manacled arm of an indigenous Australian appeared. The complaint was lodged by a person of Anglo-Saxon descent, claiming vilification of people of Anglo-Saxon origin.	The ADB found the mural did not constitute vilification of people of Anglo-Saxon descent, because the history of Aboriginal dispossession and disempowerment was accurately displayed in the mural.
Case O	A pamphlet distributed by a community organisation called multiculturalism "threatening", and referred to Asian inter-ethnic "rivalries" which threatened stability and social cohesion.	The ADB found the material unlikely to pass the hatred threshold and declined the complaint.
Case P	Newspaper articles on the issue of immigration depicted Asian immigration as a threat to social cohesion.	The ADB found the material unlikely to pass the hatred threshold and declined the complaint. It was noted the complaint would probably fall under a free speech exemption, even if it were considered to constitute vilification.

Appendix B. An outline of racial anti-vilification laws in Australian states, other than New South Wales, and federally as at 2001.

Western Australia: Criminal Code Amendment (Racist Harassment and Incitement to Racial Hatred) Act 1990 *(WA).*

Western Australia has enacted perhaps the most narrowly applicable anti-vilification law nationally. In 1988 the Law Reform Commission of Western Australia was asked by the Attorney-General in 1988 to investigate possible changes to the law to "deter acts which incite racial hatred" (James 1991:30; WA Law Reform Commission 1989). This was in direct response to a perceived rise in racist activities in and around Perth, particularly by the Australian Nationalist Movement and most commonly in the form of racist posters and graffiti (Jones in Cunneen 1997:221; McNamara 1995a; Twomey 1994c:4). The *Criminal Code Amendment (Racist Harassment and Incitement to Racial Hatred) Act*[179] was passed in 1990. The Act creates a criminal offence where a person is in possession of "threatening or abusive material" *and* intends to publish or distribute or display that material *and* intends racial hatred to be "created, promoted or increased" by its publication or distribution or display (s77). The penalty is 2 years' imprisonment (s78). A lesser penalty of one year's imprisonment applies where a person possesses (s79) and displays (s80) such material, intending only to harass a racial group (White 1997:5). All sections provide for jail terms of only 3 or 6months, or fines of up to $2000 for the same offences if prosecuted summarily (White 1997:5; Twomey 1994c:4). Prosecution under this legislation is necessarily difficult, requiring a demonstration of intent and possession of written material deemed "threatening or abusive". To date, no prosecutions have taken place under this legislation and following implementation of the law, a decline was noted in the incidence of severe racial attacks (Jones 1997:222).[180] No provisions exist in the WA legislation for civil forms of redress. The criminal provisions are focussed on the possession of written material that is racially derisive, and not on the regulation of speech-acts.

Australian Capital Territory: Discrimination Act 1991 *(ACT), ss 66 and 67.*

The *Discrimination Act 1991* (ACT) mirrors that of NSW, which has been examined in depth. It creates both civil and criminal sanctions (ss66 and 67) and similar exemptions apply, in the case of fair reporting of a public act, or academic or scientific debate, artistic works or research purposes in the "public interest", "reasonably and in good faith". Under ACT legislation a criminal offence may occur a maximum penalty of $2000 and there are no provisions for imprisonment. Up to 1995, there had been no criminal prosecutions under this legislation (Twomey 1994c:4).

South Australia: Racial Vilification Act 1996 *(SA).*

South Australia has enacted legislation designed specifically to deal with racist hate-speech-acts. The *Racial Vilification Act 1996* contains both criminal and civil provisions and defines a criminal offence as an act to "incite hatred towards, serious contempt for, or serious ridicule of" a person/s on grounds of their race *by* "threatening physical harm" or "inciting others to threaten physical harm" to that person/s or their property (s4) [my emphasis]. Possible penalties include 3 years' imprisonment and/or a $5,000 penalty for individuals, and a $25,000 fine for corporations (s4(b)). Prosecution requires the consent of the Director of Public Prosecutions (s5).

Civil provisions were also enacted. The *Racial Vilification Act 1996* (SA) created the civil offence of "racial victimisation" by amendment of the *Wrongs Act 1936* (SA) (s37). The offence of racial victimisation consists of the incitement of "hatred, serious contempt or severe ridicule" on the ground of race. The offence is subject to considerable exemptions including reporting the act of another person, publications subject to privilege, and a "reasonable act, done in good faith, for academic, artistic, scientific or research purposes" or any matter under public debate. The civil offence provide for action under tort law; that is provisions are made for individuals or their representative organisations to sue other individuals under the provisions of the *Wrongs Act* and seek damages (in the form of monetary compensation or an apology, for example) in return. A remedy is provided in allowing for the awarding of damages of up to $40,000 to an individual victim or a vilified group (s6) (White 1997:4). Rendering an offence of racial vilification actionable under tort law is a proposal supported by some critical race theorists (Delgado 1993). Since the South Australian law is relatively recent, no comprehensive analysis exists of the outcomes or efficacy of its implementation.

Tasmania: Anti-Discrimination Act 1998 *(Tas), s19.*

Tasmania has enacted the most recent racial anti-vilification legislation in Australia, passed in December 1998 in the context of broad anti-discrimination legislation. The *Anti-Discrimination Act 1998* (Tas) contains a specific anti-vilification provision (s19) which prohibits the incitement of "hatred towards, serious contempt for, or severe ridicule of" a person on the ground of race (or disability, sexual orientation or religious belief) via a public act. This offence is subject to exemptions if the conduct is a "fair report", a matter subject to privilege or an act done "in good faith", for "academic, artistic, scientific or research purposes" or any purpose in the public interest (s55). The display or any sign or notice that "promotes, expresses or depicts discrimination or prohibited conduct" is also prohibited (s20). It is possible that this clause, although not yet tested in practice, could be utilised to render the use of some emblems, such as swastikas or the wearing of Ku Klux Klan insignia, prohibited. The Tasmanian legislation is relatively new and its implementation awaits examination.

Queensland: Anti-Discrimination Amendment Act 2001 *(Qld), ss 124A, 131A.*

In 2001 Queensland enacted racial and religious anti-vilification legislation containing both civil and criminal provisions. The *Anti-Discrimination Amendment Act 2001* replaced Section 126, which had restricted the advocacy of racial or religious hatred which incited unlawful discrimination,[181] with Section 124A ("vilification") and Section 131A ("serious vilification"). The legislation was modelled on that of NSW.

Victoria: Racial and Religious Tolerance Act 2001 *(Vic).*

A committee set up in 1990 to examine the issue of racial vilification in Victoria, in light of already-existing anti-vilification provisions in NSW, Western Australia and internationally, recommended the enactment of a Racial Vilification Bill in Victoria (Grimm 1992:20).The committee's report recommended the implementation of anti-racism policies in schools and other public institutions, as well as the implementation of both criminal and civil racial anti-vilification provisions with exemptions to protect free speech (Grimm 1992:22–23). A *Racial and Religious Vilification Bill 1992* was proposed just prior to a 1992 state election which saw a change of government, and the Bill lapsed. In 1993 when questioned on the absence of vilification legislation being put to parliament, the then Liberal government cited the imminent introduction of federal legislation as rendering any state legislation unnecessary (VPDLA, 22 April 1993:1102). During parliamentary debate in 1996, a call was made for renewed investigation of the possibility of implementing racial anti-vilification legislation (VPDLA, 12 November 1996).

In June 2001 a newly elected state Labor government passed the *Racial and Religious Tolerance Act*, prohibiting the incitement of "hatred against, serious contempt for, or revulsion or severe ridicule of" a class of persons on the grounds of their race or religion. The Act creates both civil and criminal offences and is modelled on the NSW legislation. Civil penalties include fines of up to $6,000 for individuals and $30,000 for organisations. Criminal penalties include a jail sentence of up to six months.

Commonwealth: Racial Hatred Act 1995 *(Cth)*.

A *Racial Discrimination Amendment Bill 1992*, which lapsed in 1993, included both criminal and civil offences. The criminal offences were public acts intended to stir up racial hatred (with a penalty of 12 months' imprisonment) and acts intended to cause people of a certain race to fear that violence may be used against them (with a penalty of 2 years' imprisonment) (Twomey 1994c:5). The civil offence was a public act likely to stir up racial hatred. The government undertook public meetings around the country to discuss the Bill (Twomey 1994c:5), and received 646 submissions of which 563 were opposed, and 83 in support (CPDHR, 15 November 1994:3380).

When the new *Racial Hatred Bill* was introduced in 1994, it also included both criminal and civil offences. The criminal offences included threatening to cause physical harm on the grounds of race (penalty of 2 years' imprisonment), threatening to damage property on the grounds of race (penalty of 1 year's imprisonment), and committing a public act intended to and which is "reasonably likely to incite racial hatred". The first two were already covered by criminal law, but without the component of the offence being committed on the ground of race. The third offence drew criticisms not unlike those directed at the *Public Order Act* in the UK, where the looseness of definitions rendered the application of the law difficult (Twomey 1994c:8–9). Furthermore, the third offence was not subject to any of the usual exemptions, for fair reporting, matter subject to privilege, or artistic, scientific, academic debate (Twomey 1994c:10). None of the criminal provisions were retained when the legislation was enacted in 1995.

The *Racial Hatred Act 1995* (Cth) creates the civil offence of racial vilification (s18B, 18C), defined as an act "reasonably likely, in all the circumstances, to offend, insult, humiliate or intimidate" a person on the grounds of their race or nationality, broadly defined. The offence is subject to exemptions for activities performed "reasonably and in good faith" as an artistic work or in the course of academic, artistic, scientific or public debate (s18D(a) and (b)). A further exemption is permitted for fair reporting (s18D (c)(i)) and for fair comment on any matter of public interest if the comment "is an expression of a genuine belief held by the person making the comment" (s18D(c)(ii)). During parliamentary debate on the Bill, references were made to the need to "balance" free speech rights with the values of tolerance and the right to live a life of dignity (CPDHR, 16 November 1994: 3411–3412, 3428). The statutory defences to the offence are therefore considerable, and include the genuine expression of personal opinion on any matter subject to public debate. The federal offence of racial vilification requires only the demonstration of offence, insult, humiliation or intimidation, and not the more stringent requirement of "incitement" used in other statutes, or the demonstration of intent. However, the wide-ranging exemptions to this provision would appear to obviate any potential for overuse of the law. Complaints of racial vilification may be lodged with the Human Rights and Equal Opportunity Commission (HREOC) (s22) and remedies include orders to desist, apologise or retract the statements, take actions to redress damage, or to employ or promote the complainant.[182]

Following enactment of the legislation, the HREOC implemented a strategy in 1996/97 to raise awareness about the law and to promote racial tolerance more generally (HREOC 1997). The Commission noted that where education targetted a sector of the community about their statutory rights, complaints from that target group tended to increase. Overall, an increase in the number of complaints in the second year of implementation was noted (HREOC 1997:39), and a decrease in the third year which was explained as a natural subsidence following a large initial influx of complaints (HREOC 1998:38).

Index